Affective bordering

Manchester University Press

RETHINKING BORDERS

SERIES EDITORS: SARAH GREEN AND HASTINGS DONNAN

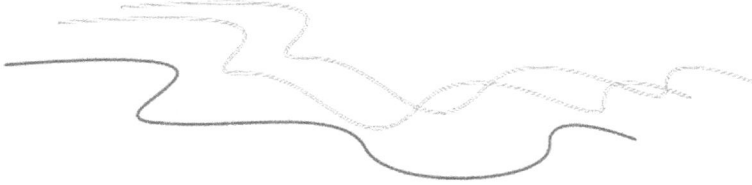

Rethinking Borders focuses on what gives borders their qualities across time and space, as well as how such borders are experienced, built, managed, imagined and changed. This involves detailed and often richly ethnographic studies of all aspects of borders: finance and money, bureaucracy, trade, law, new technologies, materiality, infrastructure, gender and sexuality, even the philosophy of what counts as being 'borderly,' as well as the more familiar topics of migration, nationalism, politics, conflicts and security.

To buy or to find out more about the books currently available in this series, please go to: https://manchesteruniversitypress.co.uk/series/ rethinking-borders/

Affective bordering

Race, deservingness and the emotional politics of migration control

Billy Holzberg

MANCHESTER UNIVERSITY PRESS

The right of Billy Holzberg to be identified as the author of this work has been asserted in accordance with the Copyright, Designs and Patents Act 1988.

Published by Manchester University Press
Oxford Road, Manchester M13 9PL

www.manchesteruniversitypress.co.uk

British Library Cataloguing-in-Publication Data
A catalogue record for this book is available from the British Library

ISBN 978 1 5261 7230 3 hardback
ISBN 978 1 5261 9627 9 paperback

First published 2024
Paperback published 2026

The publisher has no responsibility for the persistence or accuracy of URLs for any external or third-party internet websites referred to in this book, and does not guarantee that any content on such websites is, or will remain, accurate or appropriate.

This book will be made open access within three years of publication thanks to Path to Open, a program developed in partnership between JSTOR, the American Council of Learned Societies (ACLS), University of Michigan Press, and The University of North Carolina Press to bring about equitable access and impact for the entire scholarly community, including authors, researchers, libraries, and university presses around the world. Learn more at https://about.jstor.org/path-to -open/

EU authorised representative for GPSR:
Easy Access System Europe – Mustamäe tee 50, 10621 Tallinn, Estonia
gpsr.requests@easproject.com

Typeset
by Deanta Global Publishing Services, Chennai, India

Für Hannelore

Contents

Acknowledgements

This book has long been in the making and would not have been possible without the support of many. I firstly want to thank Clare Hemmings, who supervised this project from its early days. Your conceptual sharpness, generative feedback and infectious queer feminist spirit are unparalleled, and I couldn't have wished for a better mentor. Thank you also to Sadie Wearing for your generous support and incisive insights. I also want to thank Miriam Ticktin and Tina Campt for taking on and supervising this project during my time at Columbia University in the City of New York and for pushing me to think beyond the limits of the political. I am also grateful to Yasmin Gunaratnam and Éric Fassin for providing invaluable feedback, allowing me to imagine this work as a book. Thank you also to Tom Dark, Shannon Kneis and Laura Swift at Manchester University Press, who have been fantastic editors from start to finish, as well as to Sarah Green and Hastings Donnan for including the book in the 'Rethinking Borders' series and for their generative feedback on earlier drafts.

I am lucky to have been able to call the LSE Gender Department my intellectual home when first venturing into this project. I would not have been able to do this project without the queer feminist camaraderie of Aura Lehtonen, Jacqueline Gibbs, Ilana Eloit, Tomás Ojeda, Niharika Pandit, Priya Raghavan, Aiko Holvikivi and Hannah Wright. Thank you also to Hazel Johnstone and Kate Steward for making the department the caring, dynamic and convivial place that it is, as well as to the fantastic community of scholars that have helped this work in different stages of development: Leticia Sabsay, Sonia Corrêa, Alyosxa Tudor, Sumi Madhok, Dianne Perrons, Ania Plomien, Marsha Henry, Mary Evans, Wendy Sigle, Nicola Lacey, Melissa Chacón, Jenny Chanfreau, Lizzie Hobbs, Emma Spruce, Senel Wanniarachchi, Nour Almazidi, Alia Amirali, Alanah Mortlock and Zuzana Dančíková.

I am also grateful to the LSE Sociology Department and the LSE International Inequalities Institute, which provided me with another academic home from my early days as a Master's student to my later work as an LSE Fellow. Thank you to Kristina Kolbe for navigating this journey with me from the beginning and your friendship throughout. Thank you to Frank Tonkiss and Monika Krause for your guidance and supervision as well as to other colleagues in the department who provided intellectual feedback and inspiration in seminars, hallway chats and pub conversations.

I am equally lucky now to call the Centre for Public Policy Research at King's College London my academic home. Thank you to Sharon Gewirtz and Alan Cribb for the supportive interdisciplinary research environment you have created. Thanks also for your dedication to care and social justice and the feedback on earlier drafts of this work: Liz Fouksman, Tania St Croix, Rana Khazbak, Aisha Phoenix, Antonia Dawes, Francesca Meloni, Clare Coultas, Ayo Mansaray, John Owens, Melanie Cooke, Polly Mitchell, Farhan Samanani, Sara Black, Marguerite Mueller, Maren Elfert and Anwar Tlili. Special thanks also to Leonie Ansems de Vries for your careful engagement with my work that allowed me to sharpen the narrative arc of the book. I am also thankful to Queer@King's and KCL UCU Waterloo for providing community and hope in and against the neoliberal university.

This book was made possible through the personal, intellectual and activist relations that sustain me and the hope that a different world is possible. Thank you for your queer friendship, political drive and curiosity, and for putting up with (or even joining) me as I disappeared into yet another writing hole: Michelle Pfeifer, Anouk Madörin, Brell Wilson, Rebekka Hammelsbeck, Tsari Paxton, Merle Groneweg, Asiya Ahmed, Almut Poppinga, Dan Glass, Jerry Hoffman, Samira Marty, Fabio Santos, Lilli Schwoerer, Inken Büngener, Lena Kalisch, Emma and Oran Ward, Mania Godarzani-Bakhtiari, Alici Lecchi, Ellie Duncan, Alex Eisenthal, Danielle Oxenham, Zoe Rubenstein and Sophie Kloos.

Many of the ideas developed in this book I learned early from my family. Thank you, Claudia for your feminist spirit, Oskar for your unrelenting curiosity, Laura for your emotional intelligence, Nick for your political drive, Pepe for the infectious joy and Hannelore for your love and resilience. And thank you to my partner Howie Rechavia-Taylor for being there throughout the ups and downs of this project. Your intellectual drive, political rage and relentless inquisitiveness drive me absolutely mad, yet I could not think of or wish for a better person to share that madness with.

Introduction: affective bordering and the racial grammars of deservingness

Contesting the crisis

In the summer of 2015, the border regime of the European Union (EU) gave in for a moment. As a result of the persistent mobilisation of migrants from Syria and other places of war, violent conflict and destitution in the Middle East, Northern Africa and Southeast Europe, several hundred thousand people came to Germany.[1] Although the scale and dimension of these mobilisations had intensified over previous years, this moment – which came to be known as the 'refugee crisis' – was not a new phenomenon. Migrants from across the globe have entered Germany at various moments, and the country has long reacted with a deadly mix of deterrence, denial and humanitarian exceptions to people's arrival and presence in its post-war history. More than an unpredictable set of sudden events, the 'crisis' was a moment in which the entrenched racialised violence of the European border regime was revealed and the continent saw itself confronted with the results of global inequality, partly produced by its own colonial and imperial histories (Sharpe 2016; Bhambra 2017a; Danewid 2022). The war in Syria and the ongoing repercussions of the military invasions of Afghanistan and Iraq, as well as armed conflicts in African states like Eritrea and Somalia, all contributed to a growing number of people making their way towards Western and Central Europe.[2] As a result, the EU was less and less able to keep hidden its violent border securitisation practices, which, over the last decades, it had increasingly outsourced to the borderlands and externalised buffer zones of Europe (Andersson 2014, 2019; Madörin 2022).

The terminology of the European 'refugee' or 'migrant crisis', consequently, misnames the situation by constructing migration itself as a crisis. As Fatima El-Tayeb (2016) points out, the term references 'less the plight of millions trying to leave military and economic warzones than the inconvenience their arrival is causing the European Union'. What gets obscured behind the rhetoric of the 'refugee crisis' is a crisis of neoliberal racial capitalism, in which Europe sees itself confronted with the reality of escalating global inequalities that it continues to perpetuate and often actively benefits from. European nation-states like Germany have not only been complicit in the destruction brought about by the 'war on terror' but continue to profit from a global capitalist system based on the racialised division of labour, environmental destruction, and the extraction of natural resources in the Global South (Boatcă 2016; Bhambra 2017a; El-Tayeb 2017; Walia 2021). Given the longer genesis of the underlying causes for the contemporary 'refugee crisis', the current crisis is, therefore, best understood as what Lauren Berlant (2011: 761) has described as a 'crisis ordinariness': as 'a form of catastrophe a world is comfortable with or even interested in perpetuating'. The long summer of migration in Germany was a moment in which this crisis ordinariness came to national attention and some of the historical injustices and inequalities responsible for its genesis became open to contestation (Kasparek and Speer 2015; Hess et al. 2017). Migrants claimed their rights to mobility, safety and material well-being, and the questions of what Germany should do, where its boundaries lay and how it ought to be defined were and continue to be up for redefinition.

While the summer of 2015 was born out of the wider crises of war and destitution that people were fleeing from, it also marked a political opening in the migration and border politics of Germany. The then Chancellor Angela Merkel would suggest that 'we can do this' (*Wir schaffen das*) and evoked the vision of a country of hope and pragmatic hospitality. National and international media talked of the emergence of a new compassionate 'welcome culture' (*Willkommenskultur*) in Germany and marvelled at a nation determined to overcome the guilt and shame attached to the horrors of its dark past through solidarity and humanitarian action in the present (Hamann and Karakayali 2016; Fleischmann and Steinhilper 2017; Karakayali 2017). Simultaneously, migrants on their way to and across Europe unleashed their hopes, grief and anger into the public sphere. Together with solidarity initiatives, they organised marches, held vigils of public mourning and went on hunger strikes to remind the EU of the values of universal human rights, civil liberties and social equality on which it claims to be founded (Kallius, Monterescu and Rajaram 2016; Pfeifer 2018; Monforte 2021).

Yet, while some movement towards a more open and hospitable society was made, in the coming years, nationalist resentment and fearful protectionism were on the rise again. After violent attacks in Ansbach and Munich committed by asylum seekers and the New Year's Eve events in Cologne in 2015 in which several hundred cases of sexual violence were reported to the police, racist discourses of migrant criminality and sexual violence took centre stage (Boulila and Carri 2017; Hark and Villa 2020; Holzberg and Raghavan 2020). Arson attacks on asylum accommodation and neo-Nazi terrorist attacks ravaged the country; the outer borders of Europe were reconstituted and further securitised through deals with buffer countries like Turkey, Libya and Tunisia; and the once unconditional right to asylum enshrined in the German constitution was hollowed out to a point so far unseen in post-war Germany (Buckel et al. 2021; Hess 2021).[3] Éric Fassin (2017: 1) has described this period in German and wider European politics as the 'neo-fascist moment of neoliberalism' in which we witness 'the simultaneous rise of the far right and the authoritarian evolution of neoliberalism'. At the time of writing this book in autumn 2023, the far right anti-migration party Alternative for Germany (AFD) is gaining more than 20 per cent in national election polls, while the new social democratic Chancellor Olaf Scholz has declared that mass deportations and a further tightening of the asylum law are the priority of his coalition government.[4]

How did a period that emerged as a moment of at least cautious hope and compassionate solidarity turn into a period of fearful re-bordering, resentment and increased nationalism? *Affective Bordering* investigates this question through a focus on affect – understood as the emotional fuel of political action – by tracing the affective border struggles of this period. The book was written in the aftermath of the long summer of migration of 2015, and I have spent the last eight years tracing the affective dimension of border and migration politics in Germany, from the invocation of hope and empathy in the early summer to the re-emergence of nationalist fear, resentment and anger in the years following in its wake. I understand this period in German politics as a focal point through which to analyse how the political present and future are produced – a moment when naturalised forces of structural domination were up for contestation through competing forms of affective identification. Whereas liberal actors tried to defend the status quo of a murderous politics of deterrence with humanitarian exceptions, many migrants and anti-racist actors fought for a different, more open and less bordered country, and right-wing and neo-fascist groups aimed to and partly succeeded in seizing the moment to install ever more nationalist and protectionist regimes of power.

In tracing the mobilisation of different affects like hope and empathy, anger, shame and fear in the border struggles of this moment, I explore the practice I have named *affective bordering*. Put simply, affective bordering is a form of border making that reinstalls national and racial hierarchies through the mobilisation and unequal distribution of affect. The book traces how this form of border making operates, highlights its social and political effects and explores how it might be resisted.

Paradoxical politics

A key provocation of this book is that appeals to 'positive' emotions like empathy, love or hope in contemporary border politics do not necessarily form the political counter to 'negative' affect like anger, resentment or fear but often participate in shared practices of affective bordering. In fact, by continuing to centre the affective life of citizens over the concerns, experiences and demands of migrants themselves, the appeal to positive, or negative, emotions often keeps the power relations of citizen and migrant, local and stranger, subject and object of affect intact – even when aiming to undo them. At the heart of this book lies the investigation of the paradox that humanitarian, and even more radical activist, interventions that aim to challenge the ways that citizens *feel* about migration tend to re-centre citizens' affective lives as the site of political intervention and, as such, are in danger of re-inscribing the power dynamics their intervention aims to undo. This argument goes against classical approaches to affect that focus on the inherent moral and political value of 'positive' emotions over 'negative' ones in liberal social and political theory (e.g. Nussbaum 2013, 2016a; Wirth 2022). Instead, the book's central premise develops alongside queer feminist scholarship that has shown how affect is a highly ambivalent force (Ngai 2007; Hemmings 2011; Ahmed 2014; Pedwell 2014; Bargetz 2015) and builds upon the feminist insight that, in liberal regimes of power, liberatory politics are best understood as necessarily paradoxical (Scott 1996; Brown 2000; Madhok 2022).

In doing so, *Affective Bordering* breaks with accounts that simply explain the violence of the European border regime as a result of a lack of empathy or an excess of nationalist hatred and resentment. Instead, the book traces how practices of affective bordering continue to position racialised and migratised minorities as strangers to the nation – reliant on the goodwill and right feelings of the nation.[5] This paradoxical insight means that political affects, like empathy for migrants arriving on Europe's shores, do not necessarily work as antidotes but can easily emerge from and play into the same logic that undergirds nationalist fears, anger and resentment. The problem with affective bordering, therefore, is not simply the mobilisation of nationalist anger or hatred but the process by which questions of justice and rights are resolved through a focus on the feelings and sentiments of majoritarian publics. This insight is developed in conjunction with critical scholars of humanitarianism (Walters 2010; Fassin 2011; Pallister-Willkins 2022) and humanitarian sentiment (Malkki 1996; Ticktin 2011) who have drawn out the unintended consequences of humanitarian approaches to borders and migration.

More concretely, this book argues that what ties forms of 'positive' and 'negative' affect into the same dynamic of affective bordering are the shared racial grammars of deservingness underlying them. I use the concept of racial grammars of deservingness to highlight that the allocation of who deserves national protection and understanding is key to how practices of affective bordering operate. Whereas 'good' migrants are constructed to deserve empathy, love and emotional concern, 'bad' migrants should be feared or, worse, hated and resented. In other words, the politics of deservingness work through wider social discourses that mark some bodies as worthy of affective concern while others are framed as expendable, or even as direct threats to be deterred and exterminated. In highlighting how these allocations of deservingness are racialised, I am building on scholars like Leigh Patel (2015), who have pointed out that, in the context of contemporary migration politics, 'deservingness acts as a discourse of racialization, narrating across racially minoritized groups to re-instantiate the benefits for the racially majoritized'. The question of 'race' and racism consequently is key to understanding how practices of affective bordering operate and how they come to reproduce whiteness as a foundational structure of the German nation (see also Campt 2005; El-Tayeb 2016; Salem and Thompson 2016).

The book reveals that by positioning some people as more deserving of affective concern than others, racial grammars of affective bordering work to interpellate some people as the *subjects of affect*, while positioning others as the *objects of affect*. Through this process, people who are migratised and/or marked as racially different are positioned as un/deserving outsiders to the nation, dependent on the right feeling and generosity of the nation. The problem with practices of affective bordering, thus, is not only the kind of affects that it produces but the ways in which it centres the emotional experiences of citizens and sets conditions for membership in the nation based on the affective concerns and desires of its established white citizenry. In other words, affective bordering needs to be understood as a racialised practice that by privileging the (often assumed) affective fears and concerns of the majoritarian public re-cements white supremacist constructions of national citizenship. Attention to these racial grammars of deservingness helps us understand how easily affective identifications can shift in the face of migration. It explains how the initial hopefulness of the long summer of migration – which started with the granting of asylum to Syrian refugees and the celebration of a new, more compassionate German welcome culture – could easily turn into a nationalist project of re-bordering, which ended in the further erosion of the asylum protections enshrined in the German constitution and intensified the externalisation of borders into the militarised buffer zones of Europe.

I develop this insight through the analysis of the ongoing affective construction of the 'refugee crisis', ranging from the summer of 2015 to the border struggles of today. The book focuses on Germany as the economically most powerful country in the EU, the political decisions of which are crucial in shaping wider European policies. I trace the circulation of different affects by examining key events such as the mobilisation of hope in Angela

Merkel's '*Wir schaffen das*' (we can do it) speeches; the invocation of empathy in response to the publication of the photo of Alan Kurdi, the three-year-old Kurdish boy found dead on the coast of Turkey; the intensification of anger and resentment after sexual violence committed by racialised men during New Year's Eve in Cologne; and the rise of fearful ignorance and border paranoia in the current moment of pushbacks and border militarisation. I further attend to alternative affective practices aimed at subverting dominant practices of affective bordering found in migrant marches of hope, refugee hunger strikes, acts of public mourning and activist interventions aimed at shaming the European border regime. In tracing the political mobilisation of affect across these various sites of texts, images, media, activist mobilisations and political practice, *Affective Bordering* brings together critical and postcolonial border and migration studies with the rich archive of queer feminist theories of affect.

Rethinking borders

The analysis of the long summer of migration gives me a particular vantage point through which to analyse and conceptualise the affective dimension of migration control and to shift the conversation in critical migration and border studies. In times of heightened global displacement and intensified nationalism, the question of borders has moved to the centre of social and political analysis. Some of the most innovative work in this field has focused on the concept of bordering and border making to highlight that borders are not static entities, but dynamic processes aimed at the capture and containment of migrant mobility through neoliberal labour regimes, state securitisation and processes of racialisation (Tsianos and Karakayali 2010; Mezzadra and Neilson 2013; De Genova 2017; Yuval-Davis, Wemyss and Cassidy 2019; El-Enany 2020; Santos 2021; Walia 2021). What often remains underdeveloped in these theorisations, however, is that bordering is not merely a political, economic or symbolic practice; it is also an affective one that operates at the level of emotional identification and attachment. At the heart of *Affective Bordering* is the argument that the political mobilisation of affect is key to border discourses aimed at controlling migration as well as to practices that aim to contest these. In other words, the book explores how collective forms of affective attachment which sustain the deadly violence of border regimes are reproduced and contested.

The book's argument that affect is key to contemporary border politics derives from a queer feminist critique of rationalist conceptualisations of how politics operate in liberal democracies. Counter to Habermasian accounts which would hold that the public sphere is a space of rational deliberation, I understand the political as a space of affective contestation. Here I am building on the work of Chantal Mouffe (2022), who refutes idealistic notions of deliberative democracy, and abstract theories of justice, through the simple sociological observation that politics works through antagonism. These antagonisms, she suggests, are not only driven by ideological differences but most crucially by competing affective identifications. As queer feminist theorists of affect point out, affect, after all, is what moves us, what spurs us to action (Hemmings 2012; Ahmed 2014). Affect is not the opposite of rationality but the link between consciousness and action (Wetherell 2012). It is what gives texture and fuel to our thoughts and actions. The question of whether liberal, fascist, humanitarian, socialist or abolitionist ideas and practices become hegemonic in a moment of rupture, therefore, is not one of pure rational deliberation but one of affective identification, in which competing constructions of fear, anger and hope move people into (in)action.

In developing this insight, I draw on the rich archive of knowledge produced in the ongoing 'turn to affect' in social and cultural analysis. The affective turn is a highly contested project that has resulted in a multitude of often competing understandings of affect, emotion and sentiment (Gregg and Seighworth 2010; Holzberg 2018; Slaby and von Scheve 2019; Seigworth and Pedwell 2023). Amongst this multitude, I suggest that queer feminist theories of affect are the most useful as they have long focused on deconstructing gendered and racialised hierarchies between the public and private, the rational and the emotional, the mind and the body. These theories do not understand affect as a radically new concept that will draw us to the hidden aspects of the social world working beyond or outside of the reach of consciousness, discourse and the social as it has been positioned in some strands of social and cultural thought.[6] Instead, the queer and feminist theorists I draw on are primarily interested in understanding how affect comes to reproduce and contest unequal power relations (Berlant 2011; Hemmings 2011; Cvetkovich 2012a; Ahmed 2014, 2020; Pedwell 2014). This body of scholarship needs to be understood in a longer tradition of feminist psychosocial and sociological conceptualisations of emotions in relation to discourse (Lutz and Abu-Lughod 1990; Butler 1997, 2016; Wetherell 2013; Åhall 2018) and social practice (Hochschild 1979; Gunaratnam and Lewis 2001; Walkerdine and Jiminez 2012). Following this line of work, *Affective Bordering* highlights how affect works as a social and political force, how it is activated and produced, and how it might be subverted.

There continues to be heated debate about the conceptual language best used to analyse affect and emotion, or what Margaret Wetherell (2012: 4) has described as 'embodied meaning-making'. Whereas some scholars posit a sharp distinction between affect and emotion, many queer feminist scholars have argued against the usefulness of such a distinction. Clare Hemmings (2005) has demonstrated that the insistence on affect as a radically new paradigm tends to erase older, especially Black and postcolonial queer feminist, contributions that have long paid close attention to questions of how power inscribes itself in the body through emotion and feeling. In a related line of argumentation, Sara Ahmed (2014) has dismissed the distinction between affect and emotion as not only conceptually void but also politically useless and suggests that rather than getting bogged down by endless debates on what emotion *is*, we should turn our attention to what emotions *do*.[7] In the same spirit, Ann Cvetkovich (2012b) has expressed hesitation to employ the phrase 'affective turn' since it suggests that there is something novel in the examination of emotions, whereas this line of inquiry has been underway in queer feminist engagements for a considerable time.

I agree with these critiques – their proposed shift in citational practice, the focus on the political work that affect and emotion do and the collapsing of any definite distinction between the two. As such, throughout the book, I make little difference between affect and emotion. If anything, I use affect to describe the more diffuse and less defined states of intensity and bodily charge, while I tend to draw on the terminology of emotions to name concrete states of fear, anger or shame, for which there are socially agreed-upon, yet always contested, definitions. In other words, instead of fine-tuning the difference between affect and emotion, I examine their co-constitution by tracing how more diffuse affective states become ordered into more concrete emotional forces in political discourse and practice. In investigating processes of affective bordering, I am consequently not interested in the pre-social aspects of affect, nor am I making any definite statements about what emotions *individual* people actually feel. Instead, I delineate what forms of collective affective identifications and attachments are made possible in contemporary discourses and practices of bordering.

Affective bordering

A central premise of this book is that in few sites of contestation is the political power of affective identifications as evident as in the contemporary politics of migration and borders. Fear-mongering narratives of migrants as terrorists, sexual invaders and criminals, as well as resentment-driven stories that frame migrants as 'welfare scroungers' coming to take jobs and exploit social services, have long played a key role in legitimising ever more violent forms of border securitisation in Europe (Tyler 2013; Castro Varela and Mecheril 2016). Given the centrality of affect to migration politics, surprisingly little attention has been paid to the careful conceptualisation of how affect operates in contemporary practices of bordering. There is a large body of literature on the relationship of emotion, migration and diaspora, which examines the lived experience of migrants, as well as a growing body of literature on the concept of affective citizenship.[8] Although the insight that the 'affective and emotional dimensions of processes of subjectivation play a key role in both the attempts to govern migration and migratory practices seeking to subvert these' has become key to contemporary discussions of borders and migration (Casas-Cortes et al. 2015: 84; see also Bissenbakker and Myong 2019), more work is needed that conceptualises how exactly affect works as a force of bordering, and how this might be contested.

The most generative work in this regard has focused on the analysis of specific emotions such as fear (Huysmans 2006; Jones et al. 2017; Andersson 2022), empathy (Ticktin 2006; Sirriyeh 2018), disgust (Tyler 2013), love (d'Aoust 2013; Myong and Bissenbakker 2016; Scheel 2017) or grief (Gunaratnam 2013; Stierl 2015; Alonso and Nienass 2016). Ala Sirriyeh (2018), for instance, has developed a highly insightful account of how the politics of compassion and related emotions inform migration politics in Australia, Europe and the United States (US), while Hannah Jones et al. (2017) analyse how fear and suspicion are mobilised in anti-migration initiatives in the United Kingdom (UK). Leonie Ansems de Vries, Nora Stel, Nadine Voelkner (2024) have further studied how affective states of uncertainty and exhaustion are key to migration governance in France and the UK. Other scholars like Serhat Karakayali (2017), Isabel Meier (2020) and Aino Korvensyrjä (2024) have started to examine how affect operates in German border politics by tracing how emotions infuse different spaces of migration management and contestation such as asylum camps and volunteering initiatives. *Affective Bordering* is in close conversation with and builds upon this growing body of literature by examining how interrelated affective forces of hope, empathy, anger, resentment, guilt, shame and fear operate throughout and in the aftermath of the long summer of migration. This long-term focus on different emotions offers me a route into conceptualising how different instances of affective bordering connect through the racial grammars of deservingness and allows me to highlight the various ways in which the affective life of national citizens operates as the focus and target of migration politics. Through the concept of affective bordering in particular, the book embeds queer feminist theories of affect and emotion more centrally in the conceptualisation of borders and bordering.

A key example of the practice of affective bordering are nationalist discourses that conflate migration with the threat of terrorism in right-wing tabloid headlines such 'Asylum Madness: Terrorists Were Allowed to Legally Come to Us' (Bild 2018) – which became increasingly frequent in the wake of the 'long summer of migration' in Germany. As Sara Ahmed (2004) has laid out so evocatively, it is through the association of the 'bogus asylum seeker' with the figure of the Islamist terrorist in political and media discourse that fear gets stuck to the body of the migrant so that the body of the migrant itself gets read as 'fearful'. This performative production of affect – in the sense of producing what it describes – works through reiterating wider racialised, mostly Islamophobic, discourses of counterterrorism that produce the composite figure of the Muslim terrorist asylum seeker in the first place. Little must be said in the newspaper headline to conjure an image of threat in the reader's mind that marks the body of the Muslim migrant as, what Ahmed describes as a 'sticky' object of fear (p. 11). This form of affective bordering is not necessarily a conscious and intentional practice. Instead, as Judith Butler (2009) has shown in her work on frames of grievability in the 'war on terror', it is through the reiterative citation of wider social discourses that some bodies and lives get marked as worthy of mourning whereas others are framed as expendable, or even as direct threats to be deterred and exterminated.

Such practices of affective bordering have detrimental effects. The production of fear in right-wing media campaigns, as one of the most pronounced forms of affective bordering, legitimates ever more violent border policies. It helps to enshrine militaristic forms of border control that expand migration control through the wider security apparatus built in the global 'war on terror' (Bigo 2002; Huysmans and Squire 2016; Kapoor 2018; Gray and Franck 2019). From this perspective, the practice of affective bordering is best described as the governance of migration through emotional politics. It is racialised practice that helps to produce nationalist fears and affective identifications which are then used as a legitimisation for further extending policies of border securitisation. As such, the book highlights how affective bordering is not an innocent practice but part of what Ruth Gilmore (2007: 247) describes as the 'the state-sanctioned and/or extralegal production and exploitation of group-differentiated vulnerability to premature death'.

Racial grammars of deservingness

The political mobilisation of affect, however, is not the exclusive domain of the political right. While there has long been a tendency in sociological analysis for researchers to 'trot out emotions only to study Nazis, moral panics, and other movements they dislike' (Jasper 1998: 421), affect is key to social mobilisation across the political spectrum. Campaigns for less violent borders commonly evoke the promise that by feeling with people on the move to Europe, their suffering can be ameliorated. From Pope Franciscus pleading that we 'need to open our hearts to refugees' to international organisations, non-governmental organisations (NGOs) and local migrant solidarity campaigns that argue for more empathy in our approach to migration, the call to positive emotions like compassion, love and hope has become the cornerstone of humanitarian approaches to migration (Ticktin 2011, 2016; Fassin 2011; Chouliaraki and Stolic 2017). However, is empathy really what people on the move need? Can 'love' and 'hope' overcome national boundaries and ameliorate racialised hierarchies? And does 'opening our heart to refugees' really undo the unequal power dynamics that the utterance of such a call is built upon?

The book contends that calls to emotion like love or empathy often reproduce rather than challenge the power dynamics they are built upon. Even though affects like empathy or hope can work as forces that activate political dissent and create new bonds of solidarity, more often than not they work as ties that bind people to the status quo of the European border regime. *Affective Bordering* highlights that the humanitarian invocation of positive affects like hope and empathy often participates in the interpellations of some people as the *subjects* and others as the *objects* of affect. As such the call to positive emotions can *re*- rather than *un*do the dynamics of affective bordering and play into the racial grammars of deservingness that frame some people as more deserving of affective concern, life and protection than others. Such practices are racialised in the way in which the hierarchies of who counts as a desirable and undesirable subject are informed by the legacies of European colonialism (Anderson 2013; Tudor 2018; El-Enany 2020; Walia 2021; Danewid 2022). The call for empathy with less fortunate ones, often migrant children and women, for instance, needs to be understood in close relationship to civilisational and gendered discourses well alive in contemporary development and humanitarianism campaigns (Mohanty 2003; Wilson 2011; Ticktin 2017) – just like the fear of the 'refugee terrorist' discussed earlier can only be fully understood in relation to wider Orientalist histories that have imbued the figures of the 'Muslim terrorist' with fear in the first place (Said 1995; Ahmed 2004; Bhattacharyya 2009).

A key concern of this book is that this form of affective bordering means not only that the governance of migration increasingly operates through a focus on the affective life of national citizens but also that the concerns and emotional needs of people on the move fall outside of public concern. This logic can be seen most clearly in the appeals of politicians like the head of the AFD, Alexander Gauland, who posits that 'we finally need to take people's worries seriously' – calls that have become increasingly common in the context of the 'refugee crisis' in Germany.[9] Such appeals are not directed at *people* on their way to Europe, *people* affected by racist violence or *people* worried about deportation regimes within Germany – whose emotional concerns are erased and pushed outside of public consideration. Instead, the

invocation of 'the people' by right-wing politicians is based on the construction of the nation or *Volk* as a raced, gendered and classed formation. It rei-
fies the idea of the 'everyday man' (*der kleine Mann*) – white, male, middle
class – as the assumed citizen and benefiter of the state, who is presumably
worried about the changes brought about by migration.[10] Floris Biskamp
(2017) shows how such rhetoric reproduces rather than challenges racist
demands and presents 'the AFD as the representant and saviour of its own
collective' while cutting out racialised and migratised groups in and outside
of Germany from consideration.

This insight means that affective bordering works to secure borders outside as well as inside of Germany. The book pays close attention to the ways
in which affect is mobilised in relation to people coming to Europe, yet
affective bordering also works to exclude racialised and migratised minorities who have long been in Germany. Naika Foroutan (2016: 99) has shown
how contemporary border struggles are part of larger social contestations
about cultural, political and economic power in a postmigrant society. In a
context in which every third child in Germany now has a 'migratory background', the recent refugee migration highlights the extent to which homogeneous definitions of German nationality are no longer, and have never
been, applicable.[11] Strides have been made by anti-racist groups that challenge the ideas of racial and cultural homogeneity, and by queer and feminist
movements that unsettle traditional definitions of family and the nation by
enacting new forms of kinship and affective affiliations. Foroutan argues
that rather than embracing these transformations, many political actors in
Germany resist these changes to reaffirm homogeneous racial and heteronormative constructions of what it means to be German. Her argument alerts us
to the ways in which affective bordering not only works to secure external
borders but also reproduces internal boundaries and racialised hierarchies.

In grappling with these tensions, this book further traces how calls to
emotion in the face of migration are often more about resolving citizens'
own affective dilemmas than they are about actually attending to the realities of people on the move. After all, migration has become a projection
foil for wider social anxieties and tensions. It has become a key investment
point both for nationalist, right-wing groups keen to exploit the topic of
migration for neo-fascist projects of authoritarian protectionism, as well as
for the hopes and desires of activist and humanitarian groups aiming to create a more just world – my own investments included. These affective dis-
placements include the projection of anxieties caused by a world ravaged by
decades of neoliberal destitution, marked by escalating inequalities, climate
collapse, wars and armed conflict. Instead of tackling these issues, practices
of affective bordering promise to solve structural problems through an affective investment in migration and border control. As such, affective bordering

is a way to displace overwhelming problems that seem out of people's control onto the racial and migrant 'Other'. *Affective Bordering* explores these dynamics in more depth. It suggests that in the 'spectacle of the border crisis' (De Genova 2015), it is often the figure of the 'un/deserving migrants' that comes to operate as the 'figure of crisis' imbued with the emotional weight of multiple crises, environmental, economic and political, that shape the historical present (see also Holzberg, Kolbe and Zaborowski 2018).

Postcolonial Germany

The study of affective bordering contributes to the current project of establishing post- and decolonial paradigms more clearly in the study of migration and borders. Whereas migration studies and postcolonial studies have long been kept separate (Mayblin and Turner 2020), more recent work has highlighted how border regimes in Europe need to be understood as a continuation of colonial power arrangements (Tudor 2018; El-Enany 2020; Madörin 2022). Harsha Walia (2021) has effectively used the concept of 'border imperialism' to highlight how contemporary border regimes reproduce racialised distinctions, labour regimes and geopolitical hierarchies steeped in colonial power relations. This is particularly evident in the case of the European border regime that produces migrant illegality and forces migrants from the Global South to risk their lives in dangerous irregular border crossings (Van Houtum 2010; Bhambra 2017a; Sharpe 2016). In this book, I grapple with how the legacies of colonial domination live on not only at the level of law, policy or knowledge production but also at the level of affect.

I do so by examining how practices of affective bordering reconstruct boundaries between citizens and non-citizens, locals and strangers, and subjects and objects of affect and how these divisions are shaped by raced, gendered and classed imaginaries of whose emotional life matters in a neoliberal Europe shaped by the legacies of colonialism. In doing so, I pay close attention to how processes of racialisation intersect and are co-constituted with other dimensions of difference (Nash 2008; Crenshaw 2017; Salem 2018). As queer and feminist scholars of border and nationalism have shown, the nation needs to be understood as a gendered and sexualised formation which is increasingly secured through racialised discourses of national reproduction and gendered vulnerability (Yuval-Davis 1997; Siddiqui 2021), protectionist invocations of women's and lesbian, gay, bisexual and transgender (LGBT) rights (Fassin 2012; Farris 2017) and moral panics about sexual threat and contagion (Ticktin 2011; Holzberg, Madörin and Pfeifer 2021).

By focusing on Germany, *Affective Bordering* traces the ongoing affective reverberations of colonialism in a quintessential yet often overlooked context. German liberal democracy is commonly presented as the exceptional achievement of 'coming to terms' with the history of the Third Reich and the German Democratic Republic (GDR). Yet colonial histories remain largely unspoken, and if they are attended to, this is usually done through narratives of dismissal or even loss, in which it is suggested (or lamented) that unlike France or the UK, Germany never really had a proper colonial empire (Castro Varela and Dhawan 2010; El-Tayeb 2016). Although there are strong challenges to this narrative by contemporary postcolonial groups and anti-racist initiatives (Rechavia-Taylor 2023; Kolbe 2024), this sloped invocation of history tends to side-line the history of German colonisation and obscures how legacies of European colonialism shape German society and politics more broadly. It also produces troubling constructions of citizenship and difference and has contributed to what Fatima El-Tayeb (2016: 16) has described as a 'colour-blind ideology' in which race is dismissed as an exception and aberration of the Third Reich that should not be spoken. As a result, discussions of the ongoing power of racism in German social and political life are often erased or pushed to the margins of public discourse, while migrants, as well as racialised groups such as Black, Roma and Sinti and Muslim Germans, continue to be produced as *Ausländer* (foreigners), framed as a threat to the national community (see also Tudor 2015; Castro Varela and Mecheril 2016; Foroutan 2016).

The book's focus on Germany is at odds with the idea of Germany as a highly sober, unemotional and rational country. Political and media discourses in Germany seem dry in comparison to the emotive style of US political debate or the sensationalist media frenzy of the British press. Yet the national stereotype of Germany as a space devoid of affect misses that German public discourse and political practice need to be understood as a particular *emotional style* rather than as a lack of affect (Breger 2020; Frevert 2020). German border politics operates in a specific affective landscape. Since the founding of the Federal Republic in 1945, German public debate has been marked by the question of how to deal with the national guilt for the horrors of the Holocaust and the Shoa. The 'economic wonder' of the 1950s was marked by widespread denial of this history and the lingering structures of antisemitism in the country, and it was only with anti-racist mobilisations by Jewish, Roma and Sinti, Black and other activists as well as the student movements of the late 1960s and 1970s that some 'reckoning with the past' started to take place in public (Rothberg 2009; Florvil 2020; Rechavia-Taylor 2022). Since German reunification in 1989, this process of *Vergangenheitsbewältigung* – the complex German concept for describing the process of 'coming to terms' with and 'working through' the past – is increasingly developing into a newfound national pride for supposedly having 'overcome' the dark past to become a reunified country of economic success and liberal democracy (Dietze 2016a; Czollek 2020; Moses 2021b; Rechavia-Taylor 2022). This powerful narrative of *Vergangenheitsbewältigung* offers a complicated and often troubling emotional context in which contemporary debates around migration develop and need to be understood. *Affective Bordering* critically dissects the emotional effects that this national memory culture has on contemporary border and migration politics.

Abolitionist futures

The hope of this book is that understanding in more depth how practices of affective bordering operate in Germany today might help identify and augment ways to subvert and resist these. While the concept of affective bordering describes the ways in which a political focus on the affective life of citizens re-cements national boundaries and racialised hierarchies, the aim of this book is to point out ways to subvert these. Affective bordering, after all, is not the only way in which affective politics can operate in contemporary migration and border politics. This insight follows a rich body of queer feminist literature that has shown that while affect can work to cement power, it can also be the fuel of resistance and subversion (Cvetkovich 2003; Gould 2009; Ahmed 2014; Kurt 2023). Scholars like Sukhmani Khorana (2022), for instance, have shown how emotions can be harnessed as forces for positive collective change in migrant and migrant solidarity activism.

Tracing these alternative affective politics requires a shift in analytical focus. While the public debate in the wake of the long summer of migration continues to be dominated by emotive discussions about how the 'we' of the German nation should best react to the phenomenon of migration, people on their way to Europe enacted alternative mobilisations of affect in the cracks of the European border regime. Attending to these transnational counter-publics (Olesen 2010; Mpofu, Asak and Salawu 2022) highlights how people on their way to and inside Germany contest the racial grammars of deservingness by centring their own affective concerns and political demands. They organised migrant marches of hope, staged refugee hunger strikes, enacted forms of public mourning and performed political interventions aimed at shaming the EU. By paying close attention to these often overshadowed counter-mobilisations, my analysis highlights interventions by those deemed to be the object rather than the subject of affect.

The book's attention to transnational counter-publics works as a further critique of liberal conceptions of the public sphere that would frame politics as a space of rational deliberation and equal participation. Based on the bourgeois salons and coffee houses of the eighteenth century, the Habermasian (1991) imagination of the public sphere as an ideal space in which rational deliberation is had between equals continues to hold surprising sway in social and political analysis. This book pushes against such idealistic notions and shows how the struggle for hegemony in contemporary migration and border politics needs to be understood as one between highly *unequally positioned* actors. Nikita Dhawan (2014) has persuasively shown how the coffee houses in Europe were not only the domain of white, propertied men but were also made possible through the racialised labour and slavery in the colonies. Dhawan's argument asks us to attend to the racialised, classed and gendered exclusions that continue to structure the public sphere as well as to the material conditions that help explain who can appear and speak in public in the first place. Such attention seems specifically important in contemporary migration and border politics where the voices of the people most affected by such policies are often missing and little heard, whether in traditional forms of media and political discourse or digital practices of communication (Chouliaraki and Zaborowski 2017; Holzberg, Kolbe and Zaborowski 2018).

In doing so, the book pushes against the limited horizon of affective bordering and highlights practices that break and subvert the racial grammars of deservingness it is built upon. The book argues that such alternative grammars can be found, amongst others, in refugee hunger strikes that evoke scenes of horror and discomfort and which subvert hierarchies of empathetic identification; in acts of public mourning organised in the wake of racist border violence, which haunt a nation in denial about its fascist and colonial histories; and in marches of hope that envision expanded visions of affective solidarity and the commons. Miriam Ticktin (2016) has powerfully argued that if we want to counter growing nationalisms and the securitisation of borders in Europe, we need to extend our understanding of the political. She suggests that in a moment in which 'it seems the only subject position available to those who are not trying to build fences or walls is "humanitarian"', we need to make space for 'new political and affective grammars' that go beyond the 'humanitarian border' (2016: 255–56). In tracing alternative invocations of affect in the crack of the European border regime, the book responds to such calls for new imaginaries of the political in the face of intensified nationalism and border violence and is driven by abolitionist and speculative approaches to the border (Anderson, Sharma and Wright 2009; Walia 2021; Bradley and De Noronha 2022; Tazzioli 2023).

In contesting the racial grammars of deservingness that structure practices of affective bordering, I am writing out of and against my own positionality.

The impetus for this book stems from my own affective investments in and against the politics of the European border regime. It is informed by my own rage and guilt about the violence perpetuated through the border and my fear of growing right-wing nationalisms in Europe, as well as my hope that a different less bordered and nationalist world is possible. It also is informed by the queer experience of what it means to be imbued with the mark of shame, disgust and pity, as well as the belief that affective politics can alter structures of oppression as shown in the rich political histories of queer rage, grief and joy (Gould 2009; Muñoz 2009). At the same time, as a white middle-class German citizen, I am, in many ways, the assumed audience and ideal subject to be interpellated in the forms of border making that I describe through the concept of affective bordering. The book is written out of this position and operates through the reflection of what it means to be entangled in these forms of politics. In her work on white innocence in the Black Mediterranean, Ida Danewid (2017) has argued that in the current moment of murderous border violence in Europe, affective solidarity needs to start from thinking through historical complicity rather than striving for a position of innocence. My intent in this book is not to write my way *out* but *through* the interpellations of affective bordering. The hope is that by doing so, the book leads not only to a better understanding of the underlying grammars and violent effects of this form of border making, but also helps to augment affective solidarities, practices of care and politics of refusal that are able to undo these.

Structure of the book

The structure of the book follows a loose chronological order, from the initial hope and empathy in the early days of the summer of 2015, to the anger, shamelessness and fear constructed in the years following in its wake. This narrative arc is not meant as a definite assessment of the development of national affect in this period but as one possible way to make sense of the complex affective politics of this moment. Each chapter focuses on one affect – as object and analytic – through which I come to examine a specific moment of border contestation. Whereas in each chapter I focus on one specific affective force, such as anger, shame or fear, this does not mean that the affect in question is the only one that operates within the scene of analysis. My discussion of the image of Alan Kurdi in Chapter 2, for instance, would have looked different had I approached it primarily through the conceptual lens of grief rather than empathy; the analysis of great replacement ideologies in Chapter 5 would differ had I analysed them primarily through hatred rather than fear. The chapters should consequently be understood as analytical suggestions which offer a specific venture point into the analysis of affective bordering. While the chapters are focused on the analysis of one specific affect, the chapters also touch upon and reflect on related affective forces, showing how in practices of affective bordering states of empathy might turn into that of rage, guilt into pride and fear into hatred. Doing so, the book offers an intricate analysis of the various affective forces involved in contemporary border practices that I bring together in a last concluding chapter on the paradoxical politics of affective bordering.

The first chapter of the book, 'Hope: "*Wir Schaffen das*" beyond the Humanitarian Border', examines how hope for a new culture of hospitality was articulated during the early months of the long summer of migration of 2015 in Germany. The chapter starts with an analysis of Angela Merkel's '*Wir schaffen das*' speeches and the accompanying policies that were often read as the principle of hope for a new, more welcoming German nation. I argue that while Merkel opened the horizon to an open and more humane Europe, her politics of '*Wir schaffen das*' simultaneously distribute hope away from migrants and towards a nation imagined as needing protection from them. I then juxtapose this analysis with a reading of the March of Hope – in which migrants defied the restrictive policies of the European border regime by walking from Hungary to Germany – to see how the gesture of hope embedded in Merkel's '*Wir schaffen das*' was re-interpreted and reclaimed by the people most affected by her policies, namely, migrants on the move to and across Europe. These migrant cross-border marches, I suggest, enact mobile infrastructures of care and solidarity that break with the cruel logics of the humanitarian border invoked in Merkel's articulation of hope.

Picking up the unresolved threads of the last chapter, the second chapter, 'Empathy: Affective Solidarity and the Limits of German Welcome Culture', focuses on the politics of empathy to further examine the promise of German welcome culture. It does so by analysing the publication and circulation of the image of Alan Kurdi in relation to the alternative registers of empathy evoked in travelogues shot by migrants on their way to Europe. Thinking through these different registers of empathy, in this chapter, I trouble common conceptual differentiations between 'good' and 'bad' forms of empathy. Instead, the chapter argues that both invocations of empathy play into the racial grammars of deservingness that the European border regime operates through. To break this dead end of conceptual thinking, the chapter turns to the 'abject' that necessarily needs to be cut out from scenes of empathetic identification, expressed in protest actions such as hunger strikes. The self-directed staging of starvation suggests a different form of affective solidarity that, rather than emerging through feeling for or with the Other, aims for a shared discomfort in the face of the violence of the European border regime.

Chapter 3, 'Anger: The Sexual Politics of Resentment after New Year's Eve in Cologne', turns to the event that eventually put a halt to the hopeful narrative of a new, more empathetic welcome culture emerging in Germany: New Year's Eve in Cologne, after which several hundred acts of sexual violence committed by racialised men from Northern Africa and the Middle East were reported to the police. The event unleashed a wave of anger and resentment into the public sphere and led to a marked shift in the state policy and public sentiment towards migration. Analysing the political and media discourse that followed in the event's aftermath, this chapter suggests that the anger about New Year's Eve in Cologne operated as a catalyst for an already boiling resentment against the recent refugee migration and worked as an affective adhesive for feminist, liberal and right-wing nationalist positions. The chapter contends that the nationalist resentment in the wake of Cologne had little to do with any actual concern about sexual violence but worked as an echo of the colonial past in which it has long been the spectre of racialised sexual violence that has secured protectionist definitions of the white nation. Showing how intersectional feminist and anti-racist groups in Germany aimed to confront this echo, this chapter highlights the potentials and pitfalls of trying to sever anger about sexual violence from growing nationalist resentment in the historical present.

Chapter 4, 'Shame: Public Shaming in the Shadow of Holocaust Guilt', turns to the aftermath of the long summer of migration that revealed an increasingly shameless approach to migration. In this chapter, I scrutinise the utilisation of public shaming as a means to hold the European border regime accountable, with a specific focus on actions like the *Walk of Shame* and *The Dead Are Coming* that mobilise the mass murder of migrants by the EU as a site of political mobilisation. I suggest that these acts of public shaming offer ways to expose how the violence of contemporary border politics stands in direct opposition to the values of universal human rights the EU claims to be founded on; yet I also delve into the challenges that these actions encounter. I argue that practices of reintegrative shaming – shaming focused on betterment and reconciliation – can also re-cement forms of affective bordering, as they need to re-centre Europe as the locus of human rights and enlightened morality. This dynamic is particularly pronounced in Germany, where Holocaust guilt has played a key role in reinstalling new forms of nationalism over the last decade. At the same time, I demonstrate that reintegrative shaming strategies are also increasingly ineffective at a time when right-wing actors are undermining the notion that European border violence and the atrocities of the Holocaust should be considered shameful in the first place. Consequently, the chapter concludes by addressing the paradox of how to shame the shameless and shows how many activists are left with no alternative but to employ more disintegrative forms of shaming as acts of anti-fascist confrontation and despair.

Chapter 5, 'Fear: Great Replacement Ideologies as Paranoid Border Politics', traces the reverberations of the long summer of migration into the political present. In this chapter, I examine how fear is mobilised in a context in which the summer of migration itself has been transformed into a source of fear. I demonstrate that during this period, we can observe a merging of mainstream nationalist narratives with conspiracy theories such as the great replacement ideology, which suggests that the 'refugee crisis' was a deliberate strategy to replace white Germans with racialised migrants. Instead of confronting the racist fears and right-wing terrorist attacks that are propagated through such conspiratorial beliefs, politicians from various ideological backgrounds endorse them by urging the need to 'take people's fears seriously'. Deconstructing this dynamic of affective bordering, the chapter turns to how the families and friends of the victims of racist terrorist attacks in Halle and Hanau respond to this violence by centring their own experiences of grief, anger and fear. Based on this analysis, I propose that, rather than conceptualising fear as an inherently authoritarian emotion, the critical issue lies in determining whose fears are seen as legitimate and deserving of political attention in the context of deadly border violence of white nationalism in Europe.

In the conclusion, 'Shifting Grammars of Affective Bordering', I bring together the conceptual insights developed across the individual chapters and close the narrative arc of the book by identifying the underlying grammars that structure and confine dominant affective responses in the context of contemporary migration and border politics in Germany. I reveal how the analysis unsettles wider analyses of the historical present that would explain intensified nationalisms and border violence across the globe from the perspective of a lack of empathy or an excess of nationalist resentment in the political present. Instead, I show that thinking through affective bordering points us towards the shared racial grammars of deservingness that constrict affect's circulation within certain bounds of possibility. To illustrate my argument, I highlight how many of these racialised grammars of deservingness are being reproduced in current discourses around refugee migration from Ukraine. Even though the war on Ukraine opens new avenues for migrant solidarity action, I suggest that to properly shift energies to abolitionist border politics and speculative futures, we need to pay increased attention to alternative affective grammars enacted in the cracks of the European border regime.

Notes

1 To not reproduce moral, legal and political differentiations between (forced, political and therefore 'legal') 'refugees' and (voluntary, economic and therefore 'illegal') 'migrants', I refer to people crossing international borders to settle in a different country simply as migrants, or simply people or 'people on the move'. This is not to say that all migration is the same or that legal categories do not matter for people crossing borders. Rather, it is an attempt to circumvent the value-laden terminology of migration management that makes subjects governable through distinctions of deservingness (see also Casas-Cortes et al. 2015; Holmes and Castañeda 2016). I use the term 'refugees' or 'asylum seekers' only when I refer to studies or official statistics that rely on these terms as well as when they are explicitly used as self-definitions.

2 Most asylum claims in the EU in 2015 were made by people from Syria, Afghanistan and Iraq, followed by Kosovo, Albania, Pakistan, Eritrea, Nigeria and Somalia (Pew Research Centre 2016).

3 The right to asylum was enshrined in the German constitution of 1949, which states that the 'politically persecuted enjoy the right to asylum'. This basic right to asylum was first dismantled after racist attacks on refugee shelters in the early 1990s, when it was defined that asylum cannot be claimed by people from countries that the German state defines as 'safe states of origin'. It was further curtailed in late 2015 and over the course of 2016 when the Aslypakete I and II were passed, which, among others, saw harsher enforcement of deportations, cuts and changes to social provisions and stricter rules for family reunification (Pichl 2021).

4 For instance, in a key cover story and interview with *Der Spiegel*, Olaf Scholz proudly declared that 'we have to deport more often and faster' while working towards harsher asylum regulations on a national and EU level (Hickmann and Kurbjuweit 2023).

5 I use the conceptual language of racialisation to stress that 'race' is not biological reality but an ideological construction shaped by local and global forces rooted in the complex histories of European colonialism (Wolfe 2002; Gunaratnam 2003; Lentin 2020). I use the adjective racialised not to describe an inherent trait of people but to name the varied subject positions of people affected by racism and racial discrimination. I am using the terminology of migratism and migratised in a similar way, drawing on the work of Alyosxa Tudor (2018: 1062), who has developed the term to describe 'the discrimination based on the ascription of migration'. They point out how white migrants from Eastern Europe, for instance, might be discriminated against due to their migration status but not affected by racism in the ways that racialised migrants are. Migratism needs to be understood in close to relation to processes of racism and racialisation and is sociologically more useful than the psychological concept of 'xenophobia' that suggests an inbuilt 'fear of the stranger'.

6   Massumi (1995: 27), for instance, holds that 'emotion and affect ... follow different logics and pertain to different orders. Whereas emotion works on the system of quality that is consciously available and mediated through processes of signification and representation, affect works on the "unassimilable" level of intensity' (1995: 88). This level of intensity 'is not semantically or semiotically ordered' and is embodied in mostly automatic reactions (1995: 85). Arguing for a hard 'turn to affect', according to Massumi, cultural theory has (regrettably) nearly exclusively focused on the level of quality and neglected the more ephemeral, unpredictable level of intensity.

7   Counter to scholars like Brian Massumi, Sara Ahmed (2014) has suggested that even supposedly pre-discursive forms of affect such as the supposedly instinctual affective reaction to a bear are shaped by the social. She suggests that to be afraid of a bear, we must not only have identified the object of fear as a bear but also learned that the bear is fearful in the first place. Her approach goes hand in hand with more recent work in neuroscience and social psychology that has questioned the often highly selective use of natural sciences in the 'turn to affect' (Papoulias and Callard 2010; Leys 2011; Wetherell 2015) and that stresses the importance of learning, social cognition and language in how emotions are made (Barrett 2017).

8   For an overview of the vast scholarship on affect, emotion and migration, see e.g. Mai and King (2009) and Boccagni and Baldassar (2015); and for literature on affective citizenship, see e.g. Fortier (2010, 2016), Di Gregorio and Merolli (2016) and Ayata (2022).

9   The AFD was formed in 2013. It campaigns primarily on an anti-migration platform and has gained significant political power in the course of the 'refugee crisis', making it into the national parliament for the first time with 12.6 per cent of the vote in 2017.

10 The rhetoric of taking 'people's worries seriously' in the context of migration is not confined to far-right politicians but increasingly also articulated by centre-right parties like the Christian Democrats as well as prominent leftist actors like Sahra Wagenknecht from the socialist Die Linke. For a more detailed discussion of this affective construction of the 'people', see Chapter 5 on fear.

11 The awkward German term *Migrationshintergrund* derives from the fact that Germany takes no census of race or ethnicity. Instead, it differentiates people by the generation of migration. Every person who was not born or who has one parent that was not born in Germany is counted to have a *Migrationshintergrund*. While the term is also used in some critical migration and policy research, what this term effectively does is enshrining a distinction between 'real' and 'other' Germans and is often problematically used when people want to refer to people of colour or religious minorities.

1

Hope: '*Wir schaffen das*' beyond the humanitarian border

Introduction

Accompanied by images of migrants being welcomed at train stations across the country, Angela Merkel's '*Wir schaffen das*' has become the slogan for a new 'welcome culture' (*Willkommenskultur*) in Germany. When, at the end of August 2015, several thousand people on their way to Germany were stranded at the train station in Budapest, prevented from continuing their journey by the police, the German government saw itself forced to react. It is at this point that Merkel stepped in front of the cameras for her yearly summer speech and declared:

> I say simply ... the motive with which we approach these things must be: we have accomplished so much – we can do this! We can do this and what stands in our way needs to be overcome, needs to be worked at. (Bundesregierung 2015: para. 26)

In this speech, Merkel defends the right to asylum, arguing that 'universal civil rights have so far been deeply intertwined with Europe and its history [...] and are one of the founding impulses of the European Union' (Bundesregierung 2015: para. 27). As she promises Syrian refugees political asylum, Merkel's statement was often read as an act of 'opening Germany's doors to refugees' and a humanitarian slogan focused on alleviating the hardship of migrants coming to Europe (Hill 2015). Once the slogan was launched, Merkel repeated it in important speeches over the coming years, like her talk at the Christian Democratic Union (CDU) party congress and her New Year's address at the end of 2015, and she used it to defend her vision of a pragmatic and open Germany in shorter speeches after critical political events such as the terrorist attacks of Ansbach, Würzburg, and Munich in summer 2016.[1]

Merkel's speech helped to generate a wave of solidarity and welcome action in the country and gave people coming to Germany hope that they would find support and assistance in the country. While she was critiqued by the political right, liberal commentators celebrated her approach, and even some of the harshest critics of her European austerity policies of the prior years rallied to her defence. Yet as Merkel continued to invoke the hopeful vision of '*Wir schaffen das*', simultaneously border securitisations in the EU were strengthened, and the German government passed the Asylpakete I and II, which further eroded the right to asylum by, among others, implementing the harsher enforcement of deportations, cuts and changes to social provisions and stricter rules for family reunification (Pichl 2021). How can we make sense of the apparent contradiction between the humanitarian and securitising aspects of '*Wir schaffen das*', which already foreshadows some of the re-bordering dynamics of the years to come?

In this chapter, I suggest that Merkel's paradoxical invocation of hope in '*Wir schaffen das*' exemplifies the humanitarian securitisation of the border – a strengthening of borders through, rather than despite, humanitarian action and rhetoric (Walters 2010; Pallister-Wilkins 2022; Ticktin 2016). While the slogan '*Wir schaffen das*' opened the horizon to a more open and less bordered Germany, Merkel's rhetoric and policies also redistribute hope away from migrants and towards a nation imagined to be in need of protection from them. I contrast this cruel invocation of hope (Berlant 2011) with the more expansive way in which the gesture of hope inherent in '*Wir schaffen das*' was re-interpreted and enacted by people on their way to Germany in the March of Hope. Here migrants defied the restrictive policies of the European border regime by walking from Hungary to Germany and enacted hope in the everyday acts of collective organisation and living in the face of adversity. Such acts, I argue, open our perspective to a horizon of hope beyond the humanitarian border – a horizon in which the relationality of social life is not framed through threat and biopolitical control but in which collective infrastructures are valued as enabling life to flourish and persist.

Hope in queer feminist theory

Hope describes the affective force that emerges in the anticipation of a positive event or outcome to take place in the future. On a phenomenological level, it is characterised by the warm experience of joy and fulfilment, which can also be accompanied by the emotional anxiety and fear that the desired event will not take place (Coleman and Ferreday 2013). As such, the exact contours of hope remain contested, and its analysis often overlaps with that of other future-oriented affective states such as optimism or desire. However, while optimism describes the stubborn belief that things will work out because they always will or have so far, and desire the more general libidinal attachment to an object that the desiring subject craves, hope might best be understood as the affective attachment to the possibility of change in contexts of adversity (Eagleton 2019). It is based on the expectation that a desired event or object which one does not encounter in the present can and might take place in the future (Coleman and Ferreday 2013). Due to its unclear contours and its common association with religious thought, hope has long been dismissed in social and cultural theory, seen as too ephemeral and esoteric in its character and form (Smith 2006; Kleist and Jansen 2016). Yet in the current context of escalating inequalities, environmental collapse and authoritarian nationalism, hope has made a comeback in social and politic scholarship, with a range of scholars trying to understand how hope can work as a force for imagining and enacting different futures (Kleist and Jansen 2016). After all, as Lola Olufemi (2021: 12) suggests, maybe hope is nothing more than the 'whisper [of] only one promise, to remain steadfast in the belief that this cannot be all there is'.

Hope also occupies an increasingly contested location in queer feminist theories of affect, in which scholars have shed doubt on the purely positive potential of hope – especially for marginalised subjects. A key intervention in this debate is Lauren Berlant's (2011) argument that hope, in the form of what they term 'cruel optimism', can stand in the way of its own promise by re-attaching us to what hinders our own flourishing. They suggest that in a moment in which economic, social and ecological conditions in late liberal democracies like that of the US are deteriorating, what remains are hopeful attachments to the 'good life' steeped in the imaginaries of the post-war period: sentimental attachments to the nation, the nuclear family and the middle-class achievements of domesticity that promise protection from the cold embrace of late capitalism. These hopeful attachments are *cruel* as their affective appeal is rising despite, or rather because, their material realisation is becoming less and less viable. Ghassan Hage (2003: 15) has similarly shown how neoliberal societies like that of Australia function as 'mechanisms for the distribution of hope' in which hope is increasingly distributed away from the many and towards a select few. This shift, he suggests, operates not only through the concentration of wealth, the destruction of social welfare and chances for social mobility, but also ideologically through the transformation of collective hopes for solidarity and care into individual aspirations of survival and success. As a result of this redistribution to the top, he suggests, all that is left for many people are fearful attachments to 'paranoid nationalism' in which hope is derived from the promise that the nation-state will at least protect you from the demands of those who are even worse off than you.

It is in this context of shrinking and cruel forms of hope that the question of 'what alternatives remain for remaking the fantasmatic/material infrastructure of collective life?' has become paramount (Berlant 2011: 259). While some queer scholars have argued that the project of hope is a futile one specifically for marginalised subjects who never have (and never will be) promised a space in visions of futurity (Edelman 2004), I agree with Berlant (2011), who argues that what we need, instead, are new objects of hope that offer more than the worn-out promises of the past. The probably most engaging approach in this regard can be found in the work of José Muñoz (2009: 1), who insists that marginalised subjects in particular cannot give up on the futures that have so far been denied to them. Hope for him is not so much an object but a queer of colour hermeneutic based in the 'rejection of the here and now and an insistence on potentiality and possibility in for another world' (Muñoz 2009). Building on the work of Ernst Bloch (1954), he suggests that turning to hope does not mean turning to the idealism and fantastic visions of 'abstract utopias' but to 'concrete utopias', those forms and contents which are already being enacted in the cracks and fissures of contemporary society.

The implementation of such a method of hope can be observed in a small yet growing body of literature that tries to locate 'spaces of hope' (Harvey 2020) in the cracks of racial capitalism and paranoid nationalisms. In queer and feminist studies in particular, scholars have tried to decipher alternative forms of living in collective political projects and everyday moments of resistance and defiance.[2] In his own work, José Muñoz (2009) has read forms of queer futurity in the cultural practices and communities created by queers of colour in the US. By turning to projects as diverse as lesbian bathhouses and state equality initiatives, Davina Cooper (2014: 2) has similarly shown how 'everyday utopias' can help us not only understand how people live on and resist under conditions of hardship but also rethink social and political concepts such as care, justice and equality. And Kathi Weeks (2011) has suggested that outlining the conceptual work inherent in concrete utopias such as feminist strikes can help give the object of hope clearer contours – thus helping to turn more fleeting affective states into long-term political practices.

From this perspective, studying hope means enriching critiques of hegemonic structures through reading practices that are open to encountering the utopian in the quotidian. Rather than merely dismissing its object, such an approach requires looking for 'the spirit of utopia' within and around one's object of critique. This approach to the study of hope grounded in queer theory and queer of colour critique is also key for current scholarship on borders and migration in which scholars and activists are looking for visions that contest the humanitarian border and break with the nation-state as the default of social and political organisation (Anderson, Sharma and Wright 2009; Ticktin 2016; De Noronha and Bradley 2022). It is with this theorisation of hope as a powerful yet ambivalent force that I want to turn to the most prominent invocation of hope during the long summer of migration in Germany.

Hope as categorical imperative

In summer 2015, Merkel's '*Wir schaffen das*' speeches emerged as the key 'principle of hope' for a new welcome culture in Germany. While the phrase has developed a life of its own, I want to start with its initial invocation and take a closer look at the way it has been mobilised in the government rhetoric of the German chancellor. What makes Merkel's use of '*Wir schaffen das*' so remarkable is its temporality of hope. Different from classical hopeful slogans like Barack Obama's 'Yes we can', which paints the image of a bright future in which the American dream will flourish, Merkel mobilises hope from the lessons and hard work of the past. Stating that 'We have done so much, we can do this', she highlights the strong economic position that Germany is in, pointing to stability during the banking crisis, the end to nuclear energy after the disaster of Fukushima and coming together after natural catastrophes as recent moments of disaster management that her government had successfully led (Bundesregierung 2015).

Most importantly, across her speeches, Merkel refers to the national achievement of rebuilding Germany after the Second World War and reunifying East and West Germany after the fall of the wall as the two monumental efforts in modern German history, the hands-on spirit of which, she suggests, needs to be reactivated in the current moment of crisis:

> I can say '*Wir schaffen das*' because it is part of the identity of our country to do great [things], to build the country of the economic miracle out of the rubble [of the Second World War] and to become a highly regarded country of unity and freedom after the division [into East and West Germany]. (Konrad-Adenauer-Stiftung 2015: 29)

Merkel's invocation of hope here is not based on the optimistic vision of an idealised world to come, or on utilitarian calculations of potential best outcomes, but on the hard-learned lessons of history. It is a nationalist invocation of historical achievement in which hope is derived from the conviction that, as Merkel states, 'the examples of the past teach us: whenever it matters we ... are able to do what is right and necessary' (Bundesregierung 2015: para. 18). Gabriele Dietze (2016a: 1) has referred to this narrative of Germany building a successful capitalist democracy out of its fascist and socialist past as one of 'exceptional historical atonement'. She suggests that specifically the memory of the Holocaust and the Third Reich have long been a crucial mobilising force for hospitable stances towards migration, as it was in response to the histories of Nazi persecution and expulsion that the right of political asylum was enshrined in the German constitution.

Merkel's adaptation of this emotional defence of the right to asylum is a break with the political mainstream that has long been dominated by Merkel's own party, the CDU. The CDU has long refused to acknowledge that Germany is a 'country of immigration' and resisted extending definitions of Germanness beyond the racial logic of *jus sanguinis* – changed in law only by the coalition government of the Social Democrats (SPD) and the Green Party in 2000.[3] Merkel's efforts stand out as they go against the common sense of her party and contradict the anti-immigration line cemented by her former mentor and long-term chancellor Helmut Kohl. As a result, Merkel faced opposition for her decisions and rhetoric during the long summer of migration. These attacks were fuelled by key figures of the far right, like Victor Orbán in Hungary and Alexander Gauland (the co-head of the AFD) in Germany, who infamously declared that 'we do not even want to do this' (*Wir wollen das gar nicht schaffen*) (Pollmer and Schneider 2015: 1). Yet opponents also came from within her own party. Horst Seehofer, the head of Merkel's sister party the Christian Social Union (CSU) and later the Minister for Interior, for instance, refused to take on Merkel's slogan and continually pushed for limits on the number of migrants who could be granted asylum in Germany.

At the CDU congress in December 2016, Merkel directly confronted the critics in her own party by arguing that migration and international co-operation are ever more important in a globalised world in which risks of terror, war and climate change can only be managed across national borders. Most importantly, she argues that 'the CDU is a party that from the beginning knew that after the horror of the Second World War and the Holocaust our Germany could only come back to its feet politically and morally if we overcome separations and build bridges beyond the borders of our own country' (Konrad-Adenauer-Stiftung 2015: 37). Here she constructs the Holocaust as a national trauma, a moral and emotional anchor, that should guide Germany's action for the future. Her rhetoric shows how the most moving visions of futurity are formed in relation to and out of the already existing material of the past. Based on narratives of exceptional national atonement, she turns '*Wir schaffen das*' into a 'humanitarian imperative' (Konrad-Adenauer-Stiftung 2015: 26) and moves a critical, even hostile, CDU to give her standing ovations at the party delegation.

'*Wir schaffen das*' further gains particular weight through Merkel's own biography. As Joyce Mushaben (2017) points out, working her way up as a woman from a small town in the GDR to the head of a reunited, democratic

Germany lends credibility to her defending a liberal system of equality, human rights and the rule of law. To stress her point, Mushaben refers to a speech given by Merkel at a benefit concert for refugees in January 2016. Quoting the former Czech dissident who became president after the fall of the Berlin Wall, they argue that 'hope is not the conviction that something will turn out well, but the certainty that something makes sense, regardless of how it turns out' (cited in Mushaben 2017: 531). The message of hope articulated in '*Wir schaffen das*' relies less on the optimistic vision of an idealised world to come and more on the lessons of history that have taught the universal value of human rights and the rule of law.

This approach gained Merkel praise not only from critics within her own party but also from some of the harshest critiques of the government's European austerity regimes of the years prior. Étienne Balibar (2015) declared that Merkel's actions 'deserve the greatest respect' as they defend a vision of 'the right of asylum and against Fortress Europe', and even the ex-finance minister of Greece, Yanis Varoufakis (2015), argued that in Merkel's statement, he 'found hope that Europe's soul hadn't disappeared completely'. He praised 'one of Germany's grandest gifts to humanity: the philosophy of Immanuel Kant' and argued that the spirit of '*Wir schaffen das*' carries the vision for a more humane Europe. What we find in Merkel's invocation of '*Wir schaffen das*' is a Kantian understanding of hope in which the use of universal morality and categorical imperatives constitutes the best compass for overcoming the horrors of the past and enacting a more cosmopolitan politics. It is based on the universal promise to include those in the hope and achievements of the nation who have historically been excluded from it.

Disconnecting connected histories

The anchoring of '*Wir schaffen das*' in the moral lessons of the past helps explain the appeal of Merkel's rhetoric across traditional left–right political divides. As Dirk Moses and Howie Rechavia-Taylor (2021) point out, stressing Germany's special historical responsibility has become the key moral foundation of the Federal Republic, on which, except for the far right, all political parties in parliament agree. The more specific argument that the crimes against humanity of the Third Reich – which led to refugee migration as one of the only ways for Jewish people, Roma and Sinti and other perse-cuted minorities to survive – legitimises the right to asylum has traditionally been an argument made predominantly by more left-liberal voices and the anti-fascist left. Merkel's incorporation of this argument into the rhetoric of the conservative Christian Democratic Union helped to embed it in the centre of politics and animated collective hopes of a new 'welcome culture' emerging in Germany. It helped to generate solidarity and hospitality initiatives across different regions and political fractions and united large parts of civil society in the necessity of providing humanitarian assistance to people fleeing from war and oppression. Most importantly, it held out, at least, cautious hope to those coming to Germany that they would be received with assistance and be given the possibility to make a new life in the country.

The narrative of national exceptionalism that Merkel's rhetoric is based on, however, also carries the potential to reproduce practices of affective bordering which position migrants as strangers to the nation, reliant on the right feeling of the nation. While Merkel's rhetoric opens up some links of historical responsibility, she forecloses others. Merkel does mention the war in Syria, alludes to Libya, Iraq and Afghanistan and frames the current refugee migration as a 'rendezvous with globalisation' (Konrad-Adenauer-Stiftung 2015: 38). Yet any more complex engagement with the reasons why people migrate and Germany's role in destabilising the Middle East (for instance through weapons sales to Saudi Arabia or the deployment of US drones from German military posts) are eclipsed. Similarly, trade policies that keep countries of the Global South from having equal access to the world market, or Europe's central historical responsibility in contributing to the climate crisis, remain unmentioned (see El-Tayeb 2016 for a more detailed discussion of such entanglements). These omissions are further exacerbated through the 'emergency logics' in which Merkel narrates the 'refugee crisis' as an unexpected event that 'poses an enormous challenge' (Bundesregierung 2015: para. 12). By invoking migration as a problem that comes to Europe from outside, her speeches disconnect what Gurminder Bhambra (2017a: 404) calls 'connected histories' and evades transnational historical responsibility by claiming a national one. This contributes to the long-established dynamics that explain phenomena such as transnational migration through an 'internalist narrative' of Europe, in which 'Europe is able to produce from within its own borders and resources, both material and spiritual, the conditions for the next phase of social development' (Hall 1991: 18).

The narrative of exceptional moral responsibility also helped to evade actual responsibility amid the European debt crisis. As Éric Fassin and Aurélie Windels (2016: 1) argue, Merkel's humanitarian gesture allowed the German government to reframe its reputation in European politics from that of a 'technocratic tyrant' to that of a 'benevolent protector'. It stifled international criticism of Germany's role in the Euro crisis and of its support for the Troika's imposing of austerity politics on European countries like Greece. The latter destroyed social welfare systems and eroded the material ground from which migrant hospitality could be mobilised in the European South. Bernd Kasparek and Marc Speer (2015: 1) further wonder how, 'regardless of its role as architect and driving force of [the European border] regime, [Germany] wins worldwide acclaim for its humanitarian stance'. After all, Germany was one of the key drivers in implementing the Dublin system, playing a crucial role in financing FRONTEX (the European Border and Coast Guard Agency), and it has long been at the forefront of securing deals that further the externalisation of borders to regions outside of Europe.

The most troubling aspect of the narrative of exceptional national achievement, however, might be the affective tone through which it is articulated. Invoking 'a new country born from the rubble of the past', Merkel presents the process of coming to terms with the past as a relatively finished process rather than an ongoing struggle with a still-festering wound. This reframing of a history of violence, guilt and shame into one of national pride forges a dubious relation between Germany and its ongoing histories of fascism and racism (see also Czollek 2020; Rechavia-Taylor 2022). Across her speeches, Merkel praises civil society's efforts in helping migrants settle in Germany and speaks out against the 'prejudice', 'coldness' and 'hatred' that she herself encountered when she was attacked and insulted by the right (Bundesregierung 2015: para. 9). Yet any more thorough engagement with the structural and institutional racism that, among others, was so blatantly highlighted in the National Socialist Underground (NSU) murders and the cover-up by the police, state, and legal apparatus (see Karakayali et al. 2017; Nobrega, Quent and Zipf 2021) remains unaddressed.

Instead, we can discern how within Merkel's rhetoric migrants become positioned as potential threats to the exceptional achievements of the German nation. In her speech to the CDU delegation, Merkel asks:

> What effect does our way to live have on the many people that are coming to us from the Arabic world, from Muslim countries? What effect does their cultural character have on us? Will we [...] with so many people coming from a different cultural circle than ours, still be the Germany that we know, the Germany that is strong and has made us strong? (Konrad-Adenauer-Stiftung 2015: 36)

Merkel answers this rhetorical question with the vision of 'a Germany with equality between man and woman and without any form of antisemitism, xenophobia or discrimination against homosexual people' (Konrad-Adenauer-Stiftung 2015). While she invokes this vision to anticipate and counter the racialised fears of her critics, she simultaneously stirs them by alluding to Orientalist discourses that position migrants as particularly misogynistic and homophobic (e.g. Puar 2007, 2013; Farris 2017).

The affective bordering inherent in such rhetoric becomes even more clear when Merkel adds 'whoever seeks refuge with us, needs to respect our laws, values, and traditions', continuing 'to say it crystal clear, our laws are above honour codex, tribal and family rules [...] Multikulti leads to parallel societies and remains a living lie' (Konrad-Adenauer Stiftung 2015: 40). Terms like 'parallel societies', 'honour codex' and 'Multikulti' are all part of the vocabulary of the 'paranoid nationalism' of the far right, based on racialised ideas of who deserves to be part of the nation and who does not. As Alena Lentin (2014) has shown, in contemporary central Europe, it is often the idea of 'culture' as an isolated silo that works as a substitute for discourses of 'race'. Such culturalist discourse works to essentialise difference and blames structural social problems on migratised and racialised minorities without evoking the charge of racism.[4] What begins as a call for a more tolerant and open society ends as a call for tighter rules for integration and assimilation that reproduce racial grammars of deservingness. It is at this point we can see how hope operates as a distributed affective force. Hage (2003) has powerfully shown how hope is best understood as a distributed emotion which, in the context of Australian neoliberalism, easily gets shifted from marginalised and impoverished subjects to middle- and upper-class white citizens as the entitled benefactors of the nation. In the context of the long summer of migration in Germany, we can see a similar dynamic unfold in which hope is distributed away from people on the move to a nation imagined to need protection from them.

While Merkel's '*Wir schaffen das*' rhetoric, consequently, seems to open the 'we' of the nation, it also delineates the idea of a harmonious and homogeneous German nation – a family or *Volk* with concrete values, traditions and laws that need to be defended against migrants troubling its exceptional achievements. Reiterating the need for stricter rules of integration, Merkel continues that 'who seeks refuge and protection with us, has to respect our laws, values and traditions and needs [...] to learn the German language' (Konrad-Adenauer Stiftung 2015: 40). Her calls for integration evoke the political slogan of a *Leitkultur*, the idea of guiding culture that ethnic and religious minorities need to adhere to. As Jana Cattien (2021) argues, the discourse of a German 'Leitkultur' works to target racialised minorities without retreating to concepts of race and is crucially informed by the legacies of European colonialism. Merkel's rhetoric is in danger of reproducing civilisational discourse that reproduces affective borders between exceptional citizens – who have created a country of cultural and economic wonder, sexual and religious tolerance – and migrants at risk of troubling these national achievements. This form of affective bordering works through the ominous 'feel[ing] that the nation's consented-to qualities are shifting away' and recreates an affected bond between the state and its presumably worried national citizenry (Berlant 1998: 287). As a result, the hopes and worries of migrants on their way to Europe are increasingly replaced with the focus on ameliorating the presumable concerns – worries and fears – of the German nation.

Deportations 'with a friendly face'

This shift in affective focus from people on the move to German citizens is evident across most of Merkel's '*Wir schaffen das*' speeches. Merkel's iconic summer speech, for instance, starts with the compassionate appeal to 'situations and fears that refugees have to face, under which we would probably simply collapse' (Bundesregierung 2015: para. 7). Referring to the right of asylum enshrined in the German constitution, she argues that German citizens need to contribute to a 'national task' of helping migrants overcome these difficult situations (2015: para. 13). Yet she then specifies that this 'national task' is about establishing 'who has a high chance of staying' just as much as it is about declaring 'who has nearly no chance of remaining with us' (2015: para. 20) – suggesting that since Germany has a humanitarian duty to help refugees, their numbers need to be reduced. Similarly, in her talk before the CDU delegation, Merkel insists that 'we also need to focus on the people's worries, including the concerns we have succinctly expressed by stating that even a strong country like Germany is ultimately overwhelmed by such a large number of refugees' and declares 'that is why we want to and will reduce the numbers of refugees noticeably' (Konrad-Adenauer-Stiftung 2015: 30). She argues that since Germany has a humanitarian duty to help refugees, their numbers need to be reduced. Centring the presumed emotional concerns of citizens, we can see here how the state operates as a key node for the redistribution of hope. In one moment, '*Wir schaffen das*' stands for the hopeful humanitarian act of alleviating the hardship of migrants; in the next, it encompasses the securitisation of borders based on alleviating the presumable worries and hardship of national citizens.

The redistribution of hope is even more tangible in Merkel's discussion of the necessity for deportations. Clarifying her stance on deportations, she reminds the audience at the CDU party conference that 'asylum seekers need to stay in reception centres for up to six months, if they come from secure sending countries … so that at the end of their trials they can be better repatriated if their asylum cases are denied' (Konrad-Adenauer-Stiftung 2015: 32). Arguing that deportations constitute the enforcement of an asylum system implemented for the protection of the most vulnerable, she suggests that we 'can also do this with a friendly face' (Konrad-Adenauer-Stiftung

2015). Merkel's invocation of deportations 'with a friendly face' points to the securitising underside of humanitarianism. It is the articulation and production of the 'humanitarian border' in which humanitarian efforts do not necessarily resist but often work hand in hand with the securitising logics of migration control, separating the deserving few from the undeserving many (Walters 2010; Ticktin 2016; Pallister-Wilkins 2022). Deportations in this logic of affective bordering become framed as caring acts that, as Miriam Ticktin (2011) has similarly shown in her analysis of French deportations of the *sans-papiers*, are not committed in opposition to but in the name of protecting a more just and humane future.

Merkel further ties this humanitarian logic to the economic benefits that migration promises to bring for Germany. Reminding the audience that any 'country profits from successful immigration', she argues that 'no other country needs Schengen as much as Germany' (Konrad-Adenauer-Siftung 2015: 34, 40) and contends that Germany needs to be open to immigration to stay internationally competitive while warning of the economic burden that unskilled migration might cause. Lurking underneath Merkel's invocation of a universal Kantian imperative is a conditional hospitality that splits deserving from undeserving migrants according to their economic contribution to the nation (Holzberg, Kolbe and Zaborowski 2018). This conditional hospitality is structured by a double imperative: while the right of refuge is universal, there also needs to be some preconditions and limitation on who can be granted residence in the first place. These limitations are structured not only by culturalist discourses that declare the end of multiculturalism but also by material considerations that measure migrants according to their worth to the national economy. It is here that affective bordering as a key technology of the contemporary workings of racial capitalism comes to the forefront (Walia 2021; De Genova 2023).

In line with the politics of the 'humanitarian border' she invokes, already in August 2015, Merkel declared a list of policies that would need to be implemented so that Germany could fulfil its 'humanitarian duty'. Within this list, she names assistance measures – from more funding for municipalities to increased investment in social housing – yet mainly calls for policies of border securitisation. These securitising policies included implementing national procedures for making deportations a priority, changing financial support for asylum seekers to non-cash benefits and the suspension of family reunifications. Also included were foreign policies such as declaring the countries of the West Balkans safe, implementing a refugee deal with Turkey, and expanding Europe's outer border controls through border police and coastal guards (Konrad-Adenauer-Stiftung 2015: 31–34). In later speeches, Merkel would confidently assert that, thanks to international policies such as the refugee deal with Turkey and the closing of the Balkan route, 'less and less people are coming to us' ('Im Wortlaut': 1). Rather than constituting a diversion tactic or position that contradicts her humanitarian stand, the humanitarian and securitising elements of Merkel's approach are mutually reinforcing. It is a convergence that she never conceals and that her fellow party-member Guido Wolf referred to as 'two sides of the same coin' when introducing her in his welcome speech at the CDU delegation (Konrad-Adenauer-Stiftung 2015: 17).[5]

Such politics of humanitarian securitisation offer hope to migrants while simultaneously eroding the material and ideological ground that such hope is built on. This dynamic was further illustrated when, in summer 2016, Merkel would declare that she 'would prefer not to repeat ['*Wir schaffen das*']' as some people 'feel provoked by it' ('Im Wortlaut' 2016: 1) and replaced her slogan with the statement that 'Germany will remain Germany – with everything that we love and hold dear about it' (Braun and Roll 2016: 1). We could read this evolution of '*Wir schaffen das*' from a humanitarian to an increasingly securitising mantra as the result of the increasingly right-wing nationalist context in Germany and the EU that Merkel had to navigate. However, it also points to the limits of a nationalist invocation of hope in face in the context of escalating global inequalities and highlights how the Kantian appeal to hope as an act of establishing universal laws of morality embedded in universal civil rights falters as long as those rights are tied to citizenship. As Hannah Arendt (1973) has pointed out, the system of civil rights is based on the exclusion of those who fall outside of the logic of the Westphalian nation-state order: the stateless, the undocumented and precarious migrants with no nation (able or willing) to uphold their rights. '*Wir schaffen das*' redistributes hope along those lines to those who are historically assumed to be the subjects of hope: national, mostly white, citizens as the promised benefactors of the nation. In contrast, even as they seem to be the benefitting subjects, migrants, positioned as racialised strangers – pitiful yet suspicious – are the first to be materially, as well as ideologically, cut out from hope's promise of futurity.

This is not to say that Merkel's policies made no difference to the openly hostile and illiberal rhetoric and policy of European governments in countries like Poland or Hungary. Yet it does point to a wider cruel optimism – the hopeful attachment to an object that stands in the way of one's own flourishing – about the humanitarian border in liberal democracies in Europe today. Whereas Berlant (2011) has identified the objects of cruel optimism in the worn-out fantasies of the 'good life' embodied in the romantic couple, the nuclear family and the nation, we can see a similar attachment operate in relation to the humanitarian border. Here the hope is directed to the fantasy of a just or at least less violent border regime – one that successfully filters deserving from undeserving migrants, while assisting those in need.

This cruel optimism is not merely confined to Germany but can be observed across the EU and Western liberal democracies more generally, where the idea that more humane borders will be the answer to structural forms of structural inequality and racial domination remains a key tenet of liberal migration and border politics (Ticktin 2016). The cruel underside to this form of hope is that the humanitarian border does not counteract but results in more violence and suffering (Pallister-Wilkins 2022). For the humanitarian border to remain an object of hope, escalating global inequalities born from colonial histories, the ongoing realities of racism in Germany and the murderous violence of the European border regime itself need to remain repressed and erased from consideration.

This raises the question of what alternative invocations of hope there are that reach beyond the horizon of the humanitarian border. As José Muñoz's (2009) work on Erich Bloch reminds us, studying hope cannot stop at identifying cruel re-attachment. The study and cultivation of hope is not just an analytical but a political problem, as its absence is easily filled by the nationalist authoritarian positions (a process Bloch himself observed during the rise of fascism in Europe in the 1930s). Instead of just focusing on the 'cold stream' of dissecting and exposing social structures and systems of power, critical work on affect also needs to engage the 'warm stream' of how utopian desires are enacted in the everyday life of concrete utopias (Bloch 1954: 209). Given that Merkel's statement is built upon a caring gesture of hospitality and solidarity, I want to channel this Blochian spirit to examine what an invocation of '*Wir schaffen das*' might look like that does not end up folding back into the biopolitical regime of the humanitarian border. After all, in the early days of the long summer of migration, '*Wir schaffen das*' was not only a political slogan but also, at least partly, also a lived reality enacted by migrants and solidarity actors on their way to Germany.

The March of Hope

When Merkel stepped in front of the cameras for her summer speech, large groups of migrants had already made their way from Turkey through Greece and via the Balkan route towards Germany. Since the Balkan route had for several months provided a relatively safe and invisible path towards Central Europe, at the end of August the Hungarian government put an end to this. As the first Schengen country in the south-east, Hungary started barring migrants from boarding trains in Budapest and tried to forcibly relocate them to refugee camps instead. As a result, several thousand migrants were stuck at Keleti station in Budapest. Within days of Merkel's original '*Wir schaffen das*' speech, a number of migrants opted for a simple yet effective plan: they would walk to Germany and Austria on foot (Kasparek and Speer 2015). The march, which was joined by several thousand people, became known as the March of Hope.

While the March of Hope was born in relation to Merkel's humanitarian politics of '*Wir schaffen das*', the march shifts the focus from the 'we' of the nation-state to collectives of people moving in the face of adversity. Those who so often are denied the right to the public – migrants, the undocumented and the stateless – enacted what Butler (2015: 11) calls the 'right to appear that asserts and instates the body in the midst of the political field'. Probably the most dominant articulation of hope in this public appearance emerged in relation to the right to asylum. As Kasparek and Speer (2015) document in their accounts of the March of Hope, many people made their way over the border after the information spread that Syrian migrants might be granted asylum in Germany. Most news stories focused on this aspect of the March of Hope and presented the movement in line with Merkel's policies. Their stories were accompanied by the now iconic image of an injured man on crutches leading a migrant march on a highway towards Germany while carrying an image of Merkel ('Zug der Verzweifelten' 2015). Other images showed young men heading marches over the highways of Hungary and Austria while waving EU flags ('Zug der Verzweifelten' 2015). In such media stories, political institutions like the EU and German government upholding the right to asylum emerged as the objects of hope.

Other representations of the March of Hope focused on more radical political demands. Activist migrant and migrant solidarity blogs and media outlets demanded not only the right to asylum but also the 'right to move' ('March of Hope' 2015). Tweets, stories and images of the marches shared by migrant solidarity organisations were occasionally accompanied by hashtags such as #overcomingthefortress and #openborders and called for an overhaul of restrictive EU policies ('March of Hope' 2015). Within these accounts, hope was constructed through acts of defiance that resist the restrictive border policies of the EU. Crossing the border between Hungary and Austria, a border that for most EU citizens is no longer a boundary, people on the move question the regimes of (im)mobility that allow some bodies to cross freely while denying others this possibility. The unequal distribution of hope was laid bare, substituted by the egalitarian demand for redistributing the right to move, including to people beyond the border.

What gets lost in both the mainstream and the more outright activist interpretation of the March of Hope, however, are the quiet frequencies of people simply moving, waiting, eating or resting. As Muñoz (2009: 91) points out, it is often these 'quotidian gestures [that are] laden with potentiality'. We get a sense of such quotidian gestures in the genre of 'refugee selfies'. Smiling into the camera refugees positioned themselves in front of scenic views like that of the bridge over the Danube in Budapest, took group photos while having food breaks, or simply took pictures of each other walking along the highways into Germany. Images like these evoked the most furious public reactions in the German media debate and led to people being labelled 'economic migrants' in opposition to 'real refugees' who would never have access to technologies of the selfie (Madörin 2021). Given these reactions, scholars have conceptualised the refugee selfie both as a technology of symbolic bordering (Chouliaraki 2017) and an act of self-presentation (Risam 2018) that can reverse the gaze and hold the state accountable through literal face-to-face encounters – such as in the now iconic selfies that migrants took with Merkel upon arrival in Germany. Most importantly, however, these photos portray the wrong affective comportment. The seemingly careless act of smiling into the camera troubles the imperative of suffering that needs to be conveyed for people to be read as deserving refugees. Rather, in these images, movement becomes reframed as an act of travelling, an arduous journey that nevertheless also entails moments of pleasure, excitement and laughter (see also Bayramoğlu 2023).

Such selfies extend the focus of hope to the more complex and less spectacular forms of living life in conditions of impossibility. In the following section, I want to suggest that it is these less spectacular registers that gesture beyond the cruel optimism of humanitarian border. In other words, while hope is clearly articulated in the call for the right to asylum and the more outright resistance to border violence, it primarily emerges in the infrastructures of care and hospitality that enable this form of movement to be enacted in the first place. In developing this argument, I am building on the rich sociological work that has shown the importance of care and horizontal assistance in the March of Hope (Speer and Kasparek 2015; Kallius, Monterescu and Rajaram 2016) and the wider welcome initiatives that were developed in Germany during the summer of 2015 (Hamann and Karakayali 2016; Fleischmann and Steinhilper 2017).

The mobile commons

The March of Hope only came about through the material and affective infrastructures of assistance, exchange and sharing that migrants created on their way to Europe. Dimitris Papadopoulos and Vassilis Tsianos (2013: 192) call these forms of self-woven infrastructure the 'mobile commons', defined as 'resources and paths for surviving the pressures of sovereignty and capitalist exploitation'. They suggest that mobile commons are 'neither private nor public, neither state-owned nor part of civil society; rather [they] exist to the extent that people share [them] and generate [them] as they are mobile and when they arrive somewhere' (2013: 190). The mobile commons include invisible knowledges of mobility and informal economies and entail the creation of new communities of justice and politics of care (2013: 191). Here relations of sharing and assistance were created between groups of people who often did not know each other before so that as many people as possible could participate in the movement.

As Annastiina Kallius, Daniel Monterescu and Prem Kumar Rajaram (2016: 9) point out in their ethnographic account of the March of Hope, in the summer of 2015 these mobile commons were probably best exemplified in the 'migrant occupation of [parks] and other seemingly neutral nonplaces, such as highways … where people forged horizontal political solidarities'. Public parks 'evolved into hubs of habitation, smuggling, and communicative action', where people on the move shared food and shelter and exchanged maps and resources about the safest and easiest routes through the Balkans and over the border to Germany (Kallius, Monterescu and Rajaram 2016: 9). Such temporary migrant squats might best be understood as 'essential parts in the "corridors of solidarity" that are being created throughout Europe, where grassroots social movements engaged in anti-racist, anarchist and anti-authoritarian politics coalesce with migrants in devising non-institutional responses to the violence of border regimes' (Dadusc, Grazioli and Martínez 2019: 521). In these spaces, migrants excluded from political membership in the nation enact practices of care and horizontal assistance as the ground from which collective political action and hope for a better future can be generated.

This is not to say that the mobile commons are free of racialised tensions and gendered divisions of labour. Many of the people on the move to Europe organised along national lines and tensions between different ethnic and religious groups erupted at different points in their movement (Kallius, Monterescu and Rajaram 2016). In her critique of idealised invocations of the mobile commons, Carla Angulo-Pasel (2018) further points out how most of the reproductive and emotional labour during migrants' travel, especially childcare, continues to be done by women. Moreover, these spontaneous infrastructures can put women, queer and trans people at increased risk of violence and abuse. Nevertheless, in the mobile commons, there are ruptures in traditional relations of care that separate care as a private endeavour from public political action and engender new affiliations and solidarities. As Maria Puig de la Bellacasa (2017: 58) suggests, a feminist attention to care is a crucial part of the project of developing hope through 'a more radically democratic way of listening to neglected things'. It shows how seemingly uneventful practices of everyday survival carry the seeds for transformative political projects.

(2016: 28)

Acts of public mourning

A revealing example of the politics of care during the March of Hope was the vigil that migrants held before the march at the main train station in Budapest. After 71 people died in a truck that tried to cross over to Austria on 27 August, several hundred people came together in front of Budapest railway station. People lit candles and put up a large banner reading: 'Europe your hands are covered in blood'. Even after the official event was over, people kept joining the vigil, including a group of Muslims who started praying and chanting in Pashto and Urdu (Kallius, Monterescu and Rajaram 2016: 28). Migrants here rewrite the parameters of who counts as a subject worthy of mourning (Butler 2000). In doing so, these acts of public mourning operate as acts of communal care in the face of pervasive violence. They provide a sense of solidarity as, while faced with destruction from all sides, collectives of people create the infrastructures that sustain life and care in the face of death and adversity.

What makes these acts of public mourning so powerful is how they break the public/private divide and bring intimate matters of grief and bereavement into the political sphere. Migrants claimed and appropriated public space and refused to comply with the temporalities of emergency that would require them to move on and let go of the dead. Instead, the vigil retains memory by engaging the ongoingness of historical violence in the present. After all, it was at the vigil that daily protests against the state began, demanding that refugees be allowed to cross the border. Christina Sharpe (2016: 33) has described such temporality in relation to Blackness and the histories of transatlantic slavery as 'being in the wake' – a state of being in which 'the past that is not past reappears, always, to rupture the present'. This temporality, she suggests, also applies to the 'current refugee crisis' in which the killing of racially marked bodies cannot be separated from 'the continuation of military and other colonial projects of US/European wealth extraction and immiserating' (2016: 126). Acts of public mourning might be described as 'wake work', in which care is moved away from 'state-imposed regimes of surveillance' and instead enacted laterally (2016: 20). Wake work here also works as a kind of hope work – highlighting how enacting different futures is not about moving onwards from the past but requires staying with the ongoingness of political violence for subjects marked and produced by its histories.

This temporality of the wake troubles Merkel's temporal logics of hope based in states of emergency. Stating that 'we are all shocked by the awful news', Merkel's government framed the deaths of migrants in the truck in Austria, like the 'refugee crisis' overall, as a sudden state of emergency to be solved through humanitarian securitisation – assisting migrants in need while decreasing future migration through tightening migration control (Bundesregierung 2015). On the contrary, as Ticktin (2016: 268) suggests, the act of public mourning staged by migrants 'insists on going beyond the temporality of emergency to include the haunting of the dead, and to demand accountability and responsibility'. It does not cut off ongoing histories of violence through narratives of exceptional national atonement but, in Avery Gordon's (1997: 195) words, brings the 'ghostly matters' of border violence and postcolonial inequalities to the centre of public attention. Doing so, it highlights 'the living effects, seething and lingering, of what seems over and done with, the endings that are not over' (1997: 195). Forms of backward-looking affects like mourning and grief do not emerge as antidotes but as part and parcel of an invocation of hope that insists that a different world is only possible if we care for the wounds of the past.

This invocation of hope as a backward-looking affect also operates in the way the March of Hope engages with the geopolitical contexts that people are fleeing from. Rather than disconnecting connected histories and flattening complex transnational entanglements, many migrants based their demands in more complex engagements with the questions of global inequality and the unfolding wars and destitution in the Middle East and Northern Africa. Speer and Kasparek (2015) recall that one of the 'the most beautiful aspect[s of the March] is the fact that along with the refugees from Syria, the original power and hope of the Arab Spring has come to Europe for the second time and challenged its boundaries' and suggest that 'the rhythm and determination of the slogans that were chanted, for days on end ... seemed strangely familiar' (2015: 1). Syrian civil society organisations participating in the march discussed how 'coming together people can change the European asylum policy', yet they also called for more thorough support of 'those that have not fled yet and instead continue trying to build a future in Syria' (Adopt a Revolution 2015). In actions like these, migrants on the move centred their own stories, narratives and histories and highlighted the complex geopolitical realities cut out from most of the German government's public accounts of the long summer of migration.

Hospitality beyond the humanitarian border

The March of Hope was made possible by two interrelated groups: migrants on their way to and across Europe and European citizens engaged in hospitality actions. According to Kallius, Monterescu and Rajaram (2016: 3), the March of Hope would not have been possible without 'unexpected horizontal solidarities involving private citizens working with migrants, standing with them in their protests, sheltering people, and transporting them to the Western border'. Migrant solidarity organisations in Hungary assisted with legal aid and resources like tents and blankets and provided places to sleep so that 'along their way, the marchers found food and water bottles waiting for them' (Kallius, Monterescu and Rajaram 2016: 3). A variety of civil society organisations further organised car convoys, and the #MarchofHope hashtag was quickly followed by the hashtags #carsforhope and #busesforhope that people from Austria, German and Hungary used to organise private bus and car transport over the Hungarian border. These efforts created pressure on European governments to act. After one day, bus convoys were organised by the German state. Whereas many of the marchers were hesitant about this offer, which had previously resulted in migrants involuntarily being placed in asylum camps, and with the public media attention upon them, they entered the vehicles. In these moments, the humanitarian actions of the state and large NGOs merged with grassroots solidarity actions (Kallius, Monterescu and Rajaram 2016: 3).

Nevertheless, differences between the futures invoked by humanitarianism and the actions of solidarity could be observed. Whereas major humanitarian organisations mainly confined the enactment of hope to charitable action by providing blankets, food and water to migrants and pointing out human rights abuses, the more grassroots organisations like MigSzol Csoport also focused on providing alternative infrastructures of mobility by organising places to sleep, travel routes and the said car convoys. As Kallius, Monterescu and Rajaram (2016: 9) argue, their horizontal solidarities went beyond charitable action constricted by the parameters of the law and instead focused on creating the conditions for collective action that question 'distinctions between citizen and migrant or refugee and the way political agency is constricted'. They suggest that their actions also differed in the organisations' approach towards other marginalised groups within Hungary. Whereas most humanitarian organisations refused to offer assistance to homeless or Sinti and Roma populations within Hungary, groups like MigSzol framed the migrants' struggle and their own as a shared one, united against structural racism and regimes of inequality created by the Orbán regime (Kallius, Monterescu and Rajaram 2016: 7). In the context of ongoing austerity regimes, mobile commons consequently operated as a nexus for rethinking social welfare systems and as meeting points for migrant, labour and anti-austerity efforts. These more holistic visions of hope often overlapped with, but also stood in contrast to, humanitarian actions that primarily focused on the alleviation of the suffering of specific deserving subjects.

Welcome initiatives

Similar dynamics could be identified in the welcome initiatives that sprouted all over Germany and in which thousands of people volunteered to help refugees coming to Germany. Larissa Fleischmann and Elias Steinhilper (2017) have unveiled the 'myth of apolitical volunteering'. They point out that, on one hand, the volunteering work of the 'welcome culture' can reinforce and align itself with the humanitarian securitisation of the border by perpetuating established hierarchies, racial exclusions and discriminatory practices. At the same time, they show that these initiatives also have the potential to challenge and transform the existing migration regime. Given that this was the first time many volunteers had encountered structural forms of inequality and exclusion, such encounters carry the possibility for social transformation, especially 'when volunteers become aware of the powerful myth of "apolitical" help and begin to embed their volunteering activities in a wider context, instead of turning a blind eye to it'. In their work on volunteering and welcome culture, Ulrike Hamann and Serhat Karakayali (2016: 80) come to a similar conclusion, arguing that the volunteering initiatives built in the context of German 'welcome culture' carry 'the potential to enhance reflection and self-observation [as well as] the potential to constitute a space from where resistance and a struggle for rights can emerge'.

This work shows that while welcome solidarity activism overlaps and is easily incorporated into the humanitarian border, it also gestures towards forms of collective organisation that might go beyond it. Examples of hopeful solidarity initiatives could be observed all around Europe, from the migrant squats in Athens (Squire 2018) to collectively organised search and rescue alarm phones in the Mediterranean (Stierl 2015) and sanctuary cities and initiatives in the UK (Bauder 2017). Here relationality is not framed as a threat to be managed and contained but as a potential site for new forms of sociality to emerge. Being part of a mobile commons, most of these infrastructures were, however, temporary. After the media attention had faded and most of the migrants had left Keleti station, the Hungarian government built a fence on its border and Germany pushed the buffer zones of its border further out by declaring Serbia a safe country of residence. As a result, only a few months later, the train station in Budapest resembled a ghostly place, in which only faint traces of the mobilisations of the summer could be identified.

What remains in these traces is what, with Berlant (2016a: 414), can be described as the horizon of 'common infrastructures that absorb the blows of our aggressive need for the world to accommodate us [and that] ... hold out the prospect of a world worth attaching to that's something other than an old hope's bitter echo'. Whereas the humanitarian border invoked in Merkel's rhetoric of '*Wir schaffen das*' harnesses care out of an impetus to reduce suffering while keeping its racialised grammars of deservingness intact, the 'mobile commons' and wider welcome culture initiatives counteract some of these tendencies by rebuilding infrastructures of care beyond biopolitical reason. As such, the March of Hope continues to work as a simple reminder that no one suffers from a lack of care without the social failure to organise such solidarity. More than that, it highlights that such failure is not a biopolitical necessity – the spirit of '*Wir schaffen das*' does not need to fold back into paranoid nationalism and biopolitical control – but rather can also result in a more caring future of mutual assistance and solidarity.

Conclusion

In the novel *Exit West*, Mohsin Hamid (2018) constructs a world in which magic doors appear that enable immediate travel from one geopolitical location to the other. Through this narrative device, he invites us into a world that, if not borderless, is porous; people fleeing from war and destruction find their last possibility of survival in these doors, while others use them for travel and transnational connection. Throwing the international political system into crisis, the magic doors become heavily controlled by Western states and incite political violence. At first it looks like the existence of these doors will usher in war and state-led genocide. Yet a potentially more hopeful political future develops. Collective initiatives pop up in which the people assist each other in constructing new settlements of cohabitation and conviviality, from Lampedusa to the well-off boroughs of West London and the Bay area of the US. Often read as Mohsin Hamid's reflection on the 'refugee crisis', his novel does not depict a utopian vision of perfect harmony yet engages the hopeful idea that in the face of adversity and need, people will create new infrastructures of care, solidarity and the commons.

Examining the Marches of Hope in relation to Merkel's statement of 'We can do this', I have suggested that such a 'spark of hope' could likewise be deciphered in political action during the early days of the long summer of migration. Going beyond the rhetoric and actions of the state, I have shown how the enactment of mobile commons in migrant marches offers glimpses into different practices of care, solidarity and the commons that extend beyond the biopolitical regime of the European border regime. Whereas Merkel's '*Wir schaffen das*' politics engages in practices of affective bordering that redistribute hope away from migrants and towards a nation imagined to be in need of protection from them, migrants reclaim these hopes on their way to and across Europe. Highlighting the temporal dynamics through which they gain their affective power, I have shown how dominant mobilisations of hope work through narratives of exceptional national atonement that erase the transnational entanglements and colonial legacies behind global inequality and racialised border regimes in the first place. In the March of Hope, in turn, we encounter mobilisations of hope that do not cut off but stay with the wounds of the past.

My analysis aims at destabilising the cruel optimistic attachment to the humanitarian border that saturates liberal migration politics across Europe. Instead, I have channelled a Blochian spirit to decipher sparks of hope in the everyday struggles of collective organisation and living life in the face of adversity. Such acts, I have suggested, open the perspective to a horizon of hope beyond the humanitarian border – a horizon in which the relationality of social life is not framed through threat and biopolitical control but in which collective infrastructures are valued as enabling life to flourish and persist. Mobile comments and welcome culture initiatives are not without racialised conflicts and gendered injustices but, nevertheless, they gesture beyond biopolitical regimes of deservingness in which life is enabled for some at the expense of others. If hope, however, is at least partly generated through the relational encounter across social difference, the question remains: what affective forces can generate such encounter? With this question in mind, I turn to the next chapter, which examines the promise of empathy as the other key affect that was invoked in the 'welcome culture' of the early summer of 2015.

Notes

1 While its relevance continues to be debated in parliament, media and civil society today, the sentence was first uttered by Merkel's coalition partner and vice-chancellor Sigmar Gabriel from the SPD, who coined it in an online speech after visiting a refugee shelter. He stated 'peace, humanity, solidarity, justice: these are European values. Now we have to prove them. I am sure we can do this!' ('Flüchtlinge' 2015). The slogan, however, only became known and picked up as a national slogan when Merkel used it as the heart piece in her now iconic summer speech.

2 Next to the more sociological work that I review here, there is a wide-ranging body of literature that takes Bloch's theories as an inspiration in literary studies. For formative works in literary utopian studies, see Krishnan Kumar (1987), Ruth Levitas (2010) and Fredric Jameson (2005). For a discussion of the history of utopian studies in literary studies, see Peter Fitting (2009).

3 Germany's first citizenship laws were introduced during the German Empire in 1913. To curb fears of racial intermixing in the German colonies of West and East Africa, these laws defined citizenship according to one's bloodline. These *jus sanguinis* laws were reinstalled in the post-war period after the Nuremburg laws of the Nazis were abolished, and effectively they were only changed in 2000 (El-Tayeb 1999; Campt 2005). For a more thorough discussion of this history and how it reverberates in the political present, see Chapter 3 on anger.

4 The attack on 'Multikulti' has long been part of Merkel's repertoire since she infamously declared in 2010 that 'Multikulti has failed utterly'. Declaring the death of multiculturalism not only showed a clear disdain for granting minority rights to religious minorities and communities of colour in Germany but was also rather ironic given that, at the time, Germany had implemented almost none of the policies associated with multicultural politics (Kymlicka 2012: 17).

5 At the time, Guido Wolf was the head of the CDU in Baden-Württemberg and got to give the short welcome address before Merkel's speech. He stated that 'self-evidently, we have a humanitarian responsibility for those coming here who are politically persecuted in their home country ... yet it is also clear – and that is the signal of this party convention: we want the refugee flows that developed over the last months to be clearly reduced, because we cannot overwhelm the people in our communities. This is part of taking political responsibility: these are two sides of the same coin' (Konrad-Adenauer-Stiftung 2015: 17).

2

Empathy: affective solidarity and the limits of German welcome culture

Introduction

When in September 2015 the European border regime collapsed for a moment and Angela Merkel gave her famous '*Wir schaffen das*' speech, international news outlets like the BBC talked of a German nation 'driven by empathy' (Hill 2015). Pictures of people waiting at train stations in cities like Munich, Hamburg and Berlin, welcoming asylum-seekers with banners, food and clothes, circulated around the world, and public commentators heralded the reaction of the German state and civil society as a crucial defence of human rights and basic humanitarianism in the face of anti-migrant nationalism in Europe. Acknowledging the efforts made in civil society, some critics on the left questioned this perspective. They warned of 'fake' empathy that worked as a smoke screen to allow the government to clean their reputation after imposing austerity measures onto Greece and other Southern European states, helped to hide the growing racism and hostility in the country and enabled the government to simultaneously tighten the asylum law. Others posited that it was not actual empathy but cold economic rationality that was the real reason behind allowing new labour power into an ageing German society. What remained shared among all these accounts, however, was that 'real' empathy would be the adequate and desired answer to the 'refugee crisis'.

Empathy after all has long been the object of hope in across Western thought and politics. Best described as feeling with someone, or the 'affective act of seeing from someone's perspective' (Pedwell 2014a: 6), empathy is often seen as an affective capability 'that has the power both to transform our own lives and to bring about fundamental change' (Krznaric 2015: ix). It has been called the 'glue that holds civil society together' and 'the bedrock of global intercultural relations' (Calloway-Thomas 2010: 7). Most work on empathy, consequently, laments a 'compassion fatigue' in contemporary societies and focuses on how to nurture, enhance and cultivate more compassionate forms of feeling, acting and relating to each other (Moeller 2002;

Höijer 2004).[1] In border and migration and politics specifically, scholars and practitioners have focused on enhancing empathy towards people arriving in Europe, with humanitarian campaigns and images portraying their suffering, stories and travelogues that narrate migrants' border crossings, and even virtual reality experiences that put the spectator in the migrants' position (Irom 2018). The imperative to feel for others in contemporary border politics has not remained without critiques (Fassin 2011; Ticktin 2011; Sirriyeh 2018), yet it remains a – if not *the* – key affective mode for countering nationalist, racist and right-wing responses to migration.

In this chapter, I want to critically unpack and interrogate this promise of empathy. More concretely, I examine what different invocations of empathy in the public sphere (can) do in the context of the European border regime by analysing how empathy is invoked and constructed during the emergence of a new German *Willkommenskultur*, I will do so by analysing how empathy is envisioned in three different visual scenes: first, I examine the agglomeration of images of suffering represented in mainstream media, best captured by the now iconic image of Alan Kurdi, the three-year-old Kurdish boy from Syria who was photographed washed ashore dead on the beach in Turkey, which filled national and international news headlines throughout the summer of 2015. Second, I analyse migrant travelogues and self-made documentary films that were edited out of snippets that people shot with their cell phones while fleeing situations of war and deprivation and that were shown at film festivals and on national television. And third, I turn to hunger strikes that were staged by asylum seekers in Germany in the same period yet that received relatively scant public attention.

Setting this analysis in dialogue with queer feminist theories of empathy, I suggest that in the context of the European border regime, empathy might stand in the way of its own promise. Whereas the dominant public reaction to the image of Alan Kurdi re-inscribes power hierarchies through a victimising subject–object relation, migrant travelogues seem to engage in a more emancipatory subject-to-subject dialogue, opening space for a more complex engagement with power, difference and agency. Pointing out how both constructions of empathy work through racial grammars of deservingness, I contend that their differentiation is more slippery than it seems as they are geared towards national recognition and require gratitude and assimilation as the right affective response to receiving the 'gift' of empathy. In a last step, I thus turn to the abject, which necessarily needs to be cut out from these scenes of empathetic identification – expressed in protest actions such as hunger strikes – to suggest a different form of affective solidarity. This form of affective solidarity keeps the political agency with the hunger-striking subject and, rather than emerging through feeling for or with the starving subject, arises out of discomfort and a shared concern about the racialised violence produced by regimes of global inequality.

'Good' and 'bad' empathy

While empathy has become a central concern in social and political theory more generally, arguably the most intricate theoretical discussions of empathy have been developed in queer feminist scholarship. Scholars as diverse as Lauren Berlant, Saidiya Hartman, Patricia Hill Collins, Clare Hemmings, Martha Nussbaum, Carolyn Pedwell, Elizabeth Spelman and Miriam Ticktin have turned their attention to the affective modes of empathy and compassion so key to questions of intersubjectivity. If a potential common concern among different feminist scholars is how processes of social separation, marginalisation and dehumanisation work through axes of difference like gender, race, sexuality and class, empathy focused on feeling for or with others might be seen as a force that can help to alleviate this dynamic. If in a Butlerian (Butler 2009) vein, for instance, we understand the problem of structural violence and marginalisation to work through processes by which lives become grievable or not, a focus on empathy might be seen as the logical antidote that would expand the sphere of affective concern to subjects that were otherwise excluded from it. As such empathy is often discussed in close relationship to debates around relationality, care and solidarity and is explored as a potential force for developing ethical relations to others.

Empathy in feminist debates, however, is as much a site of promise as it is of critique. Therein, the critique of empathy conglomerates around three interrelated axes of contention: (1) power, (2) difference and (3) action. Firstly, queer feminist scholars point out that empathy rather than undoing can keep power inequalities intact. As Lauren Berlant (2004: 4) has posited, empathy, after all, 'is a term denoting privilege: the sufferer is *over there*' whereas the observer has the *power* to decide whether and how to help or not. Rather than breaking or transforming unequal power relations, empathy often works to reinstall these. It can buy into victimising discourses that further disenfranchise the receiver of empathy and deny their agency (see also Rai 2002; Ticktin 2011).

Secondly, empathic identification can clad over, or erase, crucial forms of *difference*. Empathy can easily appropriate the experience of others. Rather than respecting the boundaries between self and other, empathy can consume the other by projecting one's own feelings and desires onto the other. Saidiya Hartman (2022: 18–19) has called this the 'difficulty and slipperiness of empathy' and suggested that it often 'fails to expand the space of the other but merely places the self in its stead'. As such, compassionate forms of intersubjectivity often erase racialised, gendered and other differences of location that require significant work to be addressed rather than a sentimental form of affective identification that muddles them together (see also Code 1994; Nakamura 2020).

Thirdly, scholars point to the problem of *action* within the politics of empathy. Empathy can often distract or forestall political action by engendering individual responses to problems that are structurally created. As Carolyn Pedwell (2014b) has suggested, empathy can go hand in hand with a 'long articulated desire to explain social and geo-political conflict and inequity as the outcome of deficient cross-cultural understanding (rather than pervading structures of global inequality)' (para. 13). As such, empathy can work as a privatising force that, rather than directing action at structures of inequality and oppression, can become a self-referential endpoint in itself (see also Spelman 1998; Ahmed 2014).

Responding to such critiques, one could suggest that 'this is a form of lazy and false empathy in which we take the other's place' (Dean 2004: 96), instead of a more complex engagement with difference in which we work through, rather than plaster over, differences in power and positionality. Martha Nussbaum (1996), for instance, holds that most critiques of empathy ultimately critique it for being not encompassing enough. From this perspective, most critiques are not really critiques of empathy itself, but rather calls for more expansive forms of empathy. As such scholars have suggested that we need to keep empathy open as an ambivalent affective force. Whereas it can go hand in hand with racialised and gendered forms of oppression, it can likewise open new paths of solidarity and political action (Hill Collins 1993; Berlant 2004; Pedwell 2014).

As Clare Hemmings (2011: 200) identifies, most scholars within feminist research have thus made a split between 'good' and 'bad' empathy. This split often corresponds to conceptual separations between 'good' empathy or compassion as the more generic ability to feel with someone else's perspective, and 'bad' pity or sympathy as a more patronising concern for the pain of others – yet it is not limited to such distinction. Whereas bad empathy is often described as a form of subject–object relation that consumes the other and leads to privatised sentimentality, good empathy is seen as a subject-to-subject engagement in which difference is worked through rather than consumed and that redirects collective action towards changing social structures of violence and inequality. These discussions are mirrored in border and migration scholarship where scholars like Ala Sirriyeh (2018: 20) suggest that the 'pursuit and implementation of alternative models of compassion that are grounded in solidarity, rather than hierarchical power relations, offer more promising prospects for social justice'. What, however, remains open in such discussions is to what extent these forms of empathetic engagement can actually be separated out from each other. Are they really different forms of affective relationality, or do they describe co-constitutive modes of feeling with or for the other?

What, furthermore, often gets sidelined in discussions of (good and bad) empathy is the unreliability of empathy. As one of probably the most ardent critics of empathy, Hannah Arendt (1977: 65), points out, 'history tells us that it is by no means a matter of course for the spectacle of misery to move men to pity'. Her insight is as simple as it is pervasive. Empathy cannot be assumed but needs to be actively created, invoked and invited. Arendt takes this argument as a point to deny empathy (as well as emotions more generally) as an unreliable guide to social justice that impedes proper, rational action in political life. As spelled out in the introduction, I disagree with Arendt's demarcation of the political as an ideal space devoid of affect, yet her argument points us to the question of failed empathy. If empathy always carries the potentiality of staying mute and irresponsive, this muteness haunts the scene of empathy. Arendt's insight pushes us to a closer investigation into the conditions that allow empathy to emerge and be read as such in the first place. Rather than merely asking whether particular scenes evoke empathy or not, it brings attention to the larger discourses, tropes, and genres that empathy needs to comply with in order to unleash its affective pull.

In approaching the visual economy of this moment, I consequently do not try to make a judgement on the actual effect specific forms of representation have (e.g. did they actually change social and political decisions?), or their moral value (e.g. are they ethically valuable representations of suffering or not?). Instead, I ask what they reveal about how empathy is articulated, scripted and invoked within contemporary figurations of suffering. What are the narratives through which empathy develops its affective pull within these scenes? How do these relate to and potentially challenge larger discourses and practices of border securitisation? And what does this tell us about dominant articulations of empathy in the historical present?

The tragedy of Alan Kurdi

Filling global headlines, social media pages and news outlets in the summer of 2015, the image of Alan Kurdi has become the iconic photograph of the so-called 'refugee crisis'. *Time Magazine* listed it as one of the most influential photos of all time and the BBC went so far as to affirm that 'it was one of those moments when the whole world seemed to care' (Devichand 2016). Murals were painted with Kurdi's image, online petitions for better humanitarian protections were signed and a rescue boat in the Mediterranean was named in his honour. In Germany, the publication of the image concurred with Merkel's decision to defer the Dublin conventions and grant asylum to

Syrian refugees so that its publication was seen as a crucial event in generating a new 'welcome culture' in Germany. Congruently, the image constitutes the most prominent representation of what, with Lilie Chouliaraki (2006), I call the 'theatre of suffering' that unfolded in the media debate around the long summer of migration.

The photograph itself depicts the image of a young boy in a red T-shirt and blue trousers. His body is motionless, his lower body on his knees; he is lying headfirst in the waves. The image works its brutal effect through the portrayal of extreme violence in all its mundanity – if it wasn't for the location of his body in the waves, we might think he was sleeping. I remember the first time I saw the image at a train station in London. It was printed on a free copy of the *Metro* reading: 'Europe could not save him'. Overwhelmed by the sheer gravity of violence depicted on the front cover, I had to stop for a moment. I was hit by a wave of pain about the death of the unknown child I was presented with and for having allowed this violent death to happen. In this act of identification, I became a direct agent in the narrative presented by the tabloid – Europe became me, and I became Europe. And I was not the only one. A group of people had clustered around the newspaper pile and looked at the image with tangible concern. How can we understand the collective affective pull the image created in this moment?

In most media stories of the image, Kurdi's death was framed as 'failure of Europe' or the 'failure of humanity', with hashtags like #humanitywashedashore on social media being the most popular. In most of these, the image was described as the symbol for the 'humanitarian tragedy' of the refugee crisis (e.g. Bröcker 2015). I want to suggest that the choice of these words is not coincidental but highlights the genre through which empathy is invoked in these representations: *tragedy*. As Spelman (1998: 35) points out, tragedy forms a privileged genre through which scenes of empathy become narrated. She states that 'suffering that deserves to be tragic is noteworthy, in some sense exemplary, its threatening, chaotic horribleness diluted to some manageable degree by its riveting intelligibility'. Therein, she defines three main characteristics of tragedy. Firstly, tragedy describes the fate of a respectable, innocent person falling into misfortune. Secondly, the forces that have led to this misfortune are larger and outside of the control of the person or anyone else involved in the tragedy. And, thirdly, the tragic aims at a sense of catharsis through which the spectator or witness comes to reorient their approach to the world.

In the case of the image of Alan Kurdi, the first characteristic of tragedy derives its emotional force through the figure of the child as a symbol of innocence. In several news stories, Alan Kurdi's photo was juxtaposed with earlier images of him playing with his sibling or laughing into the camera next to a giant teddy bear. Several news stories further reported on the story of Alan Kurdi and his family trying to flee Syria to join their other family members in Canada via Europe after their visa was denied by the Canadian state, and focused on the pain that his family felt after his and his mother's death (Faller 2016). Haunted by the image of him smiling as a little boy, within these representational constellations, Alan Kurdi's body comes to stand in for the paradigmatic tragedy of an innocent life lost. It stands in a larger tradition of humanitarian images in which it falls to the figure of the child to be the face of suffering – ranging from starving children on development aid campaigns to anti-war iconographies like the picture of Phan Thi Kim Phuc fleeing from napalm attacks in South Vietnam or Sharbat Gula holding the gaze of the camera from an Afghan refugee camp in Pakistan. These visual representations tap into the first characteristic of the genre of tragedy in which childhood, as a category untouched by the corruption of social and political life, comes to signify innocence (Castañeda 2002; Ticktin 2017).

The parental duty of care

The figure of the innocent child activated an ethics of parental care. Media ethicist Alexander Filipović (2015: 1) poignantly recounts the power of the image by describing how he 'had tears in (his) eyes. Imagining that this could have been my son – just the idea is unbearable'. This parental response was mirrored in political speeches by figures like David Cameron, who asserted that 'as a father, I felt deeply moved by the sight of that young boy on a beach in Turkey' (Dathan 2015: 1), and memes on social media which showed Alan Kurdi in the safety of a cot reading 'this is how it should have ended' (Olesen 2018: 665). As Chouliaraki and Tijana Stolić (2017: 1168) point out, it was this sense of a failure of parental care in relation to the image of Alan Kurdi 'that challenged the Western self-description of the caring parent and shifted the news narrative of the "crisis" towards sentimental pity'. Empathy in this scene consequently did not work through an act of direct identification or feeling the same as a form of 'emotional equivalence' (Coplan and Goldie 2011), but through the affective identification with his family.[2]

Empathy in the reaction to the image of Alan Kurdi consequently was expressed and invoked through an imagined form of kinship. Drawing on the philosophy of the Stoics, Nussbaum (1996: 48) has suggested that such a logic of kinship constitutes the power and challenge of empathy by arguing that 'each of us lives in a set of concentric circles – the nearest being one's own body, the furthest being the entire universe of human beings'. She presents these concentric circles – that extend from oneself to the family, to the community, to the nation, to the world – as an universalist ontology of how empathy operates and argues that 'the task of moral development is to move the circles progressively closer and closer to the centre, so that one's parents become like oneself, one's other relatives like one's parents, strangers like relatives, and so forth' (Nussbaum 1996). Nussbaum's moral imperative relies on an essentialist ontology that affirms these concentric circles as universalist moral grammars of empathy. From a more sociological perspective, these conscription circles might better be understood as an inscription of social norms into the texture of affective life. Rather than as a fixed ontology, we might better conceptualise them as a heteronormative and racialised cultural imperatives of feeling – a 'feeling rule' (Hochschild 1979: 551) – that demarcates the lines through which affect ought to work. Whereas identification with 'strangers' is seen as suspicious, the idea of care for your family is a powerful cultural frame that we are all expected to (and mostly do) adhere to.

In the case of Alan Kurdi, the emotional template of the family works through contradictory forms of racialisation. One the one hand, the affective identification with Alan Kurdi is made more manageable for white Western audiences through the ambiguity of 'race' in the visual frame (Ibrahim 2018). As Nadine El-Enany (2016: 13) argues, it was partly 'the innocence evoked by the body of a light-skinned child that enabled the temporary, fleeting awakening among white Europeans to a refugee movement that long-preceded the media spotlight on that photo'. On the other hand, the parental relation of care that calls upon the spectator to act is further intensified through longstanding forms of racialised infantilisation in the European public sphere. Whereas Syria, as the wider Middle East, is commonly represented as a sphere of inability and helplessness, in headlines like 'Europe could not save him', Europe was imagined as the actor that, having failed its parental duty, is asked to offer a helping hand to refugees in need. The legacies of such infantilisation are steeped in colonial histories that have long framed the imperative to help as the 'white man's burden' – constructing agency as the locus of white Europeans, while framing colonial subjects as childlike people unable to help themselves (Malkki 2010; Fanon 2017 [1952]; Mills and Lefrançois 2018).

The figure who steps in to fulfil this failed parental duty of care in the image is a policeman who comes to pick up the body of Alan Kurdi and who features prominently in most publications on the death of Alan Kurdi. Represented in the figure of the police, it is the state that comes to take on the paternal and benevolent role of the saviour. We can see how in this conflation the two affect-charged institutions of the family and state merge into one powerful affective assemblage of *Vaterstaat* (father-state), who, while having failed his duty of care, emerges as the key figure of identification (see also Adler-Nissen, Andersen and Hansen 2020). This attachment, however, seems to be an unstable one given that the policeman, Mehmet Ciplan, is Turkish. Commonly positioned as both 'ally' and 'other' of Europe, the location of Turkey troubles the easy identification with Europe in this image. This ambivalence points to the complex geopolitics of the European border regime and its enforcement. However, in most accounts of the image, the question of location and context was brushed over and 'the political, or political-economic, connections that link [...] viewer's own history with that of "those people over there"' (Malkki 1996: 389) was obscured. Discussions of geopolitical relations were brushed aside and the location of Turkey and its role in the European border regime often remained a sidenote or was simply located as the coast of Europe.

It is here that the second characteristic genre of tragedy comes to the fore. Rather than pointing to global regimes of inequality, the European border regime, or the war in Syria, which led to this situation, the death of Alan Kurdi was predominantly framed as a tragedy of 'humanity's failure'. Like the chaos created by the Gods of Olympus, it is presented as the tragic outcome of circumstances that seem impossible to disentangle. As Ida Danewid (2017: 1674) puts it, it is through this focus on 'abstract – as opposed to historical – humanity, [that] these discourses contribute to an ideological formation that disconnects connected histories and that turns questions of responsibility, guilt, restitution, repentance, and structural reform into matters of empathy, generosity, and hospitality'. Whereas the image, of course, can and sometimes did redirect attention to the reasons for Alan Kurdi's death, the tragic genre it was commonly framed through diffuses the question of responsibility. This has the effect that spectators can remain in a position of innocence from which compassion and charitable action seem like the only ethically right political response.

The conditionality of empathy

The reactions to the image of Alan Kurdi, however, were also of parental concern and anger. Several of the news stories focused on stories of smugglers and human traffickers. Thomas de Maizière, the minister for interior affairs, for instance, called smugglers 'dirty criminals', and indeed the only people who were held accountable for the death of Alan Kurdi were two men from Turkey who had tried to 'smuggle' Alan Kurdi and his family over the sea towards Greece (Timur 2016). These narratives go hand in hand with longstanding discourses in which it falls to smugglers and human traffickers to emerge as handy scapegoats for the violence created by border regimes of global inequality (Andrijasevic 2007; Anderson and Andrijasevic 2008; De Genova 2015; Sirriyeh 2018). Other media stories in tabloids like *Bild* went even further and blamed Alan Kurdi's family for engaging in the dangerous border-crossing in the first place and speculated that his father himself might have been a smuggler ('Totes' 2015). In stories like these, empathy was revoked and replaced through a narrative of blame that framed the tragedy as a self-induced harm resulting from careless or even evil acts of parenting.

What these media reports highlight is how empathy induced through the assignment of innocent vulnerability is highly precarious and always conditional. This conditionality was probably nowhere more evident than in the cartoon published by *Charlie Hebdo* in January 2016 that, to the question 'what would have become out of the little Aylan had he grown up?', answers with a depiction of a young male sexual predator running after a group of women and that was shared widely in right-wing spheres on social media (see Mortensen 2017: 1156). The cartoon, which draws on long-established racist tropes of migrants as sexualised predators (discussed in more depth in the next chapter), crystallised the racial grammars of deservingness that practices of affective bordering operate through. It shows how, even in death, Alan Kurdi is still suspected of the horror of sexual abuse – renouncing not only his right of citizenship but also his legitimacy to be an object of compassion.

This leads us to the problem with liberal notions of humanism that most humanitarian articulations of empathy regarding the image were scripted in. As Anne Phillips (2016: 4) argues, although the assertion of our common humanity through affective bonds remains a powerful ethical and political ideal, 'it too often involves either a substantive account of what it is to be human that then becomes the basis for gradations, or else a stripped down, contentless account that denies important differences'. In the articulations of empathy expressed in relation to the image of Alan Kurdi, we can see how these two dynamics work hand in hand. Whereas differences in form of power and location are clad over so that humanity can be felt as one big family, the question of racial and gendered disparities slips back into the frame through the question of who deserves to be part of this affective family in the first place. Whereas an innocent, dead child seems to be the most secure figure for evoking empathetic engagement, this compassion remains fragile and is always conditional on the judgement of the spectator. What we consequently encounter in the calls for humanity that tend to accompany the image of Alan Kurdi is what Miriam Ticktin (2006: 35) has described as a 'humanity devoid of social and political content; yet [...] that even in its minimalism keeps intact racial and gender hierarchies'. It is a humanity that is based on the logic of racialised deservingness and treats difference according to the logic of 'recognize it exceptionally and deport the rest' (Ticktin 2008: 844).[3]

What is further missing from most stories around the image of Alan Kurdi are the voices of migrants themselves who, apart from short interviews with some of his family members, remained obscured and decontextualised. As Liisa Malkki (1996: 388) points out in her foundational work on representations of refugees as 'speechless emissaries', 'helplessness is vitally linked to the constitution of speechlessness: victims need protection, need someone to speak for them'. What makes this dynamic even more pronounced in the case of the image of Alan Kurdi is that there is no subject who can speak or even just look back. The child is dead and remains at the mercy of the uninvited gaze of the spectator. This erasure of voice returns us to the third tragic element in the engagement with the image that rather than as a consensual form of mutual engagement is primarily focused on the cathartic experience of the spectator. Berlant (1998: 648) has called this dimension the 'great promise and threat' of empathy, 'the possibility that through the identification with alterity you will never be the same again'. It is here that the tragic genre of the image unfolds its 'sentimental politics' which is 'performed whenever putatively suprapolitical affects or affect-saturated institutions (like the nation and the family) are proposed as universalist solutions to structural [...] antagonism' (1998: 641). While the image opened discussions about the violent border policies of Europe, most of it seemed self-referential, reproducing long-established attachments to the family of the nation as the site of security and protection.

'Bad' empathy?

The problem with empathy in regard to contemporary migration might consequently not solely be an empathy fatigue, nor forms of fake empathy that distract from violent policies being implemented behind its smokescreen. Rather the problem with dominant articulations of empathy, as represented in the reactions to the image of Alan Kurdi, seem to be that they emerge within and as part of the power relations that they promise to challenge. The assignment of vulnerability and innocence as an ontological condition of the migrant body work as part and parcel of the biopolitical regimes of European border control, rather than a necessary roadblock to their operation. And indeed, the image of Alan Kurdi was used as a justification for securitising measures such as the EU–Turkey deal that would see the reallocation of refugees from the EU in exchange for financial and political support for the Turkish government. In a news conference with Merkel, the then Turkish Prime Minister Davutoğlu, for instance, declared that 'our priority was to stop the baby Aylans from washing up on the shores, and we have made great strides in this aim'. As Adler-Nissen, Andersen and Hansen

(2020: 93) show in their analysis of this moment, here we can see here how '"Kurdi" has been institutionalised as an emotionally charged reference to be mobilised not only in defence of open-door policies, but also to prevent refugees from attempting to enter EU-Europe'.

From the theoretical discussion at the beginning of this piece, we might, thus, think of the empathy expressed in the dominant reaction to the image as corresponding to what feminist scholars have labelled 'bad' empathy – characterised in all three dimensions of *power*, *difference* and *action*. The image of Alan Kurdi emerges with the powerful Butlerian promise to extend the sphere of grievability to subjects that have so far been excluded from it, yet this promise seems to falter in the face of the border regimes it aims to undo. Rather than a genuine engagement with the other, this form of empathy seems to emerge through a subject–object relation in which the other remains defenceless to the affective inscriptions and judgements of the viewer. It preserves agency as the privilege of the spectator and obscures differences of location and power through a sentimental focus on a shared family of humanity while reinstalling questions of disparity through racial and gendered assumptions that question who deserves to be part of this affective kinship in the first place. Moreover, this form of empathy shifts attention from the need for structural transformation to the individual and enshrines vulnerability as an ontological condition of the migrant body to be managed through not only humanitarian but also securitising logics of border control.

While the figure of thought of 'bad' empathy might be a bit schematic, let me defer its deconstruction for now and try to think about what other forms of empathy could look like. In other words, if the dominant forms of empathy articulated in relation to the image of Alan Kurdi are not what most queer feminist affect and critical border and migration scholars might have had in mind, what would or could a form of 'good' empathy in the context of current migration politics then look like?

My Escape and refugee travelogues

If the image of Alan Kurdi was the dominant mode of how empathy was invoked in the European public sphere, it was not the only one. In the context of German *Willkommenskultur*, a range of 'counter-strategies in the "politics of representation"' (Hall 1997: 8) were developed that aimed to invoke empathy in different ways. A particularly prominent example of such strategies are documentaries and migrant travelogues that were edited out of films and photos that asylum seekers shot with their cell phones on their way to Europe. These range from major film productions like *Exodus: Our*

Journey to Europe (2016), *Human Flow* (2017) and *Shadow Games* (2021) to community productions like *Refugee TV* and local photography exhibitions like *Refugeecameras*. These productions coincide with the call for self-representation and the augmenting of marginalised voices in critical media scholarship on border and migration as a way to reverse the uni-directionality of more dominant representations of migration and asylum (Leurs 2017; Ponzanesi 2018; Bayramoğlu 2023).

A less spectacularised yet exemplary cultural production of this genre in the German context is the documentary *My Escape/Meine Flucht* (2016). It features the stories of ten different migrants who show and comment upon film snippets that they have shot on their way to Europe. The film was assembled and produced by the German filmmaker Elke Sasse, whose aim was to support asylum seekers to make the stories they had collected on their cell phones available to a larger audience so as to 'create understanding and empathy for what people who are fleeing go through' (Ehrenberg 2016: 1). Originally produced for West German Broadcasting (WDR), the film was screened at documentary and human rights film festivals; won several prizes, such as the German Social Prize for civilly engaged journalism; and has generally been commented upon as an 'important film at the right time' that builds bridges and changes dominant perspectives on the 'refugee crisis' (Ehrenberg 2016).

Reversing empathetic spectatorship

Ariella Azoulay (2015) argues that civil gazes are a crucial means for holding state power to account and for carving out critical counter-publics. More specifically, she identifies film and photography as weapons for marginalised subjects to make a dent in the public debate. This logic applies specifically to people without or with precarious citizenship. After all, if one of the problems with dominant invocations of empathy is the erasure of speech, self-made representations could be a powerful way to alter this dynamic. *My Escape* seems to directly follow this logic. The film focuses on the narratives of ten asylum seekers from Syria, Iraq, Iran and Eritrea who arrived in Germany in the course of 2015. This form of self-representation, however, raises what Spelman (1998: 70) calls the 'moral and political dangers of becoming the object of compassion', which bring up the question of how to 'maintain authorship of your experiences, even as you urge your audience to focus on the [...] suffering to which you have been subjected against your will'. The film tries to solve this dilemma by making use of a double-layered lens of representation. Showing the original film material, it cross-edits these with scenes of protagonists commenting upon the material they shot during their journey. As such, the film makes a conscious effort to forestall the reaction of the audience and guide the viewer's affective responses in particular directions.

Whereas the image of Alan Kurdi operates in the genre of tragedy, *My Escape* works through the more self-directed genre of the travelogue. Reversing the long colonial history of travel reports about trips into 'far away exotic lands', it offers a perspective onto Europe from the position of those who have historically been brutalised by it. Rather than an uninvited gaze directed at the cathartic experience of the viewer, it aims to present an 'oppositional gaze' (hooks 1992) directed at the European border regime. Through a focus on people's journeys, the film partly de-sensationalises the idea of the escape and shows how migration stories are a component of the lives of so many people, without diminishing or normalising the violent conditions that make this journey necessary in the first place. As such, it does not simply reverse the tragic account so common in the theatre of suffering through a heroic odyssey story but creates a more complex and ambivalent account of people's journey to Europe. It is exactly this ambivalence, I want to suggest, that marks the film's potentiality to circumvent the sentimental politics that animate dominant framings of empathy.

Starting with phone clips of bombs falling over Damascus, the film draws the viewer into the reasons why people leave the places they used to live in. The next scene presents two of the main protagonists, Mohammad and Abdullah, showing clips from their life in Damascus before the war. Talking about the metal bands they used to be part of, the cafés, bars and concert houses they used to frequent, the horror of war is not told through the gruesome images common to most media accounts but through the textures of everyday life that were destroyed by its onset. It is this shifting between the mundane and the extreme, the domestic and the grotesque, the daily and its collapse, that marks the rhythm of the film. We are introduced to the next protagonist, Omar, through a clip showing him waiting at a bus stop in Turkey. Annoyed that the bus is late, he tries to make the most out of the time by taking selfies and shooting little videos of himself. Once on his way to Izmir, he is shown cheerfully on the bus listening to music on his cell phone. A few scenes later, we see him cramped into the tank of a transporter trying to cross over the border to Hungary. Commenting upon the clips, Omar talks about how he still cannot believe how it was possible for fifteen people to breathe through a hole as large as his thumb. It is this collapse of 'ontological security' (Giddens 1991: 35), the sense of basic reliability and continuity in the world, that the film focuses on and makes affectively tangible to the viewer.

Following the protagonists through their journey, the film does not represent the collapse as a nebulous tragedy but as a socially and politically created situation, and it offers an insight into the geopolitical situations behind people's decision to leave, ranging from globally induced poverty in Eritrea to political repression in an Afghanistan torn apart by the 'war on terror'. While the film presents a general background to the reasons for migration, most of the storylines, however, focus on the violence inflicted by people's restricted freedom of movement. Following the protagonists through their journey to central Europe, it offers a sense of the complex web of 'managed inhospitality' that Europe has created, from passport checks in border regions like Libya and ship patrols and blackmailing in Turkey to border fences in Hungary and detention centres in Greece and Italy (Casas-Cortes et al. 2015). In several scenes of the film, protagonists highlight what Leonie Ansems de Vries and Elspeth Guild (2019: 2157) call the 'politics of exhaustion' as 'the felt effects of the stretching over time of a combination of fractured mobility, daily violence and fundamental uncertainty' that migrants navigate on their way to Europe. Filmed through a shaking cell phone, the protagonist talks about how he has been hiding for more than two weeks and is running out of water and food. Turning their camera at a patrolling ship on the coast of Turkey and how it hinders their movement, a counter-representation to the policeman in the image of Alan Kurdi is presented. In a similar scene, the confusion and chaos created at the border in Croatia, in which groups of people are being pushed from one place to the next, is articulated. In the midst of it, one of the protagonists collapses. The state turns from an affectively charged saviour to an object of fear and suspicion.

Representations of ambivalence

Rather than a victimised account, the film thus presents a more complex portrayal of collective agency. Throughout the film, several clips show people singing songs in Arabic that they have made up on their journey. One of the recurring ones is:

> To Germany, to Germany, we are illegally going to Germany and if we can't go over Turkey, then we will go over Spain. And don't forget from there we can go and stay in Austria or go to Hungary. Sweden is a warm welcome but they don't need more people. I swear, the most difficult is England. To Germany, to Germany, we are illegally going to Germany and if we can't go over Turkey, then we will go over Spain.

If the border regime is marked by what Anca Parvulescu (2010: 5) describes as the 'seriousness [...] as a function of gravity, a matter of oppressive weight, a lead-effect' that fixes bodies in place, this song 'is a gesture of the group responding to this exigency of life in common' through laughter and playfulness. Taking on and even cheering the term 'illegally', the song reverses the judgement of the European security regime and unmasks the brutal absurdity that lies behind any demands to 'legality'. In this gesture, the journey through European borders becomes a playful act, the success of which is fragile yet framed as inevitable. Despite the knowledge that deportation, injury and even death might occur at any corner, it opens a space of potentiality that pokes holes into the seriousness with which both European security logics, as well as sentimental forms of compassion, are usually presented. As Yener Bayramoğlu (2023: 596) similarly suggests in his analysis of refugee smartphone videos, it is the representation of 'border crossings as a joyful experience whereby migrants show agency, not victimhood – producing a countervisuality that is at odds with both humanitarian and racialized imagery of migration'.

A similar portrayal of laughter and humour features in the representation of human smugglers. Several storylines focus on how, in the face of European border securitisation, the protagonists have no choice but to cooperate with them. Contrary to the demonised representation of smugglers as traffickers in the media reports on Alan Kurdi, here we get a sense of the ambivalent position that they occupy. Hamid talks about smugglers as 'having two faces': one face that is helping you and another one that can easily exploit your vulnerable position for economic gains. Alex, from Eritrea, describes how he got stuck in the hands of a group of smugglers in Libya. Being unable to pay the money, he was held captive, threatened and abused for several weeks until his family managed to pay the outstanding money. Rather than painting a simplified image of dependent helplessness, however, in the next scene, the film shows Abdullah and Mohammed sitting at a beach in Turkey waiting to cross over to Lesbos. Filming how a group of smugglers tries to repair a boat that looks anything but fit for the trip, Mohammad shouts to Abdullah, who is holding the camera, 'come film me'. Raising his thumb and smiling into the camera, he says: 'we are in the hands of traffickers. It's great!' The group around him breaks into laughter. In this scene, Mohammed directly plays with the imagined viewer on the other side of the camera. Forestalling the pre-conditioned idea of 'being in the hands of traffickers' as a hopeless situation, he subverts the sentimental gaze of empathetic concern without, however, denying the difficult situation that they are in. Rather than feeling *for*, he hence invites the viewer to feel *with* him and the complex situation he finds himself in.

Rather than being faced with a clear-cut, one-way story, in *My Escape* the viewer is consequently presented with a multiplicity of voices that not only give different accounts of their journeys but are also internally and temporarily split and conflicted. It is this polyphony of perspectives that one might suggest keeps the film from immediately being absorbed into a sentimental tragic narrative of victimisation. As Berlant (1998: 56) argues, it is ambivalence that might form the central element of a 'countersentimental modality' that has the potential to disrupt simplified, sentimental forms of empathy. We could consequently consider this film as invoking a form of 'good empathy'. It reverses the power relations of the gaze, in which, rather than being looked at, migrants themselves navigate the stories they want to tell. It negotiates rather than obscures difference and marks clear boundaries of location that are not easily consumed by the greedy eyes of the spectator. And it directs attention to the structural conditions that induce hardship and violence while making the collapse of people's sense of ontological security a tangible experience for the viewer to relate to. Rather than a subject–object relation, empathy here hence emerges as a subject-to-subject engagement that opens up yet respects the distinctions between self and other.

Gratitude as affective reciprocity

The more ambivalent account of the film, however, seems to falter when it reaches its emotional climax. Having made it through the border in Hungary, Omar finally sits in the train to Germany. Commenting upon images of his train journey, he describes how after a while, 'welcome to Austria' was announced in Arabic through the train speakers. He states that 'this was the best moment of the entire trip; no-one so far has ever said welcome [...] It was incredible to be in a place where everyone helps you.' In the next scene, we see clips of people waiting at train stations, holding up banners, singing and cheering the arrival of the protagonists. Heba and her partner Ahmed similarly comment: 'We were really surprised. We did not expect this. We did not expect people actually being happy about us coming here.' It was this scene that was quoted in nearly all reviews of the film, with one journalist recalling how moving it was to see 'how unbelievably speechless and happy the refugees film their arrival in Germany' (Kurth 2016). For a moment it seems like the promise of empathy is unfolding and everything can be okay.

The scene stands out in its emotionality by being the climactic endpoint of a story of people in hardship finally arriving at their destination. Where before there were borders, violence and death, there now is compassion, belonging and harmony. Having made it through the border of the EU, Behnin, from Iran, is on her way from Lesbos to Greece. Filming her family sitting on the huge ferry, she talks about how she cannot believe what a difference this is from the small motorboat on which she made her way to Lesbos. The threat of death, the chaos at the border and the prison-like conditions of the arrival camp in Lesbos, which were discussed in the scenes before, recede into the background, and we get the sense of a brighter future to come. This future is confirmed in the last scenes of the film. Behnin is shown having left Iran because of the threat of an arranged marriage. Now in Germany, she is filmed learning German. Other protagonists are presented doing internships in manufacturing, protesting terrorism, engaging themselves in their local communities and building snowmen. They are shown not only integrating into the cultural life of German society but also becoming good citizens in the labour market, politics and civil society.

Telling their stories in brightly lit, large apartments in Germany, all the stories end in a happy ending of safe, national arrival. In the juxtaposition with the amateur clips of hardship and struggle presented in the self-made clips, the film thus creates a clear narrative of progression into a better and more advanced future. This is not to say that these stories are incorrect or manufactured, but rather points us to the question of which stories cannot be included in this genre. In a telling slippage at the end of the film, we are, for instance, informed that Alex is threatened with being deported back to Italy as the first place of arrival in Europe. The dawning deportation is mentioned; however, this storyline is not further explored. Instead, the film jumps to a scene of Sahmed finding her first apartment in Berlin. Whereas the violence of borders is still shown at the border zones of Europe, once arrived within Germany, discussions of the racialised policies and institutions of asylum camps, work restrictions, detentions, violent reactions of civil society or deportations are cut out from the narrative. It is at this point that the sentimental logic of empathy seems to enter the scene. Rather than including forms of violence that could shatter the viewer's notion of innocence by pointing out Germany's complicity in the production of violence, the ending presents the nation as the social and emotional solution to structural inequality.

The limits of empathy

We could now suggest that this is an omission or a slippage of the film which exposes it to the more sentimental politics of 'bad' empathy. Rather than reading this as a failure of or break in the text, however, I would suggest that the film's ending points to the trouble and limits of empathy more generally. It highlights the narrative conventions with which cultural texts need to comply to be read as empathetic objects in the first place. These are not limited to *My Escape* but can be found across the genre of the migrant travelogue more widely. In one of the scenes of the British documentary travelogue *Exodus: Our Journey to Europe*, for instance, we see Ishra's father Tarek expressing his gratitude for the welcome he received in Austria: 'Austria's welcome was very good. I send my greetings and thanks to this country ... put religion to the side. Humanity is more important.' In this scene, religion, or rather Islam, is positioned as something that needs to be left behind for people to share into the protective fold of humanity. This scene aligns with Sara Ahmed's (2004: 132) argument that integration into the humanist fantasy of a world in which we all feel for each other commonly relies 'on condition that they give up visible signs of their "concrete difference"'. Empathy is conditional on a shared humanity that means a potential stripping of rather than respect for difference.

While this is arguably a particularly drastic example of this form of conditionality, what it shows is that empathy 'is always marked by that which cannot be empathized with and draws a limit as a self-evident boundary for what (and who) can be included' (Hemmings 2011: 197). Empathy is pre-structured through the logic of recognition that, as Hemmings suggests, works through the condition of 'I recognize you; you meet my criteria for recognition' (2011: 213). Difference here, however, is put aside not only for reasons of integration, but also as an act of 'gratitude', and the affective climax of both *My Escape* and *Exodus: Our Journey to Europe* is marked by the protagonists of the film returning the 'gift of empathy' they have received. To be the object of positive feeling, one needs to reciprocate the feeling that one is the receiver of. As Sara Ahmed (2014: 135) explains 'it is [...] "having" the right emotion that allows one to pass into the [national] community'. In the case of empathy, the *right* emotion is that of gratitude, or at least thankfulness. Empathy consequently assumes a subject that not only complies with the demarcated conditions of recognition, but also reaffirms the right affective attitude to become part of the nation (Fortier 2016; Ayata 2022).

We can observe this dynamic also on a wider political level. Thomas de Maizière, the then minister of interior affairs, who had blamed Kurdi's death on smugglers, argued that German *Willkommenskultur* (welcoming culture) needed to be accompanied by a new *Ankommenskultur* (arriving culture) in which migrants must show respect and gratitude for the country that offered them asylum ('Thomas' 2015). It is this form of affective reciprocity, I want to suggest, that is the real trouble with empathy in both its 'good' and 'bad' invocations and that helps us to explain how forms of empathetic engagement so easily make way for related feelings of anger and hatred. If the object of empathy does not respond with the right affective attitude, it creates a narcissistic blow, a feeling of hurt that the gift one has bestowed on the other is not acknowledged (Kohut 1972). It is this slippery dynamic in the racial grammars of deservingness that may explain how the *Willkommenskultur* expressed in the solidarity initiatives discussed in the last chapter and the images welcoming migrants at train stations so easily made space for the intensified hostility that was unleashed into the public sphere in the years after – especially after reports about cases of mass sexual abuse committed by racialised men during the events of New Year's Eve in Cologne erupted in the public sphere, discussed in more depth in the next chapter.

Deconstructing 'good' and 'bad' empathy

Both 'good' and 'bad' might hence be difficult to sever from a logic of national recognition and inclusion. Whereas empathy might be a crucial force in enabling forms of solidary action, these remain tied to the conditions of the subject assigning the 'gift of empathy' in the first place. To enable forms of affective identification, empathy relies on cutting off the abject that could disrupt its fragile suture from the scene of compassionate encounter. Reframing Julia Kristeva's more psychoanalytic theorisation of abjection, Imogen Tyler (2013: 46) conceptualises social abjection as exercises through which 'different arms and operations of state […] determine the value of life adjudicating on who is expendable and who is of worth'. The abject consequently describes those subjects, subjectivities and forms of expression that need to be expelled for the fantasy of national harmony to remain intact. In both scenes, the racial grammars of deservingness structure who deserves to be part of this affective family in the first place and requires proof that subjects are deserving of the gift of empathy. Whereas the dominant reactions to the image of Alan Kurdi clad over structural differences through the invocation of affective kinship, in travelogues difference and potential contradiction likewise need to be forestalled for the subject to fold into the empathetic embrace of the nation.

The differences between 'good' and 'bad' empathy, thus, are more slippery than they seem. Where the two invocations of empathy seem to differ most clearly are in questions of power and agency. While the image of Alan Kurdi offers a site of uninvited spectatorship that consumes the pain of the other, in travelogues the direction of representation is counteracted by migrants filming and commenting upon their own stories. However, the empathetic subject's ability to retreat and refuse identification seems to dominate the scene of encounter even in such potential forms of self-representation. Similarly, although *My Escape* calls out the violence of the border regimes, does it not also redirect affective attachment to the nation as the site where protection and help can be sought? And is this attachment not made even more explicit in the narrative of the migrant travelogues that end in national harmony than in the figure of death of the image of Kurdi that centres loss as a potential sites for a different kind of affective engagement?

These reflections are not meant to ultimately decide the political worth of these different representations. Rather, the analysis highlights how difficult any clear demarcation between good and bad empathy in the context of contemporary border regimes is and how trying to finetune these differences might send us down the wrong path of political thinking. In the remaining part of this chapter, I thus want to think about what a different form of affective relationality vis-à-vis the border might look like by analysing what happens when the abject, the scenes of discomfort and rejection, that necessarily need to be cut out from scenes of empathetic encounter enter or even become the centre of this encounter.

The emotional politics of hunger strikes

While media discussions focused on the emergence of a new *Willkommenskultur*, groups of asylum seekers staged protests and hunger strikes in a range of cities. In the late summer of 2015 alone, nearly one hundred people went on hunger strike in Hamburg to protest the inhumane conditions of an improvised refugee camp housed in a DIY warehouse. In Hannover, fifty Sudanese refugees refused food and water to protest for the right of residence and in Munich, a long-lasting fight between refugee groups and the police erupted, highlighting the racist procedures of the asylum system. Simultaneously, protests spawned around the borders of Hungary, Serbia and Greece, and in the refugee camps of Calais and Idomeni, people refused to eat and sewed their lips together in protest of the conditions that kept them in destitution – creating a dispersed yet interrelated network of protest movements calling out the violent practices of the European border regime.

In their analysis of the cultural politics of an earlier refugee hunger strike in Würzberg, Michelle Pfeifer (2018: 466) points out that it is through the longer history of hunger strikes in Germany that refugees 'staged the encounter of horror with the abject in city centres all over Germany'. After the Iranian asylum seeker Mohammad Rahsepa committed suicide in a collective refugee housing in Würzburg in 2012, a protest wave erupted in Germany that reverberates up into the political present. Starting with a refugee tent in Würzburg, a Refugee Tent Action was started, and dozens of protest camps emerged all over Germany that called out the racist practices of the German asylum system and demanded the right to residence and improved living conditions. In one of the most powerful moments of this protest movement, people marched from Würzburg and other protest camps around the country to Berlin and created a centralised protest camp on Oranienplatz in Kreuzberg. The camp became the epicentre of migrant protest organisations and worked as a base for other actions such as occupations and larger mobilisations (Pfeifer 2018; see also Steinhilper 2021). The camp was cleared in 2014, yet its spirit and migrant protest networks remained as seen in ongoing refugee actions in Munich or sanctuary initiatives like Lampedusa Hamburg.

Whereas in the summer 2015, most of these protest actions were overshadowed by the wave of *Willkommenskultur* focused on helping people in need through more charitable action, protest actions and hunger strikes continued. A relatively small but exemplary protest during this time was staged in the city of Nuremberg. As the seat of the Federal Office for Migration and Refugees (BAMF) already in August 2015, several hundreds of migrants protested in Nuremberg and submitted a letter to the head of BAMF, in which they demanded that 'refugees, independent of where they are from or what their status is, need to be given a prospect to live' (Nürnberg 2015). More concretely, they asked for a halt to deportations, an improvement in housing and changes in the German system of *Duldung* (toleration) in which people's asylum cases are hanging and they are banned from working or moving outside of the area they are housed in (Nürnberg 2015). After the head of the BAMF did not respond, a group of asylum seekers from Afghanistan, Iran and Ethiopia went on hunger strike. Following the tradition of the Refugee Tent Action, they occupied a square in the middle of town. As their demands continued to not be heard, they escalated the situation and refused not only food but also water.

Allen Feldman (2008) posits that while hunger strikes have often been discussed as a particularly prominent practice of non-violent resistance, this classification is misleading as it works on a conception of violence that counts as such only when it is committed against others. Rather, he suggests that we should understand hunger strikes as a form of violent self-mutilation. Self-starvation starts a range of biological processes in the body. Heart and blood pressure drop rapidly, energy levels go down and the body starts breaking down protein from tissue unrelated to survival, such as the muscles in the eyes. Vision, sight and speech start to become impaired, pain spreads through the limbs and the body literally starts to consume itself (Machin 2016). From this perspective, hunger strikes might better be understood as a re-enactment of the subjugating violence inflicted by the state that one refuses to submit to. Explaining their motivation to refuse water, one of the protesters stated that 'at home they will kill me in a minute, here I am dying slowly' ('Einhundert' 2015). Hunger strikes, in this logic of self-mutilation, make the racial violence of the state visible by publicly enacting it on oneself.

The cultural politics of hunger strikes might thus best be described as 'vulnerability in resistance' (Sabsay, Gambetti and Butler 2016). Whereas in the invocations of empathy so far, vulnerability seems to have mainly been scripted as a disempowering condition that calls for paternalistic forms of protection, in this practice vulnerability is reclaimed and enacted not as the counterpoint but the source and focus of political action. In her work on Palestinian hunger strikers in Israeli prisons, Ashjan Ajour (2021) suggests that we need to understand hunger strikes as a form of 'embodied resistance' which creates collective forms of political consciousness in situations of 'living death'. Showing the potential of hunger strikes to divert biopolitical regimes of power focused on the subjugation of the body, the hunger strike in Nuremberg put the city government in a double bind – either they let the strikers die or give in to their demands. The mayor warned that 'a fundamental good of the law [*Rechtsgut*] is under threat, namely that of life itself' (Brock 2015: 1). The mayor's telling description of biopower – as the 'right to make life and let die' (Foucault 2003: 241) – reveals how the state was unable to react to the self-enacted seizing of life that questions the state's monopoly over the governmentality of life. In reversing biopolitical reason through their resistant enactment of vulnerability, the protestors consequently created a lacuna in the political response of the state.

The 'abject' of empathy

The hunger strikes also created a lacuna in the politics of empathy. Rather than calling for empathetic concern or charitable action, hunger strikers in Nuremberg asked for a political understanding of the situation they find themselves in and for people to take an active stance against it. In their protest actions, they confronted the racialised asylum system and highlighted Europe's ongoing complicities in the production of global inequality and violence. In a demonstration in front of the BAMF, protestors carried banners reading 'dictatorial countries = direct death; democratic Germany = painful death' and called for an end of 'the financial and political support of dictatorial regimes' that the European border regime collaborates with (Asylbewerber 2015). Rather than positioning Germany as the mature agent giving a 'helping hand' to the rest of the world, they pointed out how the state, too, has 'blood on its hands' and question notions of social and historical innocence (Asylbewerber 2015). Giving out flyers to people walking past, the appeal was not only directed at the government but also at citizens who asked to decide whether to stay complicit with these processes or unsettle their relatively secure position as citizens of the state and the positions of 'white innocence' from which some other humanitarian campaigns in the context of migration and borders are enacted (Wekker 2016).

At the same time, hunger strikes are highly precarious in the sense that they create a situation in which power might crack down with even more force. As such, many of the more established refugee advocacy groups like Pro Asyl have often been against hunger strikes and warn of the violent reactions from state actors and civil society that could follow. And, indeed, like in Munich, Würzberg or Berlin before, in Nuremberg, the city officials refused to give into the demands of the hunger strikers (see Pfeifer 2018; Steinhilper 2021). First, the refugee camp was pushed out of the centre of town and into a less frequented part of the city, shielded from passers-by, and a few days later the camp was evacuated. After eight days of strike, five of the strikers were hospitalised, and the protest was ultimately dissolved. Given the 'failure' of the protest to meet their demands, what do we make out of the affective politics of the hunger strike? By attempting to circumvent dominant forms of biopolitical control attached to the invocation of empathy, does it not create an even more violent enforcement of power?

Read through the lens of empathy, I want to suggest that what emerges in the space opened by hunger strikes is the suggestion of a different form of affective solidarity that does not emerge through a form of feeling for or with, but a shared outrage at and concern for the structures productive of violence and death. I am building here on the work of Michelle Pfeifer (2018), who has conceptualised the affective potential of hunger strikes in Germany through the concept of 'becoming flesh'. Drawing on Black feminist theories of refusal, they suggest that hunger strikes express a form of becoming minor that not only unmasks the racialised German asylum system but also enacts a refusal of the biopolitical reach of late liberal state power. They argue that hunger strikes operate as 'a politics of refusal that subverted the logics of recognition, empathy, and suffering liberal rights discourses rely on and, instead, performed an embrace of the refugees' abjection' (2018: 461). Therein, they suggest that the idea of abjection should not be understood as an ontological category but rather as a social location that is induced by the racialised asylum system, which positions the body of the refugee in conditions of 'living death'. An embracement of this abjection refuses both the inscription of power through regimes of biopolitical control and 'evades the labouring of the racialized body's suffering' that 'white empathy' commonly relies on (2018: 465).

Following Pfeifer's line of argumentation, it is the potential of circumventing the hierarchical encounter of empathy that marks out hunger strikes as a specifically potent political practice. Rather than through the genre of tragedy, it is the genre of horror through which hunger strikes unfold their affective power. The performative re-enactment of the violence inflicted upon the body is not meant to evoke compassion or empathy but rather a shared ground of discomfort from which to call out the processes that made this act necessary in the first place. As Hayley Rudkin (2012: 309) suggests, in a best-case scenario, hunger strikes enable an empathetic rupture that throws spectators into a position of discomfort and puzzlement: 'since we cannot help but recognise that suffering, and eventual death are on display before us, do we have a responsibility as witnesses to intervene? What has caused the subject to starve themselves?' They suggest that 'while starvation elicits empathy, self-starvation both confounds and cries out for understanding' (Rudkin 2012). Even in their 'failure', hunger strikes hint at an affective disruption in the power relations and dynamics that fuel the European border regime.

Alternative affective solidarity

In trying to find a different ground from which to consider affective solidarity, Hemmings (2012) suggests a similar line of argumentation. Disputing dominant approaches within feminist theory that would try to ground feminism either in fixed identity categories or processes of empathetic identification, she suggests that what might potentially unite feminist subjects is not their shared womanhood or empathetic concern for each other, but rather an affective dissonance between the world as it is and how we imagine it to be otherwise. In order for this discontent to emerge, however, she argues that first 'an affective shift' must occur that makes dissatisfaction a felt and acknowledged reality (157). Such an affective shift will always depend on the standpoint of the subject and as such keeps conflict and antagonism at the heart of any form of unified political action. Hemmings is further careful to point out that no one event would necessarily create such an outcome: 'Affective dissonance cannot guarantee feminist politicisation or even a resistant mode. And yet, it just might …' (Hemmings 2012).

Bearing witness to hunger strikes can create a dissonance that generates such an 'affective shift' in the spectator by troubling all three dimensions of power, difference and action. Being witness to a self-directed form of mutilation reverses subject–object relations and keeps agency with the striking subject. Producing radically negative affects of shock, horror and disgust, hunger strikes keep difference intact by grounding the perspectives of people affected by border violence and their experiences from being consumed through simplistic forms of affective identification. Instead, they point to the wider racialised structures and systemic injustices that have created this encounter of horror in the first place. Most importantly, hunger strikes centre the affective concerns of those deemed the object rather than the subject of empathy, reversing the logics of affective bordering by keeping political agency with the striking subject.

This does not mean that bearing witness to hunger strikes necessarily leads to states of anger, shock or grief, which might engender other forms of affective solidarity in the witness of hunger strikes. Quite the opposite; they can lead to dismissal ('they should be happy to be here!') disengagement ('I can't watch this!') or protectionism and hostility ('someone deport them!'). The generation of affective solidarity through actions like hunger strikes, therefore, is highly precarious and can always fail. It does not necessitate any form of anti-nationalist politicisation or even resistant mode. And yet, it just might …

Conclusion

In her 2019 exhibition at Tate Modern, artist Tania Bruguera created a *Forced Empathy Room*. Adjoining the grand turbine hall, she built a 'crying room' filled with tear-inducing air. Before entering, visitors pass a security guard who stamps their hand with a constantly changing number. When I enter the space, it was 10,110,926 – the number of people who migrated to another country in the last year plus the number of migrant deaths counted since the start of the project. In the description outside the space, the room is advertised as a place in which 'a shared emotional response' will be created that might combat a social 'sense of apathy' towards migration. Walking inside, however, all I encounter are perplexed people standing in a white cubicle, rubbing their eyes, and looking slightly embarrassed. Coffee table books on contemporary art in their hand, two people next to me stare at the stamps on their hands. Like me, they seem to wonder whether they are engaging in the right affective response. How is this empathy supposed to feel? What does it enable? And are we engaging in a politically transformative act of affective relationality or a largely self-referential gesture of sentimentality that we can at least later tell our friends about? The artwork takes no ultimate decision on the value and promise of empathy. Yet we all leave with a sting in our eyes.

This analysis intends to leave a similar sting. Through an analysis of three affective scenes, I have tried to complicate some of the optimistic attachments to the promise of empathy that seem to permeate late liberal knowledge production in both its mainstream as well as feminist modes. Therein, I have suggested that the split between 'good' and 'bad' empathy in the context of the European border regime might not be as easily established nor as theoretically helpful as it might seem. Whereas images of migrants circulating within the theatre of suffering seem to mostly invite empathetic responses that might be labelled as 'bad' empathy (in which power hierarchies are re-inscribed through a victimising subject–object relation), travelogues might seem to invoke forms of 'good' or at least 'better' empathy (a subject-to-subject dialogue that opens up spaces for a more complex engagement with power, difference and agency). Questioning how, within the context of contemporary migration and European border regimes, both seem to circulate within the same frames of liberal recognition and national belonging, I remain hesitant about how easily they might be disentangled. Rather, I have suggested that empathy, in either articulation, folds into the biopolitical modes of humanitarian securitisation that work exactly through caring for some deserving subjects while relegating others into spheres of non-intelligibility in detention camps, border points and the mass grave of the Mediterranean.

Instead, I have tried to think and feel through what other forms of affective attachments are made possible when we try to move beyond the warm pull of empathetic engagement and turn to scenes of the abject that usually need to be cut out from scenes of empathetic encounter. Thinking through what it means to bear witness to hunger strikes, I have suggested a different form of affective solidarity that, by keeping agency with the striking subject rather than emerging through feeling for or with others, arises out of a shared concern for the border regimes and systems of global inequality that are productive of violence, death and precarity. Such an affective solidarity might emerge through a politics of difficulty, discomfort and outrage, a feeling for the ultimately shared yet highly unequally distributed conditions of vulnerability or maybe even through forms of empathetic engagement. In any case, its emergence might play a crucial role in how an increasingly violent present of nationalist anger and resentment – discussed in the following chapter – might be able to be resisted.

Notes

1 There are two forms of compassion fatigue discussed in current literature. One describes the wearing out of compassion as a result of a 24/7 news cycle that is seen to desensitise the public to the fate of others, the other a psychological condition that affects many people in care work roles such as nursing and social work (for a review of the literature on the latter see Sorenson, Bolick, Wright and Hamilton 2016). While the two are interrelated, I am mainly referring to the social condition described by the former.

2 This could be seen in the mostly negative reactions to the photographs of Ai WeiWei, in which the artist restaged the death of Alan Kurdi, lying face down on a beach in Lampedusa, for an art fair. While Ai WeiWei's direct appropriation of Alan Kurdi's pain and similar actions were widely called out for their insensitivity and crudeness, parental identification was mirrored in most media accounts of Alan Kurdi's death (see Mortensen 2017: 1155).

3 A straightforward application of this logic of deservingness in relation to children can be observed in current moral panics of refugees 'claiming to be underage' in the UK and other European contexts and the newly implemented regimes of age-measurement and surveillance that are aimed at identifying whether people are actually minors and thus classify for specific asylum protections. For an early discussion of this practice see Liz Fekete (2007).

3

Anger: the sexual politics of resentment after New Year's Eve in Cologne

Introduction

Whereas in summer 2015 national and international media still reported about Germany as a bastion of humanitarianism, a nation that opened its door to refugees, and published pictures of citizens waiting for migrants at train stops with blankets, balloons and welcome signs, in January 2016 this discourse took a drastic turn. After New Year's Eve in Cologne, in which several hundred cases of sexual violence, theft and intimidation by racialised and migratised men were reported to the police, a wave of anger and indignation was unleashed into the public sphere. CDU Vice-Chancellor Volker Bouffier famously declared that 'Cologne changed everything' and captured how New Year's Eve night in Cologne operated as a turning point in the social climate and official government policy of Germany (Birnbaum 2016). Media stories evoked the image of a country overrun by groups of violent, mainly Muslim, migrants from North Africa and the Middle East who take advantage of a weak and overwhelmed state – abusive foreigners who do not respect sexual freedom and gender equality and mistreat the generosity that they have been offered. Political actors from across the political spectrum called for tougher border restrictions and speeding up deportations and even international media like *The New York Times* argued for 'closing Germany's borders to new arrivals', 'beginning an orderly deportation process for able-bodied young men' and 'giving up the fond illusion that Germany's past sins can be absolved with a reckless humanitarianism in the present' (Douthat 2016: 1).

In this chapter, I analyse how 'Cologne' came to operate as a catalyst for the shift in public discourse and national sentiment. Whereas the two last chapters examined the paradoxical politics of hope and empathy in the emergence of a German 'welcome culture', in this chapter, I analyse how anger and resentment accumulate in its wake. How can we understand the growing hostility expressed in the outrage about migrants misusing the hospitality of the German nation? What can the reaction tell us about the workings of anger in contemporary border politics, and what is it about *sexual* violence in particular that generates this nationalist resentment? In doing so, I bring together scholarship on the convergence of sexual and nationalist politics in Europe (Campt 2005; El-Tayeb 2016; Farris 2017; Hark and Villa 2020) with queer feminist scholarship that has identified anger and resentment as key forces behind the rise of nativist nationalism today (Nussbaum 2016a; Kimmel 2017; Eribon 2018; Hochschild 2018).

In doing so, I argue that to understand anger, we need to follow closely how it is socially and historically scripted. Anger does not describe a universally dangerous force, but an unequally distributed emotion that is imbued with the mark of racial and gendered histories (Lorde 1997; Ahmed 2014). Based on this understanding, I suggest that while anger about New Year's Eve in Cologne operated as a catalyst for an already boiling resentment against the recent refugee migration and worked as an affective adhesive sticking together feminist, liberal and right-wing nationalist positions, it might best be understood as a 'resonant echo' (Campt 2005: 53) of the colonial past that reverberates powerfully in a time of growing challenges to enshrined entitlements in the nation. Contextualising Cologne in a longer series of sexualised panics around racially marked Others, I show how anger aligns itself along sedimented grammars of racial deservingness that secure German conceptions of nationality and citizenship through heteronormative constructions of whiteness. As long as these grammars are not uncovered and unsettled, I suggest, little will or can be done in trying to challenge anger as a force for growing violent nationalism in the historical present.

Anger, resentment and ressentiment

Anger is often identified as the emotion that defines the political present. It is commonly discussed as a key force behind the re-emergence of nativist nationalism, white masculinity and authoritarian politics in the current moment, with scholars like Martha Nussbaum (2016b: 1) warning that there currently is 'no emotion that we need to think harder and more clearly about than anger'. Nussbaum defines anger as an emotional response to a significant damage to something or someone one cares about, a damage that the angry person believes to have been wrongfully inflicted. What makes anger a problem for liberal feminist thinkers like her is that anger asks for payback and retaliation. Anger can also develop passively and eat itself into body and mind, as in the case of holding a grudge or silent resentment, yet Nussbaum asserts that anger mostly comes to be projected outwards and asks for retaliation for the hurt that has been inflicted.[1] To underline her argument, Nussbaum evokes the story of the Furies in Ancient Greece – female underground deities of vengeance usually represented as beastly creatures – who, after the reformation of the Athenian law system from a cycle of blood vengeance to a formalised legal system, are transformed into the human Kindly Ones – gentle, eloquent and wise protectors of justice. For Nussbaum, the retaliatory nature of anger is therefore opposed to actual justice, which would engage with forms of reconciliation and repair, rather than retaliation, to heal and move beyond the site of injury. Wendy Brown (1993) has similarly suggested that anger and resentment are politically unhelpful emotions. She argues that resentment keeps us attached to the object of hurt rather than helping us to move beyond it and warns against building feminist politics and identities upon such 'wounded attachments' (1993: 390).

The problematisation of anger as a dangerous political emotion is supported by a range of queer feminist work that has identified anger as a key force in reproducing gendered and racialised structures of domination. Michael Kimmel (2017) has identified anger as the key affective force for producing and protecting white masculinity, in which anger works to shield white men's location of privilege and structural domination from critique and transformation. His work alerts us to the fact that anger is more likely to push down than up as it is crucially linked to expectations – as an event is more likely to be perceived as a loss or hurt when the person has the expectation that it is not supposed to happen (e.g. a waiter serving you the wrong dish). Expectations as a sense of entitlement lead to stronger feelings of being treated unfairly and a larger likelihood of acting even more forcefully upon them (e.g. demanding to speak to the manager). Kimmel calls this psychosocial dynamic 'aggrieved entitlement' and suggests that feeling entitled and not getting what you expected is a recipe for humiliation that easily ends in bursts of outrage and retaliation (2017: 31). It is this form of anger and resentment that scholars like Arlie Hochschild (2018) have identified in the voting for Donald Trump in white downwardly mobile communities in the US. She suggests that anger in this context emerges as a reaction to a perceived threat of loss of status and privilege and works to keep social inequalities intact and helps to further augment them.

Given this assault on anger as a dangerous political emotion, a range of queer feminist scholars have tried to halt the slaughtering of the Furies on the altar of negative affect. Audre Lorde (1997) has powerfully shown how the general devaluation of anger has often meant a silencing of Black women in politics. Although anger might be read as a sign of strength and insistence in white men in power, Black women are often marked as excessively angry and beyond rational thought and so are excluded from the sphere of presumably rational political debate. Speaking against such epistemic violence,

Lorde defends anger as a crucial resource in her fight against racism, sexism and homophobia and affirms that 'anger is loaded with information and energy' (1997: 280). Building upon these insights, Sara Ahmed (2014) similarly suggests that anger and resentment do not necessitate a simple politics of retaliation but can likewise be the fuel and messenger of an ongoing critique of the worlds we inhabit. While they can attach to the source of hurt, they might likewise go beyond it and gesture at different worlds beyond the site of injury. Anger from this perspective is not the opposite of proper justice but is part and parcel of the move towards righting the wrongs of history.

What we get in contemporary discussions of anger in feminist theory is a bifurcated theoretical terrain in which anger is framed as a crucial force for seeking justice and redress, on the one hand, and a defensive force that cements power and secures inequality and entitlements, on the other hand. Integrating the ideas of Didier Fassin (2013) into this debate helps to solve this deadlock in political thinking. Fassin has usefully suggested that to fully understand anger's political force, we need to pay attention to the related affective states of *ressentiment* and *resentment* and the social and historical positions they emerge from – arguing that there is an important distinction between the two that is often overlooked in contemporary scholarship. *Ressentiment* describes an affective condition born out of direct hurt and a lived past and present of oppression and domination – a condition exemplified in the experience of Black people living under South African apartheid, as well as racialised minorities in the banlieues of Paris. *Resentment*, in contrast, emerges from a more diffuse social position of frustration and acrimony. Fassin suggests that this condition can, for instance, be seen in the resentment harboured by French police who feel themselves oppressed, disliked and misunderstood by the public, yet operate in positions of power in society overall, and often take out their anger on more marginalised subjects in society. Both conditions might feel like similar responses to an injury, whether real or imagined, on a phenomenological level, but they differ in their moral value and the structural experience they derive from.

This differentiation helps us to untie the Gordian knot of anger's bifurcated position in feminist theory and enables a more nuanced analysis of the aftermath of 'Cologne'. As Fassin (2013) suggests, in current political discourse, *resentment* and *ressentiment* are often falsely equated, such as in discussions that frame the anger expressed in protests in the banlieues and the resentment enacted in racialised police violence as spirals of equivalent affective retaliation. In the following, I want to suggest that a similar equation, or rather merging, took place during the night of New Year's Eve in Cologne in which the actual *ressentiment* of women affected by sexual violence was taken over by an already simmering *resentment* against the recent refugee migration. Fassin's distinction gives us an entry point into examining how articulations of ressentiment based in the actual experience of sexual violence that several women suffered during New Year's Eve in Cologne became entangled and overdetermined through the more diffuse states of resentment directed at migrants and racialised minorities in Germany expressed in the aftermath of Cologne.

New Year's Eve in Cologne

In the aftermath of Cologne, resentment was articulated in ways that align with Nussbaum's (2016a) conceptualisation of anger as a retaliatory affect. Actors from across the political spectrum unleashed a volatile debate about migration and Islam – in which the crimes of Cologne were primarily linked to Muslim migrants and asylum seekers from the Middle East and Northern Africa. Right-wing figures who had long been critical of the welcome culture of the summer of 2015 saw themselves confirmed in their worst nightmares and revelled in having been right about the 'dangers of migration' all along. The head of the far-right party AFD, Frauke Petry, triumphantly claimed that the events were 'the appalling consequence of a catastrophic migration and asylum politics' ('Köln' 2016), and Patriotic Europeans Against the Islamisation of the West (PEGIDA) organised several marches in major cities including Cologne, carrying 'rapefugees not welcome' signs that likewise popped up in forms of stickers in bars, lamp posts and other urban surfaces across the country. The debate following Cologne directly intertwined with calls for border securitisation and nationalist fears of the 'Islamisation of the Western World' that groups like PEGIDA and the AFD had successfully been stirring up for several years now (which I will discuss in more depth in Chapter 5 on fear).

Calls for harsher border controls, however, were not confined to a few voices on the political right but were apparent across the political spectrum. Oliver Kehrl (2017: 1) from the CDU evoked the dehumanising language of floods and waves so common to securitising discourses of migration to warn that 'the loss of control, that we experienced in 2015 along the German borders, now swept over to Cologne'. The minister of Justice Heiko Maas from the SPD spoke of a 'break of civilisation' (*Zivilisationsbruch*) (Fried 2016), which is not only a term that invoked evolutionary understandings of civilisation pertinent to colonial discourses, but also that in Germany had until that point been confined to discussions of the Holocaust.[2] Boris Palmer from the Green Party asserted that 'our generous help has been abused' (Kade 2016), and even Sahra Wagenknecht, head of the socialist party Die

Linke, who still had an unconditional right to asylum enshrined in their party manifesto, declared that 'who misuses their right to hospitality loses their right to hospitality' (Hagen 2016). Within this affective logic of narcissistic injury (Kohut 1972), rather than crimes to be punished by legal procedure, the events of Cologne became framed as signs of ungratefulness that justify the revoking of the right to asylum and legitimise practices of deportation and detention.

And indeed, the events in Cologne catalysed a range of legislative changes. In the months following the attacks, asylum laws were tightened, deportation procedures accelerated and the rights to family reunification further eroded. Simultaneously, the attacks of New Year's Eve 2015 in Cologne set in motion an overhaul of the sexual violence legislation that feminist activists in Germany had long been demanding, thus far without success. New laws were prepared by the German parliament, colloquially known as the 'No means No' legislation, which were ultimately passed in 2017. These laws directly tied new laws on sexual violence to the German Residence Act, so that under these laws, asylum seekers convicted of sexual violence could be deported more easily (Holst and Montanari 2017). The green and left parties that had initiated the motion to amend the sexual violence legislation eventually abstained from the vote, and anti-rape activists questioned whether this reform could be viewed as a feminist victory (Holst and Montanari 2017).

Given the repercussions of the events of New Year's Eve, it is nearly impossible to talk about Cologne without affirming a particular construction of the crimes committed that night. As Sabine Hark and Paula-Irene Villa (2020: 35) have pointed out, Cologne has become an 'epochal signifier' – an event that everyone seems to have a clear judgement on, and that yet remains notoriously unclear and contested. By 18 January 2016, official police protocols recorded 821 criminal charges out of which about 359 involved charges of sexual violence on the night of New Year's Eve in Cologne (Landtag Nordrhein-Westfalen 2017: 15). Whereas only about 100 charges were made on New Year's Eve night and the immediate days after, most of the charges were brought up after 4 January when the media discussion had already ensued. Given the delayed accusations in the context of heated anti-migration discussions after Cologne, a range of commentators have questioned the accuracy of the official numbers and argued that the media attention and the racialisation of the perpetrators had lowered the threshold for reporting and potentially led to several false accusations. Other commentators suggested that the few perpetrators who were arrested and convicted did not exclusively come from Northern Africa and the Middle East, and that many of them had been in Germany long before the recent refugee migration.

While these arguments are important, the sometimes implicit suggestion that the reported cases of sexual violence in Cologne did not really happen is not only empirically untenable but also politically vexed. As activists fighting sexual violence have long pointed out, one of the biggest roadblocks for feminist critiques of sexual violence is that victims' accounts are dismissed and not taken seriously (Holst and Montanari 2017). Moreover, accounts that simply dismiss cases of sexual violence easily buy into the common romanticisation of subjects on the receiving end of migratism and racism, in particular refugees, who come to be framed as eternal victims that cannot do any harm and are denied complex, agentic subject-positions (Phipps 2020; Villa and Hark 2020). At the same time, many commentators exaggerated numbers and argued that Cologne was an excessively violent event, representing an unseen scale of sexual violence – and the police department was commonly quoted as confronting a 'completely new dimension of crime' (Burger 2016). Feminist critics have rebutted such argumentation and pointed out that, while the attacks on women were horrific, similar cases of sexual violence have happened every year at Carnival or the Oktoberfest. If perpetrators are white Germans, however, sexual violence and harassment are played down and seen as trivial – a 'gentleman's offence' (Lohaus and Wizorek 2016: 1). Official numbers that attest a high prevalence of women experiencing sexual violence at some point in their life – mostly at home and by people they know – further highlight that large-scale sexual violence in Germany is by no means a problem that emerged with Cologne (Wieners and Winterholler 2016).

From ressentiment to resentment

My aim in this chapter is consequently not to dismiss the allegations nor to establish exactly what happened; instead, I explore how – in a context in which sexual violence is commonly belittled and played down in public discourse – reports of sexual violence became a topic of national concern. Building on the work of Villa and Hark (2020) and Stuart Hall (1978: 18), I suggest that there is 'no simple "event" here to be understood, apart from the social processes by which such events are produced, perceived, classified, explained, and responded to'. Instead, we need to examine the affective and political dynamics – the conditions of possibility– that enabled Cologne to become an 'event' in the first place. It is at this point that Didier Fassin's differentiation between *ressentiment* and *resentment* is key to understanding how the ressentiment about real occurring sexual violence became the catalyst for the wider nationalist resentment about migration and the welcome culture of the prior months. While Cologne at least partly emerged from the actual ressentiment of women experiencing sexual violence and harassment, in the debates it was overtaken and overshadowed by a more mobile and diffuse resentment about refugee migration.

Next to Islam and migration, this resentment came to target the state, the media outlets and the 'feeling rules' of welcome culture that were made responsible for the attacks. Firstly, the heated debate around Cologne intertwined with the longstanding resentment against a state believed to have turned its back on its citizens. Even before Cologne, several media outlets had set the state's expenditure for migration in competition with other welfare programmes asking, 'Who should pay for this?' and asserted that the state was putting citizens at risk by letting criminals and terrorists into the country (Raffelhüschen 2015). In the wake of Cologne, this resentment found an outlet and focused specifically on the failure of the police. The head of Cologne's police force, Wolfgang Albers, was fired days after the event, and at the following year's New Year's Eve celebration in Cologne, new surveillance systems were implemented, police presence increased and racial profiling was explicitly endorsed – on New Year's Eve 2016, the police in Cologne proudly tweeted how they were successfully inspecting hundreds of 'Nafris', a racist short term for 'Northern African intensive offenders' (Boulila and Carri 2017). Moreover, right-wing commentators called for Merkel to take full responsibility and step down and attacked Hannelore Kraft, the social democratic head of Nordrhein-Westfalen, who had long been heralded as a potential future chancellor. She was ridiculed for her soft approach in handling the situation and lost the coming state elections in the heartland of the SPD.

Second, anger was directed at the media. Although newspapers and radio and TV stations seemed to report about little else than Cologne, public commentators like the member of parliament Hans Peter-Friedrich from the CSU complained about a *Schweigekartell* (silence cartel) of the public broadcasters. He referred to public TV stations that – given the ethical standards of the German journalism association – did not immediately report the ethnic and religious background of the perpetrators ('Ex-Minister' 2016). Particularly in right-wing forums, these arguments cemented the conspiratorial notion that Germany was held captive by the *Lügenpresse* (lying press), which intentionally keeps their audiences misinformed about the real costs of migration.[3] But also liberal newspapers like *Der Tagesspiegel* asserted that 'radical feminists and great moguls of political correctness relativize the crimes of Cologne' and *Der Spiegel* cheered that 'Cologne is the beginning of the end of political correctness' (Martenstein 2016). Here commentators attacked not only anti-racist feminists who tried to question the conflation of sexual violence with race and religion but also the 'politically correct' debates of welcome culture in which people were supposedly not allowed to voice what they had suspected the whole time: that migrants were criminals, sexual aggressors who do not respect the values and rules of the host nation.

Third, the events intertwined with a longstanding resentment against *Gutmenschen* (do-gooders) and the 'feeling rules' (Hochschild 1979) of welcome culture during the summer of 2015. In the context of the US, Lauren Berlant (2016b) has suggested that what made Donald Trump so successful was how he embraced anger as a force of anti-repression that would free people from the shackles of liberal feelings like empathy, shame and mutual respect. This dynamic (which I examine in more detail in the next chapter on shame) could similarly be observed in Germany in the aftermath of Cologne, where anger was enacted as a freeing from the feeling rules that demanded empathy, respect or at least quiet retraction in relation to migrants arriving at the shores of Europe. Cologne was seen as the event that would unmask these misguided attitudes so that now people could finally call things what they are, and politicians like the Minister of Interior Thomas de Maizière (CDU) called for finally taking the worries of 'common people' seriously (Sauter 2016). Discourses around Cologne offered an outlet for anger while also providing legitimisation for its uninhibited expression in the public sphere.

As a result, Cologne not only allowed right-wing actors to claim that their racist fantasies had been confirmed. It also enabled some liberal and leftist actors to resolve the moral duty and responsibility that the arrival of people in Germany demanded of them without appearing ethically questionable or compassionless. If migrants are after all – as always secretly suspected – criminals and sexual aggressors, 'we' need not be so moral and politically correct anymore but can fall back into the fantasy of an imperfect but ultimately just global order. Even though 'we' have tried our best, 'they' are threatening us and show no respect or gratitude – allowing people to reverse a structural power relation into one of individual hurt and threat. Similar dynamics of affective bordering fuelled by the grammars of deservingness could be observed after the terrorist attacks of Paris and Berlin, in which refugees shifted from being framed as 'victims of terror' to 'terrorists under disguise' (Holzberg, Kolbe and Zaborowski 2018: 543). Yet, while Cologne was less the trigger than the catalyst of already existent resentments, a simple release model would underestimate the role that gender, race and sexuality played in the emotional construction of Cologne. After all, it was not just any form of crime but *sexual* violence around which the discussions following Cologne revolved.

Feminist and nationalist convergences

What made the forms of affective bordering in the night of Cologne so powerful is how they were produced through the intersection of feminist and nationalist discourse. Major conservative newspapers like *Die Frankfurter Allgemeine Zeitung* blamed the events on a 'toxic mixture of North African–Arab culture and religion' (Schirmbeck 2016), and *Die Welt* declared that 'migration imports an archaic image of women' (Ghadban 2016). Within these narratives, sexual violence was framed as a new form of gendered violence introduced by racialised intruders. Statements like these mobilise a clash of civilisations discourse in which Europe is imagined as a sexually liberal place of gender equality threatened by the misogynist, backwards and rather nebulous migrant 'Other' (Puar 2013; Farris 2017; Holzberg, Madörin and Pfeifer 2021). A wide array of sources further framed the sexual violence in Cologne through the concept of '*taharrush*' – a term popularised in the context of group sexual assault of women during the protests on Tahir Square in Cairo. Angie Abdelmonem et al. (2016) have traced how this term came to travel from feminist activist spaces in Cairo – expressing their anger, pain and ressentiment about structural sexual violence – to the mainstream discourse in Germany and highlight how the German use of the term relied more on orientalist tropes than any actual transnational engagements with the problem of sexual violence. They argue that in Egypt, the term was used to call out practices of mass sexual violence on Tahir Square, which were often politically motivated and organised acts to crack down political dissent, while in Germany they came to be framed primarily as cultural practices located in the hardwired behaviours of racially marked subjects.

In the aftermath of Cologne, such racial and orientalist framing of sexual violence was probably nowhere more evident than in the cover pages of the conservative *Focus* and the traditionally leftist liberal *Süddeutsche Zeitung*. They respectively depicted a naked white woman covered in black handprints, and a black arm reaching into the crotch of a white female silhouette. The accompanying subtitles directed blame at 'sex-attacks by migrants' – the subtitle of the *Focus* cover – and 'young Muslims [who] cannot face the other sex in a relaxed way' – the accompanying text of the *Süddeutsche Zeitung* cover (see 'Nach' 2016).[4] Here anti-Black racism (e.g. the association of dirty/black handprints in the *Focus* cover) merges with orientalist and anti-Muslim tropes that are resurfacing in the war on terror. What these images show is how representations of race (black hands/handprints, white body/silhouette), religion ('young Muslims') and nation and citizenship ('sex attacks by migrants') are conflated into one unholy assemblage of the racialised 'sexual aggressor' (see also Dietze 2016b). Given its unclear contours, this figure ultimately remains what Ahmed (2004: 124) has referred to as an unclear 'ghostlike figure in the present, who gives us nightmares about the future, as an anticipated future of injury'. According to Ahmed, the 'impossibility of reducing [negative affect] to a particular body allows [it] to circulate' and attach to all kinds of racialised bodies deemed to be a threat to the nation (Ahmed 2004). Rather than blocking the accumulation of affect, the shifting and muddled constructions of race, religion and nationality make this form of affective bordering very powerful and allow rape to be framed as a more general threat to the nation.

While the images position the Black and/or Muslim sexual intruder as the object of anger and fear, empathetic concern is directed towards the helpless and abused white female body imagined as the innocent body of the nation. This slippage from the white female body to a nation in peril was also mirrored in the wider collusion of feminist and nationalist discourse. In her book on the events of New Year's Eve in Cologne, *The Shock*, the public face of feminism in Germany, Alice Schwarzer, frames sexual violence not as a structural form of gendered violence but as a strategic weapon used in geopolitical conflicts. She positions sexual violence as a conscious strategy of war used by 'Islamist enemies of the nation' and argues that the state needs to react with similar force. In this rhetoric, she was supported by figures like the self-described 'new feminist' Birgit Kelle who argued that we need 'new heroes' – men 'who would defend their women with the fist' (Kelle 2016). Rescue came in the shape of Björn Höcke from the AFD who, even before Cologne, had shown his concern for 'growing spaces of fear, especially for white, blond women' (Zschaler 2015), as well as high-ranking politicians like the head of the CSU, Horst Seehofer, who asserted that Germany needed a 'zero tolerance approach towards criminal migrants' and a harsher legal system 'with grit and punch' ('Seehofer will' 2016).

More liberal voices in the public sphere tried to question this militaristic rhetoric, suggesting that people need to show concern for migrant women who are also the victims of sexualised violence. In articles such as 'It's not just after Cologne that women lock their doors' (Heidenreich 2016), a range of newspapers covered incidents of sexual violence and abuse in asylum centres. While these reports try to centre the ressentiment of affected women over the resentment of the nation, within these reports, women are often represented as voiceless victims whose problems stem from their communities rather than the situations of war and deprivation they are fleeing, or the European border regimes that put them in this position in the first place. As such, they become positioned as the creators of their presumably oppressive situation. For instance, in an article entitled 'Be angry with Muslim women', Femen activist Zana Ramadani (2016) argues that Muslim women, as mothers, pass the 'Islamist values' to their sons, which are framed as the driving force for misogyny and sexual violence. These discourses similarly cement discursive borders between the sexually liberated host nation and the sexually uncontrolled migrant by appealing to a more humanitarian discourse in which empathetic concern and distancing anger emerge as two sides of the same coin. As in public debates around the veil (Korteweg and Yurdakul

2014; Şahin 2014), Muslim women are framed as victims who are likewise to be blamed for their presumably oppressed position.

An affective adhesive

Moreover, and perhaps paradoxically, the invocation of feminist rhetoric in the discourse after Cologne emerges in relation to a virulent surge of anti-gender discourse in which, next to Islam and migration, 'gender ideology' and 'gender-mainstreaming' are featured as common threats to the nation (Hark and Villa 2015; Kuhar and Patternotte 2017; Holvikivi, Ojeda and Holzberg 2024). Within the last years, discussions around issues such as gender-neutral language, trans rights and the visibility of queer politics have created growing anxiety within both right-wing and liberal circles. Far from this happening in opposition to the nationalist invocation of feminist rhetoric after Cologne, these discourses often intertwine. As Villa and Hark (2020) point out in their analysis of the event, Birgit Kelle, for instance, who blamed Cologne on archaic forms of patriarchy, has long warned of gender-mainstreaming as a 'mad ideology' whose ultimate goal is the destruction of the family. Similarly, the infamous essayist Harald Martenstein argued that 'it is about Islam, stupid' and warned of the dangerous image of women that this 'ideology' perpetuates (Martenstein 2016).

Defending women against Islam, however, did not keep him from continuing his weekly tirades against feminist, queer and trans politics in his weekly column in Germany's most influential weekly, *Die Zeit*, in which he consistently critiques gender studies as an 'anti-science' that tries to erase the natural difference between the sexes. The uptake of feminist positions for nationalist argumentations within Germany simultaneously reinforced conservative ideas of the family and a biologically essentialist, mostly heterosexual, gender binary. As Clare Hemmings (2021: 30) has shown in her analysis of anti-gender politics, these forms of argumentation commonly rely on claiming the 'sane middle ground' in which it is suggested that 'while "gender ideology" goes too far on the one hand, the *patriarchal control* of Islam threatens to pull us back into an excessive past'. Commentators like Kelle and Martenstein work to protect the status quo by constructing gender equality along ethnic and racial lines while simultaneously cementing the heterosexual family and a naturalised gender binary.

The racialised discourses of sexual violence in the wake of Cologne worked as an affective adhesive that stuck together right-wing, feminist and liberal voices and perspectives. All three positions framed sexual violence through colonial tropes that have long positioned sexual violence as a pathology of the Global South while marking the West as a space of progressive gender equality (Spivak 1988; Dhawan 2013; Kapur 2013; Farris 2017). More so, in the context of Cologne, discourses of sexuality itself worked a 'method of bordering' (Holzberg, Madörin and Pfeifer 2021: 1487) in which it was specifically the threat of sexual violence that came to operate as the 'language of border control' (Ticktin 2008: 863). This shows how border discourses of sexuality need to be understood as a key force in reproducing the racial grammars of deservingness. Whereas the nation is associated with the white purity and innocence of the normative female body and felt in need of protection, migrants are figured as primordial threats – sexual aggressors which need to be kept from abusing it.

In line with the racialised framing of the event, sexual violence is figured as a recent threat – a danger that arrived in Germany with the recent refugee migration – to a problem that Germany had presumably already overcome. This progress narrative imagines Germany as a bulwark of gender equality, confronted with the patriarchal practices of people stuck in primordial temporalities. As I will demonstrate in the next section, however, neither sexual violence nor any of the discourses mobilised in its aftermath are recent phenomena. Professed attachments to the narrative of a nation free from gendered and sexual violence not only erase the reality of structural gendered and sexual violence in Germany but also conceal that the figure of the racialised sexual aggressor and disciplinary sexual protection is constitutive of the German nation. The attacks in Cologne fall into a pattern woven through a long (post-)colonial history of the appropriation of the imperilled white female body as a powerful site of nation-making. In fact, these convergences of feminist and nationalist rhetoric are amendable for the evocation and mobilisation of anger *exactly because* they link back to well-established histories that secure the nation through sexual imaginaries of racial abuse and contagion.

A resonant echo

The anger following the attacks of Cologne unfolded within, and must be understood in relation to, a long and persistent history that fundamentally shapes the ways in which sexual violence and its harms are understood in Germany. Cologne stands in a long line of racialised sexual panics in which the threat of sexual violence played a key role in reaffirming the racial and cultural borders of the nation. In the following, I thus want to suggest that we might best understand the outrage around cases of sexual violence in Cologne as what Tina Campt (2005: 53) describes as a 'resonant echo' – a sound that clearly reverberates in the present but the past origin of which has been lost and is no longer recognised. The metaphor of the echo illuminates the fact that while these histories reverberate powerfully in the current moment, their noise simultaneously erases the traces of their own production. Tracing this echo back in time, we can see how much of the resentment expressed around Cologne mirrors long-established anxieties of national impurity, in which it was nearly always the trope of excessive sexuality that helped re-establish clear lines between who does and who does not belong to a national body defined in racial, gendered and sexual terms.

This long line of sexual panics links back to the first German citizenship laws during the German colonial Empire, when citizenship was established to enshrine a clear boundary between white Germans and colonised subjects in the colonies of German South-West Africa and German East Africa. As Fatima El-Tayeb (1999) points out in her incisive analysis of the racial history of citizenship laws in Germany, questions of sexuality were key to the implementation of these first citizenship laws. They surfaced most strongly in discussions around 'miscegenation' and 'racial mixing', because it was through marriage that white German men extended the rights of the polis to their wives and children. As a result, in 1913, interracial marriages were outlawed by decree in most colonies, and a first nationality law was established that enshrined the principle of *jus sanguinis* – defining citizenship based on bloodline.[5] The alleged threat of Black men raping white women was crucial in justifying such legislation in both parliamentary and public discussions. From its inception, then, definitions of nationhood in the German empire were based on gendered and sexualised discourses of racial purity that framed Germany as 'a raced and gendered body' made vulnerable through 'the female body as the vehicle, conduit, or site of entry for potential pollution' (Campt 2005: 41).

From then on, moral panics about racialised sexual aggressors and interracial sexual relations would resurface regularly, rearticulated in various configurations. One of the most (in)famous of these came to be known as the 'Black Horror of the Rhine'. After the French army stationed several colonial soldiers of colour in western Germany at the end of the First World War, a range of civil society groups started a campaign that circulated 'the image of the "primitive African beast" that roamed around the streets of a civilized nation raping and killing' (El-Tayeb 1999: 164). Even more drastic in their racist portrayal of Black men abusing and kidnapping helpless white women, images from this period published in satire magazines and propaganda drawings show uncanny resemblances to the title covers appearing after Cologne. Tina Campt (2005: 64) argues that this panic around mostly consensual relations between white women and Black soldiers here similarly worked as a 'national adhesive' for a nation in search of repairing a wounded national pride and identity. Colonial tropes of Black sexuality as excessive, animalistic and threatening were evoked to gain sympathy from other European powers and helped to reframe Germany's position from that of an aggressor responsible for the First World War to that of an unfairly treated 'victim of black aggression' (El-Tayeb 1999: 164).

The logic of a community of blood that was enshrined in the national-ity laws of 1913, and underlined most of these panics, was taken to an extreme during the Third Reich, when race became the key organising tenet of governance. As Dagmar Herzog (2007) points out, before the Nuremberg laws and the systemic extermination of non-'Aryan' life in the concentration camps, racial policies such as sterilisation and hygiene laws were imple-mented, and white German women faced laws which circumscribed their choices of sexual partner to only those of pure Aryan heritage. Particularly in the early days of the Reich, it was again through figurations of sexual violence that Jews and other racial and ethnic minorities were invoked as sexual predators coming to threaten the innocent Aryan female body, and that played a crucial role in the early days of antisemitic pogroms and the mass mobilisation for national socialism. Antisemitic sexual propaganda published in magazines like *Der Stürmer*, a popular antisemitic national weekly, showed how a 'relentless obsession with "documenting" Jewish sex criminality and the prevalence of "race defilement"' offered an excuse for pornographic indulgence and gave a 'crucial moral permission to hate with-out guilt' (Herzog 2007: 39–40). Here again the body of the white woman, this time attacked by monstrous Jewish men with tentacles, emerged as the symbol for the white and innocent German nation.

After the horrors of the Holocaust and the end of the Second World War, the hope for a new beginning, a *Stunde Null* (hour zero), was on the horizon, which would have seen the construction of a new democracy freed from the racial logics of the past. However, while the Nuremberg laws were abolished and a programme of denazification implemented by the Allies, the old colo-nial laws *of jus sanguins* were reinstalled (El-Tayeb 1999; Chin et al. 2010). Race was officially sidelined as a relic of the past, yet already during the process of denazification, scandals about interracial relations between Black American GIs and white German women again filled parliamentary and public discussions. These not only rearticulated fears of Black male sexual-ity, but also enabled white German men and the white troops of the US army to bond as they 'both agreed upon the necessity to "defend" white woman-hood and police white women' (Fehrenbach 2005: 34). As a role model for the young German democracy, the racially segregated US military reasserted that democracy was still a notion meant primarily for white Europeans. As Fatima El-Tayeb (2016) highlights, Germany clung to a 'colour-blind' ideol-ogy that hinged on 'the firm conviction that [Germany] would be free from structural racism', while enforcing it in most spheres of political, economic and social life (El-Tayeb 2016: 7). Citizenship remained an ethnic and racial category in which 'native' white Germans were socially and legally differentiated from all 'Ausländer' (foreigners); this found its expression in policies such as the guest worker initiative of the 1960s and 1970s, which expected workers to eventually return to their home countries – and who, as Naika Foroutan recounts, were likewise suspected of raping blond women after their work shifts (Krüger 2015).

After mobilisation by migrant groups, people of colour and other activists from the left in the 1980s and 1990s, citizenship and naturalisation laws in Germany were eventually altered in 2000, and children born in Germany to non-German parents were given the chance to claim formal citizenship (Howard 2008; Kaya 2013). Despite these legal changes, the narrative of the German people as an ethnically homogeneous population persevered, and 'race' continues to operate, often under the disguise of 'cultural difference' as seen in moral panics around the 'Islamification' of Europe (El-Tayeb 2016; Lentin 2020). While the ongoing effects of 'race' and racism can mainly be identified in the history of the German Federal Republic as the state whose citizenship laws were adopted after reunification, the GDR was structured similarly. Aleksandra Lewicki (2018: 63) shows that despite its identification as an anti-fascist state, the GDR also treated migrants who mainly came as guest workers from other socialist countries like Vietnam and Mozambique as 'foreigners' who were meant to return home and concludes that both 'German states claim to have overcome the legacy of racism, but project and normalise a myth of ethnic homogeneity, and nurture a sense of superior entitlement in their citizenry'. As such, also after reunification, and migratised communities in both West and East Germany continued to be treated as anomalies in a country imagined to be racially and ethnically homogeneous. Sexuality and gender continue to play a crucial role in these debates, producing emotive discussions around issues such as honour killings, forced marriages or the Muslim veil (Yurdakul and Korteweg 2009, 2014; Şahin 2014).

This condensed historical overview demonstrates that the anger provoked by the Cologne attacks needs to be understood in relation to long-standing colonial anxieties around racialised sexual threat. As Ahmed (2014: 11) affirms so evocatively, affects sediment over time and come 'to reside in objects, only through an erasure of the history of [their] production and circulation'. In a context in which race has become 'buried alive' (Goldberg 2009: 1), the traces of its sexual history have likewise been submerged. Tracing this resonant echo back in time, however, we can see how many of the fears around Cologne mirror long-established anxieties about national impurity, in which it was nearly always the trope of sexual threat that helped re-establish clear lines of who does and who does not belong to a national body defined in racial, gendered and sexual terms. The metaphor of the 'resonant echo' highlights that these histories should be understood not as a clear-cut 'colonial continuity', but as a more contingent, contextual reverberation – a sound that can alter, one that resonates according to the context of its articulation.

What the figure of the echo further highlights is how the defence of the nation in presumably feminist terms is not new either. Lora Wildenthal (2001) points out how white women played a crucial role in empire building. While only very few of them identified as feminists, several of them stood up for women's rights and highlighted their unique importance for white racial purity and the inculcation of German culture and the family. As such they campaigned against interracial marriage and circulated an image of African and Pacific women as sexually promiscuous and inferior. These efforts continued into the Nazi regime, and also after the Second World War, women's groups have repeatedly been engaged in nationalist endeavours, often in opposition to the presumably backwards and patriarchal practices of the Global South. The collusions of feminist and nationalist discourse in the aftermath of Cologne, therefore, need to be understood in a longer historical perspective in which narrow conceptions of citizenship and nationality have long been protected by recourse to the protection of proper femininity and the white heterosexual nuclear family. The use of nationalist argumentation for the protection of women paired with simultaneous attacks on feminist struggles as dangerous, mad and excessive are not paradoxical but mutually reinforcing discourses that have long been key for the construction of the nation.

The question of forgiveness

As in historical moments before, the sexual panic about racialised threat worked as a welcome outlet for reversing the opening of national borders that had taken place in the months prior, and for questioning the authority of the state and civil society actors seen as facilitating this. Feeling the nation as a victim in need of defence allowed people of different political affiliations to come together and reaffirm racial and heteronormative constructions of what it means to be German. This moment of intense affective bordering worked to unite the diffuse resentments of various sections of society around the affective fiction of a nation leaving the safe fold of heteronormative whiteness. It shifted the racial grammars of deservingness from framing refugees as people in need who require empathy and assistance to positioning them as sexual threats who need to be fended off. As this nationalist resentment took hold of the public sphere, however, what happened to the actual ressentiment of women experiencing sexual violence that had incited the debate? How did they and intersectional feminist activists who had long fought against the normalisation of rape in society engage in this moment? And where was the anger and frustration of people who were on the receiving end of the racist outrage that was produced in the wake of Cologne? How could they voice their concerns without being branded as excusing or facilitating acts of sexual violence? In other words, how could ressentiment and resentment be disentangled in this moment of affective bordering?

Martha Nussbaum (2016b: 20) suggests that to rework anger and resentment into lasting forms of justice and equality requires a focus on 'compassion and a forward-looking spirit of generosity and cooperation'. She argues that 'inflicting pain on the wrongdoer does not help restore the thing that was lost' and points out that payback easily leads to violent spirals of retaliation. Trying to break this cycle of retaliation in the aftermath of Cologne, a range of organisations focused on counteracting the anger that they saw themselves confronted with more positive emotions. In the cities like Cologne, Berlin and Stuttgart, organisations like the *German-Turkish Union Cologne*, *Tunisian Youth* and *Syrian Men for Fairness* gave out roses to women and distributed letters and flyers titled 'not in my name', in which the authors distanced themselves from the perpetrators and condemned the crimes of the New Year's Eve night ('Syrer demonstrieren' 2016). Many of those statements highlighted how the attacks in Cologne had nothing to do with Islam or Arab culture and how they should not be used to divide society. Similar accounts can be found in interviews published by newspapers such as *die Süddeutsche Zeitung* that offered Syrian men the space to write about their perspective on the event and put them in the position to affirm statements like 'I have been here for a year and have never done anything' (Schlüter 2016: 1). In subsequent actions, several activists from organisations like *Avaaz*, primarily white German women, reciprocated the action and handed roses back. They framed this as an act of thankfulness for their prior gestures and a sign against racism and xenophobia.

These initiatives created moving media representations that highlighted positive acts of love and understanding hidden in the shadow of Cologne. Doing so, they hark back to the emotive language of welcome culture and reactivated earlier representations of people welcoming each other at train and bus stations. This form of activism, however, is confronted by the paradox that in order to undo the culturally essentialist framing of the event, it likewise needs to reaffirm it. In a revealing scene, in one of the YouTube videos of the events, an elderly woman asks the man giving her the rose 'but what do you have to do with this?' The problem with such actions is that they implicitly take on the stigma of 'collective guilt' that is put on racialised minorities, in particular Muslim communities, and re-inscribe the idea that Cologne indeed arose out of specific religious and cultural practices. As such, actions like these do not necessarily contest the established racial grammars of how sexual violence is constructed in the German imaginary and can further entrench dangerous dynamics of who deserves to be part of the nation and who does not.

Nussbaum's strategy of forgiveness seems to falter in the face of the racialised grammars of deservingness that structure forms of affective bordering. It underestimates the power of racial and sexualised hierarchies in the scene of forgiveness. Love and harmony, after all, are hard to create in a context in which some subjects are marked as threats to be excluded from the nation altogether. Moreover, these actions tend to elide the violence of the heart of 'chivalry' through a normalising gesture of heterosexual romance as such, plastering over rather than addressing the structural problem of sexual violence. The move to love and forgiveness too easily clads over the well-justified forms of ressentiment that women who are affected by sexual violence feel. These after all are not simply dangerous but potentially useful affects in a society of endemic sexual violence. In her defence of anger in political life, Audre Lorde (1997: 280) argues that 'every woman has a well-stocked arsenal of anger potentially useful against those oppressions, personal and institutional, which brought that anger into being'. Anger from this perspective is not the opposite of justice but is part and parcel of enacting structural transformations and the move towards a more just and less violent society. In activism reminiscent of such argumentation, feminist activists tried to counter the swelling resentment after Cologne by grounding it in the actual ressentiment of women who experienced sexual violence, while contesting its appropriation through nationalist discourse.

Confronting the echo

The biggest initiative in this regard was the campaign #Ausnahmslos (without exception). Initiated by a collective of journalists, academics, artists and other public figures, the group organised several demonstrations and an online petition that was signed by several hundred supporters, which argued that 'the sustained fight against sexualised violence of any kind of is of highest priority' and warned that 'it is harmful for all of us if feminism is exploited by extremists to incite against certain ethnicities, as it is currently done in the discussion surrounding the incidents in Cologne' (Gümüşay et al. 2016). #Ausnahmslos employed an explicitly intersectional approach and spoke out against nationalist appropriation of their arguments while focusing on the problem of sexual violence and called for 'stronger support of rape crisis centres and counselling support', 'increased educational work and awareness campaigns' and 'gender and sexualised violence sensitivity trainings' for the police and law enforcement (Gümüşay et al. 2016). The group organised counterdemonstrations to those of PEGIDA and the AFD, spoke against the appropriation of feminist discourse through nationalist argumentation and declared that feminism is and needs to be anti-racist.

Rather than aiming for states of love and forgiveness, #Ausnahmlos resisted the nationalist appropriation of feminist affect by centring the actual ressentiment about structural sexual violence that women in Germany are subjected to as well as the anger and hurt of people who experience racialised police and border violence on an everyday level. They did so by pointing out how the right-wing appropriation of feminist discourse furthered border violence and fuelled racist right-wing violence in the country. They also pointed to the hypocrisy of the debate in which conservative politicians like Horst Seehofer, who now called for harsher punishments against the perpetrators of Cologne, had still voted against rape in marriage being a crime in 1997. As Stefanie Boulila and Christiane Carri (2017) point out, as a result, they were attacked by political commentators like Martenstein who suggested that feminists trying to initiate a more intersectional debate around the night of Cologne were relativising the crimes and compared them to Holocaust deniers.

Despite these attacks, #Ausnahmslos continued their activism and lobbied for a reform of the sexual violence laws in Germany, in which the guidelines of the Istanbul conventions of 2011 would finally be implemented. In trying to push through a reform of the sexual violence legislation in Germany, feminist activists, however, found themselves in tricky terrain. They operated in a discursive landscape that was dominated by echoes that directly linked sexual violence to race, religion and nationality and the carceral logic of the state. As Angela Davis (2000: 4) has asked so poignantly in a speech on Black feminist responses to sexual violence, 'can a state that is thoroughly infused with racism, male dominance, class-bias and homophobia and that constructs itself in and through violence act to minimize it in the lives of women?' Her question alerts us to the fact that anger and resentment can open new forms of justice in response to sexual violence and racism yet might likewise fuel state policies that come to hit the subjects who already are most affected by structural violence. In June 2017, the German parliament passed a set of new laws known as the 'No means No' legislation, that included several demands long made by feminist activists. While conservatives attacked the reform, activists from the left had seemingly finally achieved what they demanded.

The laws, however, were directly tied to harsher migration and deportation law. This meant a twofold punishment for asylum seekers not applicable to German citizens, which also makes it more difficult for victims to file charges – particularly if they come out of the immediate families or surroundings of the perpetrators. Moreover, the law included a separate legal category for sexual abuse committed by groups, which, according to feminist activists, does not only speak to the targeted implementation of the reform but might also be unconstitutional as it easily leads into forms of collective punishment (Holst and Montanari 2017). The mobilisations of #Ausnahmlos show the potentials and difficulties of disentangling feminist ressentiment from national resentment. By highlighting the actual forms of ressentiment that were overshadowed in public debate post-Cologne, #Ausnahmslos refused the terms and frames through which women's bodies are placed as metaphors and sites of reproduction for the nation. Fully breaking out of the racialised grammars that tie the defence of women to the defence of the nation, however, seemed difficult in a context haunted by colonial echoes that have long tied feminist ressentiment about sexual violence to nationalist resentment about racialised Others. At this point, for many activists involved, anger seemed like the only answer left.

Conclusion

In *Scandal in Togo*, Rebekka Habermas (2016) recounts the story of Geo Schmidt, an officer in German colonial Togo who became infamous for sexually assaulting Black women in the colonies. While his case troubled the self-image of the German colonial Empire supposed to bring civilisation to Africa, Rebekka Habermas suggests that Geo Schmidt's story was not exceptional but an everyday episode in colonial domination, in which the control over colonised sexuality was an incremental part of imperial rule. Her book challenges common conceptions of sexual violence in which sexual aggression is assumed to originate from racialised colonised subjects and emerges as part of a larger post- and decolonial movement in Germany that tries to deconstruct and reshuffle the politics of racial and gendered violence. In these actions, people not only mobilise their own anger and hurt about historical forms of oppression but also reframe the narratives through which the nation is constructed.

This chapter emerges in relation to these efforts by highlighting histories that help us to explain the current sprouting of resentment in Western democracies. While I have suggested that anger might well be understood as a catalyst for an already boiling anti-migrant sentiment that stuck together feminist, liberal and right-wing positions, I have argued that we might best understand the outrage about New Year's Eve night in Cologne as a resonant echo of the past. Cologne needs to be understood in a longer series of sexual panics about racialised sexual attackers that have helped the nation to come together in times of perceived national crisis. This dynamic seems to be activated today, not only fuelling practices of affective bordering that position racialised minorities and migrants outside the nation, but also working to enshrine gendered and heteronormative hierarchies. While this echo reverberates powerfully in the current moment, its noise simultaneously erases the traces of its own production.

More specifically, I have shown how the affective bordering after Cologne works through the appropriation of feminist ressentiment about sexual violence for the mobilisation of nationalist resentment about migration and racialised minorities. This entanglement of feminist and nationalist feelings and discourse provides a key challenge for intersectional activists aiming to contest sexual violence as well as the racialised violence of nationalism and the European border regime. Initiatives like #Ausnahmslos provided key efforts and lessons in the potentials and difficulties of engaging this disentanglement in contemporary practices of affective bordering. With these lessons in mind, let us have a look at how else activists tried to affectively challenge bordering practices by turning to actions aimed at shaming Germany and the EU for the murderous effects of its border policies.

Notes

1 Nussbaum takes this definition from Aristotle's *Nicomachean Ethics* as probably the most common theoretical source for defining the term *anger*. Based on this conceptualisation, *anger* is often defined as the general term for a range of closely related sub or sister emotions such as resentment, outrage and wrath. These are sometimes differentiated in the hurt that they react to. Anger, for instance, might be described as a more general affective reaction to having been wronged or offended, usually directed towards people of equal standing, resentment is directed towards a hurt inflicted by higher-standing individuals, while contempt is directed at lower-standing individuals. On a social and phenomenological level, however, these distinctions are difficult to make so I prefer a more open conceptualisation and suggest that it is most helpful to think of these affects as differing mainly in terms of intensity, expression and duration. Whereas resentment describes the long-term and silent lingering of anger when it is not or cannot be expressed, fury and wrath mark intense outbursts of anger's explosive charge.

2 The concept of '*Zivilisationsbruch*' was popularised by Dan Diner (1996) to describe the Holocaust as an exceptional crime of universal human importance. For a critical discussion of this concept, its history and some of its tensions, see Dirk Moses (2021b) and Aram Ziai (2016).

3 The term *Lügenpresse* is closely tied to the history of National Socialism. The Nazis used the term in the early 1930s to attack the international press and to propagate antisemitic conspiracy theories. It has made a sinister comeback in contemporary conspiracy theories and the discussions of 'fake news'.

4 Whereas the editors of the generally left-leaning *Süddeutsche Zeitung* later apologised for the racist imagery, the chief editor of the more conservative *Focus*, Ulrich Reitz, defended their cover by asserting that who says that the cover is sexist or racist 'is afraid of the truth' ('Rassistische Titelbilder' 2016).

5 These laws are based on the Prussian citizenships laws, established in 1871, that were likewise based on the logic of *jus sanguins* and that became the basis of the legal system of the German Empire. However, during this time different federal citizenship laws still played a crucial role, and a German citizen was anybody who held citizenship of one of the states of the German Empire. The first national German citizenship laws are, therefore, usually traced back to the legislations of 1913 (for a more detailed history see El-Tayeb 1999).

4

Shame: public shaming in the shadow of Holocaust guilt

Introduction

After New Year's Eve 2015 in Cologne, the hope and empathy of the early summer of migration increasingly turned into nationalist anger and resentment. I have analysed the affective dynamics of this development in the last three chapters and have questioned the potential of 'positive' affective forces like hope and empathy to overcome the racial grammars of deservingness that structure practices of affective bordering in the wake of the long summer of migration. Yet positive emotions were not the only affective forces that activists and other actors mobilised to challenge the European border regime during this time. Already in August 2015, members of the European United Left staged a *Walk of Shame* in the European parliament. They rolled out a 100-metre-long carpet reading the names of migrants who had died because of the border policies of the EU (Leboucq 2018). The carpet consisted of an excerpt from the *List of Refugee Deaths*, compiled by the anti-racist coalition United for Intercultural Action, which documents the deaths of people who died crossing the Mediterranean, in detention camps and following deportations since the establishment of the EU in 1993 ('List of Refugee Deaths' 2023). The *Walk of Shame* was one of many actions in which the *List of Refugee Deaths* has since been used as a political tool for shaming the European Union.

Simultaneous to these cross-European actions, in Germany, the artist-activist collective the Centre for Political Beauty organised a range of actions aimed at shaming the German government for the murderous border violence it perpetuates. In September 2015, the Centre organised the activist performance *The Dead Are Coming*, in which they staged a mass burial in front of the Bundestag to call attention to migrants killed at the borders of Europe. As part of this multi-sited action, the collective brought the bodies of two deceased migrants from the borderlands of Europe to give them a dignified funeral in Germany. After the burial – to which state officials like the Chancellor, Angela Merkel, and the Interior Minister, Thomas de

Maizière, were officially invited – a group of protestors stormed the lawn with shovels and dug up symbolic graves for the people killed at the borders of Europe ('The Dead' 2015). Sharing similar affective and political strategies, both actions were focused on shaming political authorities by bringing the murderous violence of the border into the centre of public attention.

Through the analysis of the *Walk of Shame* and *The Dead Are Coming*, in this chapter, I examine public shaming as a strategy for holding the European border regime to account. I suggest that these actions enact reintegrative forms of shaming – shaming that focuses on betterment and reconciliation (Braithwaite 1989, 2000) – by pointing to the EU's commitment to universal human rights and Germany's dedication to undoing the racial legacies of the Third Reich. While these strategies open ways to expose the hypocrisy of contemporary border politics, I also inquire into the problems they face. On the one hand, these forms of reintegrative shaming can re-cement practices of affective bordering as they need to re-centre Europe as the locus of enlightened morality, especially in Germany, where Holocaust guilt has played a key role in reinstalling new forms of nationalism over the last decade. On the other hand, I show that strategies of reintegrative shaming increasingly stay mute in a moment in which right-wing actors are eroding the idea that European border violence and the horrors of the Holocaust are indeed shameful. The chapter consequently ends with the question of how to *shame the shameless* and shows how, in a moment of shamelessness, many activists have no other choice but to enact forms of disintegrative shaming – shaming focused on ostracisation and stigmatisation (Braithwaite 1989, 2000) – as an act of anti-fascist despair and confrontation.

Reintegrative and disintegrative shaming

The use of shame in contemporary migrant justice and anti-border campaigns follows a long and complex history of public shaming in social justice activism. The political potential of shaming is based on shame being a public emotion that relies on making something that you do not want to be revealed known to the outside world and open to a negative judgement. While it can be enough for oneself to know about the shameful act that one has committed, shame is augmented in the face of others judging the subject for their action (Sedgwick and Frank 1995; Sedgwick 2003; Probyn 2005). Shame, in other words, requires a public audience or a witness. The public character of shame can already be seen in its etymology, meaning to be clothed or covered – highlighting the act of being exposed, of having revealed what one does not want the public to see, as the key dynamic behind shame's affective force (Ahmed 2014). In queer feminist scholarship, shame is commonly thought of as an unbearable feeling that inscribes normative power constellations into the body. Whether it is through misogynist forms of 'slut-shaming' or the homo- and transphobic ridiculing of queer sexualities and non-normative gender identities, shame is that which marks, produces and controls marginalised gendered and sexual subjects (Eribon 2004; Stockton 2006; Halperin and Traub 2009; Munt 2017; Shefer and Munt 2019).

At the same time, queer feminist scholars have provided powerful reflections about the potential of reclaiming the affective power of shame, with scholars like Elspeth Probyn (2005) highlighting that 'shame is immensely productive politically and conceptually in advancing a project of everyday ethics' (Probyn 2005: 326). Probyn suggests that the ethical potential of shame derives from shame emerging in the gap between the reality of who one is and the ideal of what one aims to be (or at least pretends to be). Social justice movements have exploited this ethical potential and turned shame into a tool for holding states to account for the actions they commit and by highlighting the gap between the ideals they claim to aspire to and the violence they commit. Deborah Gould (2009), for instance, has shown how in the history of ACT UP, activists mobilised shame away from the queer bodies infected with the disease and towards the political and economic institutions that stayed inactive in the face of their death. Imogen Tyler (2013, 2020) has similarly illustrated how states of shame and stigma are key to contemporary austerity regimes in the UK and reflects on how stigma can be attached to the institutions that produce precarity and poverty rather than the subjects affected by it. Redirecting shame away from the body of the marginalised to structural forms of political domination offers a powerful way to question and redraw boundaries of what counts as politically appropriate and ethically right in specific a historical conjuncture.

The use of public shaming for social justice movements, however, is not without problems and difficulties. In her work on state apologies for the genocidal violence enacted on Aboriginal and Torres Strait Islander people in Australia, Sara Ahmed (2014), for instance, has shown how the acknowledgement of shame can also work to clad over rather than address forms of historical responsibility. Ahmed shows how, in the context of Australia, state apologies did little to actually address the ongoing forms of oppression and material inequalities that mark the lives of many Indigenous people, while allowing the government to claim a position of ethical feeling and even pride for having acknowledged the crimes of the past. As such, she argues that 'expressions of shame about histories of violence work not only as a narrative of "recovery", but also as a form of "covering over"' (2014: 197). In other words, the acknowledgement of shame for wrongdoings in the past can work not primarily as a form of historical redress but as a way of 'feeling better in the present' (Ahmed 2014: 197). What Ahmed's work shows is that shaming can stay mute. It can fail to have the effect – or can even have the opposite effect – we intend it to have.

At the same time, shame can also be met with hostility and backlash. Rather than leading to people or institutions changing their behaviour, it can usher in rejection and retaliation and as such produce even harsher forms of political violence (Snyder 2020). If shame after all is an unbearable feeling, subjects will find ways to reject it. To understand this dynamic of shaming in more depth, we can draw on the work of John Braithwaite (1989), who, in his work on crime and punishment, makes a distinction between *reintegrative* and *disintegrative* shaming. He argues that reintegrative shaming 'communicates disapproval within a continuum of respect for the offender; the offender is treated as a good person who has done a bad deed' (1989: 281). Reintegrative shaming is forgiving; it is focused on betterment and rehabilitation to enable perpetrators to rejoin the social fold. Disintegrative shaming, in contrast, is based on stigmatisation as a disrespectful way of shaming in which 'the offender is treated as a bad person' (Braithwaite 1989). It targets the person as such rather than the wrongful action they have committed. He argues that disintegrative shaming is dangerous and can easily lead to further crime as 'stigmatization is unforgiving – the offender is left with the stigma permanently'. As such, Braithwaite argues that reintegrative forms of shaming are way more likely to be successful in altering deviant or criminal behaviour and should always be favoured over disintegrative shaming. While Braithwaite's ideas are developed in the field of criminology, this logic can also be transposed to political activism in which, as I will suggest in the following, most public shaming of the European border regime has, in line with Braithwaite's suggestions, tried to be reintegrative.

Shaming the European Union

From this perspective, the *List of Refugee Deaths* can be understood as a tool for reintegrative shaming that brings the murderous violence enacted at the borders of Europe to public attention and, in the case of the *Walk of Shame*, into the heart of political power. Rolled out in the halls of the European Parliament, the list forced members of parliament to walk over the fate of people who have died through policies that they have helped create or made little effort to alter. By 7 June 2023, the *List* had recorded the deaths of 52,760 people killed by the European border who were not even considered important enough to be counted by a border regime otherwise so concerned with surveillance and documentation ('List of Refugee Deaths' 2023). The list is compiled and presented in the dehumanising language of statistics, so common to the governmental logics of biopolitics (Tazzioli 2015; Pfeifer forthcoming). Rather than aiming to flatten the historical and social relations that caused these deaths in the first place, however, the *List* uses numbers as an act of witnessing aimed at generating shame and responsibility by presenting people's fate in the language the EU supposedly understands best: the cold objectivity of numbers and statistics.

Next to being used during the *Walk of Shame*, the *List* has become a crucial tool in border activism and has been supported by more than five hundred NGOs and anti-racist and migrant grassroots groups across Europe who have deployed it in their efforts to highlight the mass killing of migrants as 'the shame to Europe's civil conscience' (United for Intercultural Action 2006: 9). Organisations associated with UNITED use the *List* to detach shame from the body of the illegalised migrant and instead highlight the state apparatuses responsible for their abject position. The *List* has helped grassroots organisations solicit a public affective response and gain support from established institutions, national newspapers, art galleries and political parties. With the help of the artist Banu Cennetoğlu, the *List* has since been put up in public places all over Europe – hung in the metro in Hungary, shown in train stations in Austria, and displayed on advertising surfaces in Germany, the UK and the Netherlands. This support is paramount to public shaming as a political strategy, given that shame augments in the face of a witness we respect or deem important.

The necessity of reintegrative shaming

Probyn (2005) points out that shame is only felt and acknowledged *as shameful* in relation to something we deem important and valuable. She argues that 'whatever it is that shames you will be something important to you, an essential part of yourself'. If, for instance, neither I nor other witnesses agree that heteronormativity is something to aspire to and that being queer is shameful, calling me so will fail to create the shame it intends. This means that shame can only be mobilised within an (at least partially shared) system of value. More concretely, it needs to be invoked in relation to a shared ideal of who, or what, one aims to be. In psychoanalytic vocabulary, we could say that shame emerges in the gap between the ego and the ego-ideal – the inner image of the ideal self that the ego aspires to.[1] In other words, one can only be truly shamed for something one would like to be or believes oneself to be. In the *Walk of Shame*, the gap between the ego and the ego-ideal is created by pointing out the mismatch between the EU's self-mythology as the birthplace of universal human rights and the guarantor of equality and justice and the murderous machine of the European borders regime that migrants encounter at, and within, its borders. The *List* contrasts such idealised self-understandings of Europe as the seat of human rights with the Arendtian (1973) insight that human rights have only ever really counted for certain European citizens and mean little without a state able, or willing, to enforce them.

Since shaming actions like the *Walk of Shame* critique the self-idealised notion of Europe as the carrier of universal human rights and equality, they simultaneously reaffirm, or rather *have* to reaffirm, this notion. After all, carrying the *List* into the EU parliament works on the assumption that while the EU is the originator of this violence, it might also be the place where this violence could be resolved. In their associated campaign information 'Fortress Europe: Death by Policy', UNITED ask for such a resolution by pointing out that the refugee deaths are not tragic accidents, but the results of political decisions made by EU member states. They highlight that 'all these deaths are due to policies that criminalise a fundamental human right: freedom of movement' and draw attention to processes of migrant criminalisation, border externalisation, deportation and detention regimes as key to this process ('Fortress Europe' 2016: 1). UNITED traditionally holds a day of action on 20 June as World Refugee Day. The day was declared by the United Nations (UN) in 2001 on the fifty-year anniversary of the Geneva Refugee Convention of 1951, in which the international community vowed never again to allow the atrocities of the Second World War. Highlighting border deaths on this day reminds the EU of its commitment to international law that many of its member states played a key role in drafting in response to European refugee migration after the Second World War.

The necessity of affirming Europe as the arbiter of human rights in acts of public shaming becomes clear through Braithwaite's (1989, 2000) distinction between *reintegrative* and *disintegrative* forms of shaming. Whereas disintegrative shaming formulates critique as an attack on the person or institution (border deaths are a result of the structural constitution of the EU), reintegrative shaming focuses on actions and is followed by gestures of acceptance and reparation (border deaths are a problem created by the EU that might be overcome through a renewed commitment to human rights and international conventions). The *List* could be and is also being used for acts of disintegrative shaming that would confront the idea and institution of Europe as the outcome of colonial domination which diligently protects its relative affluence and assurances of liberty. This form of shaming would focus on a more structural and radical critique of Europe and highlight the global inequalities it is entangled in. However, disintegrative shaming, as Braithwaite (1989) argues, leaves little place for betterment and is commonly met with resistance, retreat or further violence. Given this logic, shaming actions like the *Walk of Shame* and the *List* are commonly mobilised in a more reintegrative manner that affirms the notion of Europe as at least a potential haven of democracy and universal human rights.

Mobilising Holocaust guilt

If, on a European level, reintegrative shaming usually operates by pointing to the gap between self-idealised notions of the EU as a human rights bearer and the brutal reality of its borders, in Germany shame is often mobilised in relation to historical guilt about the Holocaust. The German daily newspaper *Der Tagesspiegel*, for instance, published the *List* not on International Refugee Day but on 9 November – a date that occupies a central position in the national collective memory. It marks Hitler's first attempted coup in 1923 and the *Reichspogromnacht* of 1938, which is now commemorated to honour the victims of antisemitism and the Nazi terror during the Third Reich. Moreover, 9 November marks the fall of the Berlin Wall in 1989 and denotes the beginning of German reunification. In explaining why the editors published the *List* on this 'fateful day for the Germans', they suggest that having made it through these histories 'is a gift, after everything that was. Yet it is also an obligation, to again and again live up to and do justice to this gift' (Casdorff and Marold 2017: 1). Here the article taps into the anti-fascist notion of 'never again', in which responsibility for altering the fate of migrants and confronting racialised state violence is explained in the context of Germany's dark historical past. It is articulated out of an ongoing sense of guilt for this history as well as a sense of gratitude for having received another chance at creating a more just society in the present.

Shame and guilt are closely related emotions that are commonly differentiated in relation to the source of negative feelings that they derive from. Often discussed as self-conscious affective forces, both pertain to people's self-perception and their awareness of how others respond to them. Whereas shame is a negative feeling about who one is (a not-so-just and equal Europe), guilt is associated more with one's actions (the crimes of Germany's past). Focused on action rather than being, guilt has an even more moral character than shame. Here the negative feeling does not only emerge from a mismatch between what one aims to be and actually is, but also from a deep feeling of moral doubt and remorse for actions that have trespassed one's ethical code (see also Ahmed 2014: 105). In psychoanalytic vocabulary, this means that if shame arises out of a mismatch between the ego and the ego-ideal, guilt emerges in the gap between the ego and the super-ego as the internalisation of cultural and moral rules that guide one's ethical conduct. As such, mobilising guilt might be an even more potent affect for holding people and institutions to account for their actions as it cuts into the deep layers of morality and ethics associated with social and political action.

Given this affective logic, the mobilisation of guilt – and particularly guilt for the Holocaust – has long been a crucial motor for and target of social justice activism in Germany. The mobilisation of Holocaust guilt in Germany operates in close relationship to processes of *Vergangenheitsbewältigung* – the act of coming to terms with the past. Since public intellectuals like Karl Jaspers (1946) and Theodor Adorno (1959) demanded that Germany cannot just disavow, but needs to work through and confront, the antisemitic crimes of its past, the mobilisation of guilt for the Holocaust has been a crucial affective grammar through which German politics has been animated and contested.[2] As Howie Rechavia-Taylor (2022: 210) highlights, it was through the mobilisation of 'grassroots anti-fascist, Jewish, and Roma and Sinti activists' that some reckoning with the past took place amongst the denial and avoidance that marked social and political life in post-war Germany. Initiated in the early post-war period, *Vergangenheitsbewältigung* needs to be understood as 'the result of struggle on the part of Germany's historical victims and the children of perpetrators – a struggle to recognise the importance of antisemitic genocidal policy to National Socialism' (Rechavia-Taylor 2022: 210). While the history of *Vergangenheitsbewältigung* was and continues to be a fraught and complex process, since the early 2000s it has become part of German *Staatsräson* (reason of state). All democratic political parties in parliament, except for the far-right AFD, have committed themselves (at least rhetorically) to honouring the memory of the Holocaust, as seen amongst others in the building of the Memorial to the Murdered Jews of Europe in the centre of Berlin.

The Dead Are Coming

A specifically telling invocation of this national guilt in relation to contemporary border regimes could be seen in the activist intervention *The Dead Are Coming*. In this action, the activist-artist collective the Centre for Political Beauty staged a mass burial in front of the Bundestag to call attention to migrants killed at the borders of Europe – echoing the *Walk of Shame* in its affective and political strategy. In explaining the rationale for *The Dead Are Coming*, the Centre for Political Beauty declared that:

> The group's basic understanding is that the legacy of the Holocaust is rendered void by political apathy, the rejection of refugees and cowardice. It believes that Germany should not only learn from its history but also take action. ('Political resistance' 2016)

In this invocation, the Centre for Political Beauty draws on Holocaust guilt as a source for political accountability and reparative action. Growing up with Holocaust education in school and public institutions, I myself was formed as a political subject by such affective commitment to the politics of 'never again'. I grew up with the faint – because shameful – knowledge that both of my grandfathers had fought for the Wehrmacht at the *Ostfront*, while listening to my grandma's stories of Jewish suffering and survival. Classified as a 'Mischling' (half-caste) by the Nazis because of her then-deceased Jewish father, she lived through the fear of deportation and daily terror of the Third Reich. The question of how this past can be addressed in the present formed my own political subjectivity and partly motivated this project. And so, I was there in front of the Bundestag, lured by my own commitment and interest in what a sense of historical responsibility could do. Guilty, angry and hopeful, I joined the other protestors digging graves in front of the Bundestag. Several hundred people stormed the lawn in front of the Bundestag. Armed with shovels, sticks and flowers, people dug up graves until the entire area in front of the parliament resembled a cemetery. Like in the *Walk of Shame*, it was only by walking over 'dead bodies' that politicians could return to parliament.

Guided by what the Centre of Political Beauty describes as their philosophy of 'aggressive humanism', the digging was a transgressive act that attracted a lot of media attention and was followed by other spectacular political actions by the Centre in which they, amongst others, took the White Crosses used to commemorate people who were killed trying to flee the GDR from the Reichstag to the outer borders of Europe. Maurice Stierl (2016) has lauded the Centre's confrontational style of shock and transgression that goes beyond the sentimental politics of humanitarian empathy and confronts people with the horrors of the past. Samuel Merrill (2018: 161) further stresses the historical element of the action and suggests that it constitutes a form of 'activist remembrance'. He points out that weeks after the action, anonymous graves dedicated to migrants would continue to appear in parks and flower beds in cities across Germany. These graves resembled the golden *Stolpersteine* (stumbling stones) that are put in front of houses in Germany to commemorate the victims of the Holocaust who were deported from their homes. In actions like these, the Centre for Political Beauty staged complex forms of 'multi-directional memory' which highlight contemporary racial state violence in relation to the histories of the Third Reich and that of the GDR (Rothberg 2009). Yet their actions also open questions about the inherent problems and difficulties of affective memory activism in the shadow of the Holocaust, which I want to turn to in the following.

The question of singularity

A key question that has long haunted the mobilisation of Holocaust memory in relation to contemporary migration and border politics is the question of singularity. The tenet that the Holocaust is singular in its horrific violence relates back to the Historikerstreit, in which Jürgen Habermas (1986) famously pushed against the conservative historian Ernst Nolte trying to relativise the Nazi Holocaust by making an equivalence to the crimes of state socialism. Insisting on the singularity of and particularly of the Shoah in this regard was an important intervention against Nolte's relativisation and his intent to distract from confronting antisemitism and structural state racism and to focus on left-wing extremism in the post-war Federal Republic (see also Rechavia-Taylor 2022; Rothberg 2022). In recent, years, however, the argument of singularity has been taken over by more conservative (as well as some left-wing) voices in German political debate to stifle any form of relational critique (Rechavia-Taylor 2022; Rothberg 2022). Dirk Moses (2021a) has called this tenet the 'new catechism', in which any analytical link or comparison of the Holocaust to other forms of genocide and state violence is dismissed as a form of relativisation. In line with this new catechism, some commentators critiqued the Centre for Political Beauty's actions as relativistic and disrespectful to the memory of the Holocaust, suggesting that the link between the violence perpetuated during the Third Reich cannot and should not be put in relation to contemporary forms of border violence.

Such critiques open important questions about how the memory of genocidal violence can be mobilised for social justice activism in the present. Yet the insistence on singularity tends to misconstrue the anti-fascist lessons of 'never again' into a narrow and often exclusive focus on antisemitism and an unquestionable identification with the state of Israel, and misses how the history of antisemitism is intertwined with colonial racism and European nationalism more generally (Czollek 2020; Rechavia-Taylor and Moses 2021; Samudzi 2021). As Tiffany Florvil (2021: 1) has shown, the memory of the Holocaust has been a key to anti-racist mobilisations for decades as it, amongst others, enabled Black Germans 'to use Holocaust memories to address parallel violent practices of power and exclusion in postwar Germany'. She shows how Black feminist writers and activists like May Ayim understood contemporary anti-Black violence in relation to the wider colonial and fascist histories of the state without arguing for a form of equivalence that would diminish the horrors of the Shoa. Similarly, actions like *The Dead Are Coming* are not about arguing for equivalence. Instead, they aim to unveil the hypocrisy of a German state being celebrated internationally as the *Erinnerungsweltmeister* (the memory world champion) (Assmann 2012), which repents the crimes of the past while committing racist violence in the present.

Nevertheless, the question of whose pain is mobilised to shame who remains paramount. If in Tiffany Florvli's account of Black feminist memory politics, it was self-organised directives like the Initiative Schwarze Menschen in Deutschland (Initiative of Black People in Germany) that fought against anti-Black violence in Germany, in *The Dead Are Coming*, we witness mainly white and Christian German citizens mobilising shame in the name of dead refugees, and most actions were staged and enacted by the leaders of the Centre for Political Beauty. In the burial that precluded the storming of the lawn, for instance, the Centre brought over the bodies of two Syrian migrants who had died in the Mediterranean to give them an actual burial in Germany. While their families were present at the funerals, the family members had scripted roles in this enactment that largely followed the plans of the artists. As Aleksandra Lewicki (2017) argues, some of this dynamic can be explained by the legal privilege of citizenship that allows EU citizens to act, while the families of the buried had to remain silent and anonymous so as to not have their asylum cases jeopardised. Yet it also shows how the people affected by the murderous border violence mainly worked as supporting casts in an action structured around their pain.

The agency of 'great souls'

The question of *whose* affect is mobilised by *whom* cuts to the heart of some of the problems with mobilising national Holocaust guilt in the historical present. After digging up the graves in front of the Bundestag, activists put up little white crosses so that soon the lawn would turn into a cemetery filled with hundreds of wooden symbols of Christianity. While the actual burial the day before was done by an Imam paying respect and attention to the religion of the deceased, the use of crosses highlights the unspoken assumptions carried by many of the mostly white Christian German activists on the lawn. Rechavia-Taylor (2022) has shown how memory culture in Germany often comes to reaffirm what they call 'Lutheran whiteness' or 'the traumatized Christianity of the perpetrators' as the dominant moral and aesthetic through which national memory culture in Germany operates. They recount how both the national recognition of the horrors of the Holocaust in Germany and that of colonial atrocities such as the genocide committed on the Herero and Nama at the beginning of the twentieth century is often made through white Christian frames of engagement.[3]

The Dead Are Coming was similarly enacted through white Christian frames of atonement. In their analysis of the activist performance, Jennifer Gully and Lynn Mie Itagaki (2017) engage this dynamic in more detail. They suggest that *The Dead Are Coming* was a powerful way to bring the border into the heart of political power in Germany to make it impossible for people to deny responsibility. Yet they point out how, simultaneously, the dead migrant body under the cross became a 'new symbol for the nation, an ethical symbol that reminds Europe, but especially Germans, of the sacred obligation their privileges of life and security demand' (2017: 296). As such, it also emerged as a symbol that enshrines new borders between the 'human citizen rescuers' [and] the less human migrant survivors' (2017: 283). Gully and Itagaki's analysis highlights points to the intricate relationship between the representation of migrant suffering and the reinforcement of existing racial and national hierarchies. More concretely, it shows how the mobilisation of the pain of others lends itself to the re-inscription of the racial grammars of deservingness that keep living migrants out of the sphere of political action.

If migrants remain supporting casts in an action staged around their suffering, who is the political subject of national shame and guilt? In his political manifesto, the founder and mastermind of the Centre for Political Beauty, Philipp Ruch (2015: 277), asks, 'who else if not the country of Holocaust perpetrators is morally obliged to lead an offensive battle against genocide and human rights violations and unjust regimes?' The implicit answer to this rhetorical question is that the leaders of the battle are the descendants of the perpetrators, citizens who identify with Germany and who share and have been constructed as the carriers of Holocaust guilt in the first place. It is them who are interpellated as the moral agents of national guilt. Max Czollek (2020) has critiqued the way in which the horror of the Holocaust and the depths of human suffering have been idealised and distorted in national memory, presented as a shared experience in German history. He argues that the Jewish victims of the Shoah have become a symbol of identification for the descendants of the perpetrators, turning guilt and responsibility into pride and national self-affirmation. This dynamic is mirrored in *The Dead Are Coming*, in which the identification with the past becomes the source of exceptional political agency for German citizens.

In the formulation of Ruch, after all, it is not any nation that is created through shame and guilt, but an exceptional one. He suggests that people who take up the moral duty of the Holocaust and fight against current injustice are 'great souls' of 'exceptional moral beauty' who rise above 'unaffected common souls' (Ruch 2013). We have come across this narrative of exceptionalism already in the analysis of Angela Merkel's '*Wir schaffen das*' speeches in Chapter 1. In invoking a new country 'born from the rubbles of the past', she similarly turns the invocation of historical guilt into a source of pride for having dealt so well with these histories. In her analysis of state apologies for settler colonial genocides in Australia, Sara Ahmed (2014: 101) has shown how shame can not only work to repair historical wrongs but also that 'declarations of shame can work to bring the 'nation' into existence as a felt community. In other words, shame and guilt do not only work to confront historical injustices but can also interpellate bodies into the felt community of national shame. In *The Dead Are Coming*, we see the construction of such national exceptionalism in which it is the guilt of the Holocaust that bestows certain subjects with an exceptional political and ethical agency.

This formulation of Holocaust guilt as an affect to be acted upon by 'great souls', however, also leaves the space open for people who do not identify with this guilt to be positioned as 'unaffected common souls' – subjects who have not yet learnt the lessons of the Holocaust as a precondition for their moral exceptionalism. While Ruch uses the term 'unaffected common sense' to call out German citizens who do not act in a moment of structural racial dominance and violence, the term remains open and can also be filled with migratised and racialised people often positioned outside of national memory culture. In her work on Holocaust Education, Esra Özyürek (2023), for instance, reveals how Turkish- and Arab-Germans are increasingly positioned as obstacles to Germany's national reconciliation with its Nazi past. Over the last decade, the German government has supervised specialised NGOs and Muslim minority groups to create customised Holocaust education and antisemitism prevention programmes for Muslim immigrants and refugees so that they learn to embrace Germany's fundamental post-war democratic values. Özyürek points out that while such initiatives are often well-intended, they also lead to migrants being positioned as the 'subcontractors of guilt'. In other words, these initiatives play into wider dynamics in which it is the Muslim migrant who becomes positioned as the key source of antisemitism in Germany today (see also Doughan 2022; El-Tayeb 2016).

Such anti-migrant mobilisation of Holocaust guilt is not intended by Ruch's philosophy of 'aggressive humanism' and the digging of graves in front of the Bundestag. Yet it shows some of the paradoxes at the heart of dominant Holocaust memory in Germany. For reintegrative shaming to be effective, it must draw on dominant values and national discourses. In a context in which exceptional narratives of shame and guilt are key to German nation-making, practices like *The Dead Are Coming* need to reaffirm these while critiquing them. Michael Rothberg (2021: 1) describes the paradox of dominant Holocaust memorialisation in Germany by suggesting that 'to be German requires remembering the Holocaust and confronting the Nazis' genocidal policies. Yet such a confrontation risks simply repeating the original problem if it does not challenge the very notion of Germanness that made genocide possible in the first place.' He suggests that 'migrants and minorities in Germany know this problem all too well' as they confront what he describes as the '*migrant double bind*: to be German requires remembering the Holocaust, but if you are a migrant or racialized minority, you are repeatedly told that this is not your history' (see also Rothberg and Yildiz 2011). It is in this dynamic that we can see practices of affective bordering take place that reproduce racialised grammars of who can be the subject of shame and who cannot. These grammars re-inscribe borders through narratives of national exceptionalism that again imbue citizens of the nation with special moral agency while pushing the people who are most affected by the European border regime to the sidelines of political action.

The politics of shamelessness

As shown so far, practices of reintegrative shaming in contemporary border and migration politics confront the paradox that they need to reaffirm that which they critique. At the same time, however, they also encounter the problem that not everyone will be shamed by the act of shaming. Given that shame only works within a shared system of value, shame might fail to produce the affect it intends – after all, not everyone agrees that border violence is shameful or shares the historical guilt that constructs the German nation. Such a rejection of shame could be seen when the *List of Refugee Deaths*, which was shown in Liverpool as part of the Biennale 2018, was vandalised and destroyed. The *List* that was exhibited on a public mural not far from the centre of town was torn down and spray-painted with slogans like 'invaders not refugees'. After the organisers of the Biennale repaired and reinstalled the installation, it was destroyed and vandalised a second time (Pidd 2018). Shame for the death of migrants, in this instance, was outright rejected and dismissed.

In Germany, similarly, a backlash against the action of the Centre for Political Beauty formed. Björn Höcke from the AFD called the Centre of Political Beauty a 'terrorist organisation', and the artist-activist collective would later be put under investigation by the district of attorney of the state of Thuringia for the potential 'formation of a criminal organization' ('Staatsanwaltschaft' 2019). In his work on the potential of naming and shaming in human rights activism, Jack Snyder (2020: 645) describes these dynamics and warns of the inherent potential for backlash in practices of public shaming – arguing that 'shaming commonly provokes a self-reinforcing syndrome of anger, resentment, evasion, and glorification of deviance'. These dynamics can leave social justice movements and human rights advocates in danger of retaliation and show how even the most reintegrative forms of shame are highly fragile given that they rely on both the subject and object of public shaming identifying with a shared set of values and interests.

The backlash to the *List of Refugee Deaths* and *The Dead Are Coming* needs to be understood as part of a growing politics of shamelessness emerging in the wake of the summer of 2015. This politics of shamelessness is spurned by the far right and in Germany works both in relation to the politics of migration and the memory of the Holocaust. In 2017, the AFD politician Björn Höcke conjured the right-wing spectre of a *Schuldkult* (cult of guilt) imposed on the country and proclaimed that 'Germany has to make a 180-degree turn in its memory politics' (Hofmann and Meister 2017: 1).[4] He branded the Memorial to the Murdered Jews of Europe in Berlin as a 'monument of shame' – framing not the murder of six million Jews but the memorialisation of the Holocaust as the source of shame (Hofmann and Meister 2017). In this, he was backed by the head of the AFD, Alexander Gauland, who a few months later would posit that 'Hitler and the Nazis are only a *bird shit* in 1000 years of successful German history' (Petter 2018). When shortly after, neo-Nazis stormed through Chemnitz attacking people of colour and vandalising a Jewish restaurant, senior political figures like Wolfgang Kubicki from the liberal party the FDP blamed the attacks on the refugee migration of the summer of 2015 by arguing that 'the roots of this violence lie in the "*Wir schaffen das*" of Chancellor Angela Merkel' (Weiland 2018). Rather than defending her position, Angela Merkel would give into this assignment of shame and increasingly let go of her '*Wir schaffen das*' rhetoric. As discussed in the first chapter, she would now insist that 'Germany will stay the same with everything that we love and hold dear about it', seeming to now be more ashamed of her decision to guarantee asylum to refugees fleeing Syria than Europe's refusal to assist people in need or Germany's brutal history that she so powerfully conjured in her summer speech of 2015.

The growing politics of shamelessness expressed in these instances is based on shifting the moral values and political consensus that underlies the construction of national guilt in Germany. As part of this process, we see a reversal of victim–perpetrator dynamics. It is no longer the German nation that is to blame for the Holocaust but the everyday German man that is oppressed by the enforced 'Schuldkult' of national memory. It is not the border regimes killing migrants in the Mediterranean but common citizens who are being attacked by 'sex mobs' and 'criminals' coming into the country. This reversal of power dynamics means that shame can be felt not as an ethical corrective to be attended to but as an imposition that needs to be fought and resisted. In the context of the US, Lauren Berlant (2016b: 1) has similarly argued that one key driver behind the election of Trump was that 'mainly [people] seek freedom from shame'. They suggest that 'the Trump Emotion Machine is delivering feeling ok, acting free. Being ok with one's internal noise, and saying it, and demanding that it matter' (Berlant 2016b). This form of unrepression, the 'freeing' from the shackles of 'politically correct' feeling, takes on murderous forms in the current conjuncture, in which it unleashes the racist subconscious of the nation out into the open. It can be seen not only in the US but also in Germany where, in July 2018, the then Minister of the Interior, Horst Seehofer, revelled in sixty-nine deportations to Afghanistan taking place on his sixty-ninth birthday (Vu 2018).

The emotional dynamics of this emerging regime of shamelessness can be witnessed across Europe in the wake of the so-called 'refugee crisis'. The proudly self-declared illiberal regimes of Poland and Hungary proclaimed that they would refuse to take in any refugees, conflating refugees with disease and degeneration (Follis 2019; Thorleifsson 2017); the UK extended its 'hostile environment' policies (El-Enany 2020); and states like Italy and Greece would try to hinder rescue missions in the Mediterranean and instead focus on pushbacks and the criminalisation of migrant solidarity activism (Mainwaring and DeBono 2021). Ruth Wodak (2020) has analysed this 'post-shame era' across European liberal democracies by pointing to the 'shameless normalisation' of right-wing discourse in public political debate through the repeated and conscious transgression of shared political norms and values. Her analysis underlines that right-wing forces gain support because of and not despite their transgressions of agreed norms of political discourse and feeling. After all, right-wing agitators like Victor Orbán, Marine Le Pen and Heinz-Christian Strache, as well as international figures like Narendra Modi, Jair Bolsonaro or Donald Trump, all are, at least partly, elected for their promise to destroy the normative foundations of moral and political feeling.

We can understand the force of these politics of shamelessness by attending to the phenomenological quality of shame as an unbearable emotion. Shame triggers an intensely distressing sensation, akin to an encroachment or violation that jeopardises a person's sense of security and overall wellbeing. It is for this reason that it is such a feared emotion and is often seen as the toxic force that progressive social justice movements need to address. Yet while the experience of shame can make people want to resolve the source of shame through different action in the future, it can also push people to hide and disappear, or to resist this affective sensation by fighting and rejecting it. This pushback against shame does not mean that emotions of shame and guilt are absent from the contemporary political debate. Trump loves to shame the women and minorities he assaults and Gauland tries to turn the memorialisation of the Holocaust itself into a shameful act. What marks the new regime of shamelessness is thus not the absence of shame in contemporary politics, but the destruction of the shared values and moral codex that underlies it. The politics of shamelessness aims to do away with a liberal political consensus in which representatives would commit, or at least pay lip service, to foundational values of rights, equality and democratic procedure and honour the memory of the Holocaust. Like the 'deep state' that fascist strategists like Steve Bannon aim to destroy, right-wing politics of shamelessness aim at destructing the 'deep stories' (Hochschild 2018) that structure collective forms of ethical feeling in the contemporary moment.

Shaming the shameless

What this development confronts us with is the question of what shame can still do in the context of shamelessness. How, in other words, do you shame the shameless? It is in this context of the politics of shamelessness, I want to suggest, that practices of *disintegrative* shaming become paramount – shaming that does not aim at betterment and forgiveness but that aims to ostracise subjects and actions through the force of stigmatisation. After the *List of Refugee Deaths* was vandalised in Liverpool, the artist Banu Cennetoğlu decided to keep the torn list hanging as 'a manifestation and reminder of this systematic violence exercised against people' (Pidd 2018). The destroyed *List* stands as a symbol both against the border violence and against the eroding ground on which acts of shaming meant to counter such violence can be enacted. Shaming here is no longer reintegrative as there is no subject that can or wants to be reintegrated into the social fold. There is no forgiveness for a subject that is not looking for forgiveness, no respect for politics built on disrespect. All that is left is the destroyed *List* as a reminder and accusation of the normalisation and shameless celebration of border violence.

A similar technique can be identified in Germany, where the Centre for Political Beauty built a Holocaust memorial in the backyard of the AFD politician Björk Höcke. After Höcke had branded the Memorial to the Murdered Jews of Europe a 'monument of shame', the Center built a 'monument against the creeping normalisation of fascism in Germany' next to his house in a small town in Thuringia ('Holocaust Memorial' 2019: 1). After acquiring some of the neighbouring land, the Centre put up grey blocks similar to those of the memorial in Berlin, explaining that

> The Holocaust Memorial is a monument to our shame. We need it so that we don't forget what we are capable of. Every single one of us needs it. The Center for Political Beauty has erected a private monument in the backyard of one of those people who would like to close their eyes to this reality. ('Holocaust Memorial' 2019)

Given that the rehabilitation of Björn Höcke is an impossible endeavour, the idea behind this action is not to reintegrate him or other leaders of the AFD back into the social fold, but to ridicule and ostracise him from the political community. To augment this dynamic, the Centre is organising public tours of the memorial, inviting tourists to visit the memorial and confront the shameless politics of the AFD. Disintegrative forms of shaming here thus work both as a tool to stigmatise neo-fascist figures like Höcke, while reaffirming a community of shame that is committed to honouring the memory of the Holocaust.

Braithwaite (2000) argues that disintegrative shaming is inherently dangerous and needs to be avoided for the retaliatory violence that can follow. However, what if reintegrative shaming is likewise rejected? What if there is no shared consensus of moral and political values that rehabilitation could operate from? Or what if, as in this case, such values are actively attacked and deteriorated? In her reconceptualisation of stigma, Imogen Tyler (2020) describes the 'stigma machine' that is operative against marginalised subjects from colonial power regimes to the austerity politics of neoliberalism today. Her work invites us to wonder what happens if this 'stigma machine' could not only be deconstructed but could also be reverted to call out the shameless action of the state. The forms of disintegrative shaming discussed here intend such a reversal. They enact a confrontational understanding of 'never again' as an antagonistic anti-fascist action, carried out not out of pleasure or mischief but as a last resort in an emerging moment of neo-fascist shamelessness.

After his 'bird shit' speech in parliament, anonymous activists would steal the clothes of the AFD head Alexander Gauland while he was having a swim in the lake. Stealing his clothes, the activists screamed 'No bathing fun for Nazis' (Fröhlich 2018). Unclothed, Gauland had to walk home in shame, accompanied by the police and a media campaign focused on his embarrassment. In this largely unplanned action, activists enacted a form of shaming that aims not at betterment but wants to stigmatise and shun to mark the boundaries of what is morally and politically acceptable. This shameless action in the face of shamelessness is an intent to reverse the racial grammars of deservingness by framing right-wing figures like Gauland as undeserving of inclusion in the moral and political foundations of society. It aims at enshrining a border not along racial or national lines but along that which can have no place in a historical present built out of the horrors of the Holocaust.

Conclusion

In early 2021, a discussion on national shame and historical guilt stirred the public debate in Germany. In an online talk, the artists and social scientists Moshtari Hilal and Sinthujan Varatharajah proposed the term 'people with a Nazi background' (*Nazihintergrund*) to describe descendants of Nazi supporters and those who had benefited from the crimes of the Nazi regime (Kunz 2022). Their suggestion was a wordplay on and reversal of the term 'people with migration background' (*Migrationshintergrund*), which is commonly used to describe and stigmatise people living in Germany whose families were born in a different country. The term aimed to mark the often-hidden histories of Nazi perpetrators and to show how the legacies of the Third Reich continue to structure material and social inequalities in Germany (see De Jong 2023). The term performed a reversal in the public assigning of shame – moving the social stigma attached to racialised and migratised communities in Germany onto white majority groups. Their intervention sparked a heated debate. Some praised it for breaking the ongoing silence on how the unequal material legacies of the Third Reich reproduce themselves through the intimate sphere of the family, with people sharing testimonials through the hashtag #MeinNazihintergrund (Hoffmann 2021; Rothberg and Hauenstein 2021; Rothberg 2022). Others critiqued the assignment of *Nazihintergrund* as being too identarian and thus unhelpful in fostering a pluralistic memory culture in Germany (Mendel 2021), while far right-wing outlets rejected the action as misjudged 'self-righteousness' against prior generations (Krautkrämer 2021).

Hilal and Varatharajah's intervention and the ensuing debate highlight the centrality of shame and guilt for contemporary migration politics in Germany. They show the political potential of shame as an affective force to hold actors benefiting from structures of power to account, while also highlighting the difficulties and dangers of mobilising shame in this political conjuncture. In this chapter, I have examined some of the complexities of public shaming in regard to migration and border politics today. By analysing prominent activist campaigns that aim to shame the European border regime, I have interrogated what the mobilisation of shame and historical guilt can do in contemporary border politics. I have suggested that while the reintegrative mobilisation of shame opens ways of exposing the racial violence of the European project, reintegrative shaming can and needs to re-centre Europe as the locus of enlightened morality and benign patronage. Such re-centring of national values and narratives can contest but also reproduce practices of affective bordering, specifically in Germany, where guilt in relation to the Holocaust has helped to reinstall new forms of nationalism over the last decade. It can reproduce the racial grammars of deservingness that mark national citizens as the subjects of historical guilt imbued with exceptional moral and political responsibility, while pushing racialised and migratised people to the sidelines of political agency.

At the same time, in this chapter, I have shown how shame might lose much of its power in a context in which shamelessness is emerging as an increasingly dominant motor of migration and border as well as national memory politics. I have charted how right-wing actors aim to shift and erode the moral foundations on which shame about European border violence and guilt for the Holocaust are based. Without such shared moral foundations and political values, I have suggested, activists have little choice but to enact forms of disintegrative public shaming – shaming through stigmatisation and ostracisation – as an act of anti-fascist despair and confrontation. These forms of disintegrative forms of public shaming aim to reverse racial grammars of deservingness by marking certain subjects as undeserving of inclusion in the moral and political foundations of the nation. Having charted the emerging politics of shamelessness as a key force of neo-fascist politics, in the next chapter, I want to look at what other affective forces far-right actors are conjuring in migration and border politics today. To do so, I will examine how fear is mobilised as a key force in right-wing conspiracy theories and racist violence in Germany in the wake of the long summer of migration.

Notes

1 The concept of the ego-ideal was developed by Sigmund Freud in his early writings *On Narcissism*. The central role of the ego-ideal for making sense of shame was developed in more depth by Gerhart Piers and Milton Singer (1954), whose ideas still shape many contemporary psychoanalytic understandings of shame.

2 Jaspers was a German philosopher and psychiatrist whose 1946 lectures on the 'Question of German Guilt' triggered important discussions about how the nation should relate to its past. Adorno, the key figure of the Frankfurt School, gave a similarly influential lecture on 'what it means to come to terms with the past' in 1959. Jaspers is more forgiving in his ideas and argues that the question

of guilt depends on how involved a particular individual was in the crimes of the Holocaust. Adorno has a more encompassing understanding of what *Vergangenheitsbewältigung* means and suggests that 'the past will have been worked through only when the causes of what happened have been eliminated. Only because the causes continue to exist does the captivating spell of the past remain to this day unbroken' (Adorno 1959: 103).

3 Rechavia-Taylor (2022) conceptualises Lutheran whiteness through the analysis of the restitution of human remains returned by the German government to representatives from Namibia. They recount how this act of state acknowledgment took place in the Französische Friedrichstadtkirche in Berlin as a religious rather than a government institution and was enacted through Christian terms of historical atonement that lacked legal enforcement and actual political accountability.

4 The term *Schuldkult* is a popular term used in right-wing nationalist debates in Germany. It was popularised by the literary writer Martin Walser in his acceptance speech for the Freedom Prize of the German Book Trade in 1998, in which he claimed that the 'imposed shame' around the Holocaust is mobilised by leading intellectuals 'to hurt all Germans and prevent them from being a normal people' (cited in Rensmann 2004: 184). For a more thorough discussion of this history and the denial of collective guilt in Germany see Lars Rensmann (2004).

5

Fear: great replacement ideologies
as paranoid border politics

When in August 2021 the US and their allies pulled their remaining troops out of Afghanistan and the Taliban took control of the country again, many people were trying to flee. Rather than proposing ways of solving this situation – caused by the military intervention that the German military was directly involved in – the CDU Chancellor candidate and successor of Angela Merkel, Armin Laschet, declared that '2015 cannot repeat itself' (Kappert 2021). His statement was not about improving the asylum system for people fleeing Afghanistan but constructed migration as a crisis that needs to be avoided at all costs. Instead of contradicting Laschet's position, several high-ranking CDU politicians repeated his statement, while the SPD candidate and now Chancellor Olaf Scholz had already expressed the same sentiment in his 2017 book *Hoffnungsland* (country of hope), in which he argued that 'of course, it was not good that back then we temporarily lost full control over who came to us' and suggested that this should not happen again. The assertion that '2015 cannot repeat itself' shows how, in its wake, the summer of migration of 2015 was turned from a symbol of at least cautious hope and compassion into one of fear. This shift in official rhetoric was accompanied by an increasingly paranoid border politics focused on invisibilising border violence and making migration to central Europe an impossibility through clandestine pushbacks, the further externalisation of borders into the buffer zones of Europe and the criminalisation of migrant solidarity (Andersson 2022; Madörin 2022).

Fear is a protective emotion. Focused on identifying and preventing possible threats, fear might best be understood as an affective alarm system aimed at keeping the self safe from danger. This alarm system is easily abused and manipulated for political aims through the construction of certain objects and bodies as inherently fearful. Given this logic, scholars have identified fear as the driving force of post-9/11 security regimes. Brian Massumi (2010) has described how fear works to legitimate the pre-emptive logics of the 'war on terror', in which it is the mere possibility that a threat will have taken place that legitimises ever more strident forms of state surveillance. Martha Nussbaum (2019) has conceptualised fear as the affective condition productive of authoritarian forms of government. She argues that fear is a primordial emotion that turns humans into childlike states in which they will fall for political strongmen offering protection from the threats that they themselves construct. And Sara Ahmed (2004) has made fear the central emotion of her theory of affective economies showing how fear comes to 'stick' to specific bodies, such as that of the 'terrorist' and the 'bogus asylum seeker', through repeated association in security discourse. She argues that fear not only plays a key role in cementing social boundaries but that it also 'create[s] the very effect of borders' by producing distance between the national bodies that fear and those that are constructed as fearful to the nation (2004: 132).

Fear consequently is a key affective force in driving militarised security policies, authoritarian politics and increasingly violent border regimes in the political present, and it might be key to understanding how increasingly authoritarian and neo-fascist politics are born from the ruins of late liberalism. In his reflections on the rise of Nazism in 1930s Germany, Erich Fromm (2021 [1941]) has identified the 'fear of freedom' as a key force in the shift to fascism. He argues that the advent of liberal capitalism does not only give rise to individual freedoms but also creates notions of individualised risk and diffuse forms of anxiety that easily become misplaced onto racially constructed minorities. He suggests that fear can be exploited to produce authoritarianism, destructiveness and conformity as the three key pillars of a fascist politics. His work highlights that the fear and anxiety produced by liberal capitalist democracies carry the authoritarian potential that can subvert democracy and turn into illiberal, and even outright fascist, projects of governments. Paul Mason (2021: 382) builds on this work to suggest that the fear of freedom helps to explain 'the turn to fascism [that] is triggered when a group of people who are supposed to be subservient suddenly gains power and agency, and begins to revolt in ways, that might actually embody freedom, and might show what it looks like' and that it can also be observed in the current advent of authoritarian politics across Europe and the globe.

As a result, fear remains with few friends in social and political theory. Even within queer feminist work on affect, in which most negative emotions like disgust, shame, rage or even hatred have received critical reinterpretations as potentially productive affective forces (e.g. Halperin and Traub 2009; Cvetkovich 2012; Ahmed 2014; Kurt 2023), fear seems to remain an exception – too dangerous in its authoritarian potential, too sticky in the way it marks certain bodies. It is increasingly eschewed not only for its political effects but also for its limiting epistemic potential, with scholars like Eve Sedgwick (2003) pondering on how to move beyond 'paranoid reading' practices in queer feminist scholarship. Here the idea is that we need to move beyond the fearful and well-rehearsed critiques of racism, sexism and heteronormativity that leave little space for reparative forms of engagement, which could help us identify potentialities and enact new world-making practices.

What then to do with fear in contemporary border and migration politics? In this chapter, I interrogate how the politics of fear operate in a context in which the summer of migration itself has been turned into an object of fear. I show that during this time we can see a bleeding of far-right discourse and conspiracy theories like that of the great replacement – the idea that the misnamed 'refugee crisis' was part of an intentional plan to substitute white Germans with racialised migrants – into dominant political discourse and policymaking. The murderous power of these conspiracy ideologies was shown brutally in the racist terrorist attacks of Istha, Halle and Hanau, yet rather than confronting the racist fears constructed in such conspirational ideology and counteracting the neo-Nazi terror that they fuel, representatives from across the political spectrum legitimise these by calling for 'taking people's fears seriously'. After analysing how this process of normalisation takes place, I turn to how the families and friends of the victims of racist terrorist attacks in Halle and Hanau contest the violence by centring their own grief, anger and fear. Based on this analysis, I suggest that rather than appeasing fear as an inherently authoritarian emotion, the question of whose fears are seen as legitimate and worthy of political consideration is paramount – showing how the fear of those constructed as the object of fear can work as the fuel for world-making practices against and beyond the murderous violence of white nationalism and the European border.

Conspiracies of *Umvolkung* and *Überfremdung*

In the wake of the long summer of migration of 2015, fear operated as a key emotion in migration politics. In this heated political climate, actors from across the political spectrum continued to construct migration as a crisis and mobilised well-established tropes of migrants as threats to the economy, national security and gender equality (Holzberg, Kolbe and Zaborowski 2018). A particularly vicious discourse that was constructed during this time is the conspiracy ideology of the great replacement. This conspiracy ideology suggests that the ongoing 'refugee crisis' is orchestrated to gradually substitute white populations in Europe and North America with immigrants from non-white, predominantly Muslim nations. It alleges that this replacement of the white German population is being executed through a combination of intentional migration policies and declining white birth rates in Europe, which are orchestrated by influential 'replacist elites'. These elites are believed to have support from governments, the media and migrant solidarity movements, as well as LGBT and women's rights organisations in Europe.

I have written elsewhere about the gendered and sexual politics of this conspiracy, illustrating how the *demographic anxieties* and *eugenic desires* of this conspiracy are animated by anti-gender discourses that focus on cementing a naturalised sex/gender binary and positioning the white nuclear family as the foundation of the nation (Holzberg 2024). Here I focus on how this conspiracy ideology crystallises wider fears around migration and the end of European civilisation that were normalised in the wake of the long summer of migration. While this white supremacist nationalist ideology has long been popular in neo-Nazi networks and racist online forums, it is in the context of the misnamed 'refugee crisis' that it takes hold in wider public discourse. Starting in 2014, right-wing groups such as PEGIDA gained popularity and began promoting this conspiracy theory. They organised marches across various German cities, voicing concerns about the overforeignisation (*Überfremdung*) of society and the perceived decline of white Christian culture in Germany. Following the events of 2015, the AFD, a right-wing anti-immigrant party, entered the German Bundestag for the first time during the 2017 election and brought this ideology into the parliamentary arena.

In doing so, right-wing factions rely on the intertwined German vocabulary of *Umvolkung* and *Überfremdung* to promote narratives of the great replacement. *Umvolkung*, which can be loosely translated as 'population exchange', is used to incite fears of the racial substitution of white Germans. *Überfremdung* serves as its cultural equivalent, roughly meaning 'over-foreignization'. This term expresses apprehensions about a perceived inundation by migrants, often portrayed as 'foreigners' or Ausländer, who are seen as threats to established national values, traditions and ways of life. Both these terms trace their origins back to early German imperial nationalism in the late nineteenth century and gained notoriety as Nazi terminology in the 1930s, associating the concept of the national territory with racial purity and eugenic policies (Schmitz-Berning 2010). Both *Umvolkung* and *Überfremdung* are mobilised explicitly in neo-Nazi and far-right nationalist contexts to stir up apocalyptic fears to legitimate racist violence. Different to classical fear-mongering campaigns that construct migration as a mostly uncontrolled threat to jobs or national security, the great replacement presents migration as the key element in a carefully planned conspiracy meant to destroy the German nation.

Replacist elites, the conspiracy theory suggests, are engineering falling birth rates and mass migration to purposefully replace the white German population. It is here that the antisemitic dimension of the great replacement comes to the fore. As Stephen Eric Bronner (2020: 371) points out, since the *Protocols of Zion*, antisemitic conspiracies have focused on Jews as the 'harbingers of an all-encompassing world conspiracy bent on hastening the destruction of Western civilisation in general and white Christendom in particular'. This dynamic is reproduced in the great replacement conspiracy ideology, in which it is 'replacist elites' that work to destroy the fabric of white Christian society. It is this conspiratorial element that makes the conspiracy so amendable to the production of fear and white supremacist feelings; constructing *Umvolkung* as a threat steered from above enables an affective power reversal, in which racist violence can be experienced as an honourable defence rather than murderous aggression.

Right-wing terrorism

The deadly consequences of this conspiracy theory are evident in a series of right-wing terrorist attacks that occurred in Germany in the wake of the longer summer of migration. On 2 June 2019, Walter Lübcke, a Christian Democrat politician, was shot in his garden in the village of Istha. He was singled out by a neo-Nazi assailant for his support of Angela Merkel's asylum policies. During Yom Kippur in October 2019, a neo-Nazi attempted to attack the synagogue in Halle, intending to open fire on the Jewish community. Failing to gain access, he killed Jana Lange, a passer-by, and also fired shots at a nearby kebab shop, resulting in the death of one of the patrons, Kevin Schwarze. On 19 February 2020, a racist terrorist killed Gökhan Gültekin, Ferhat Ünvar, Mercedes Kierpacz, Said Nesar Hashemi, Sedat Gürbüz, Fatih Saraçoğlu, Hamza Kurtović, Kaloyan Velkov and Vili Viorel Păun in the city of Hanau. The white supremacist assailant targeted his victims in a shisha bar before proceeding to a small supermarket to open fire.

All three killers subscribed to elements of the great replacement ideology. The conspiracy theory was most clearly expressed in the manifesto of the killer of Hanau, which proclaims that the central problem facing Western nation-states today is the presence of people of colour, framed as inherently inferior, about to out-populate white people. The manifesto asserts that they need to be pushed out of Europe through anti-immigration politics and annihilated through imperial wars led by the US. The murderer of the CDU politician Walter Lübcke similarly ascribed to ideas of the great replacement. The politician was targeted for his defence of Angela Merkel's asylum politics of 2015. Critiquing racist attacks on an asylum centre, Walter Lübcke argued that values of hospitality, tolerance and respect are key to the social contract in Germany and suggested that 'who does not share these values, could leave the country at any point' (Steinhagen 2021: 1). In neo-Nazi networks, this quote was misconstrued as proof that the great replacement of the white German population was being planned by the political establishment in Germany. The conspiracy that the population swap is led by powerful elites was also articulated by the terrorist behind the shooting in Halle who, in live footage of the attack, blamed mass immigration on Jews and evoked an antisemitic conspiracy of Jewish elites aiming to weaken Western nation-states (Schüßler 2020).

This series of Nazi terror attacks needs to be understood as the latest chapter of a long history of racist violence committed in the name of paranoid constructions of the white nation in Germany. While many established Nazis remained in power in the 1960s and 1970s, counteracting and exposing the largely inconsequential project of denazification, it was in the 1980s and 1990s that increasingly expansive neo-Nazi groups and networks formed that dedicated themselves to the National Socialist model by adapting racial terror and violence. They attacked and killed, organised white supremacist groups and spaces and connected with neo-fascist parties like the NPD. How widespread their ideologies and tactics were was revealed in the early 1990s, when racist arson attacks on refugee centres in Solingen, Rostock and Mölln became the centre of political debate (König and Jäckle 2023; Schultz 2021). Nazi terror continued over the coming decades, most explicitly in the murderous activities of German neo-Nazi terrorist cell the NSU. Between 2000 and 2007, the group killed nine people of Turkish, Kurdish and Greek descent and a policewoman in different cities in Germany (Karakayali et al. 2017; Schmincke and Siri 2013). Police and state institutions remained inactive, they criminalised families and communities of the deceased and they were complicit in the cover-up and continuation of the murder series – exposing a longstanding dynamic of racist denial and active complicity that I will come back to later in this chapter.

Despite this history, many commentators have and continue to revert to individualistic psychological explanations and have described far-right terrorists like the killer of Hanau as a 'lone wolf' perpetrator acting in isolation rather than as part of a wider terrorist cell.[1] Pointing to his paranoid writing in which he fabulises about being observed by a secret state surveillance organisation, Germany's Federal Criminal Police Office suggested that the murderer of Hanau did not act out of clearly racist motives, arguing that there was no indication that he was part of a right-wing group or political disposition and instead suggesting that he acted out of psychotic paranoia and the desire to spread his own conspiracy theories ('Rassismus bei Rathjen' 2020; Edwards 2021). Such 'lone wolf' explanations trivialise the collective power of the internet in which right-wing terrorists like that of Hanau and Halle are organising and crafting conspiracies transnationally.

They also play into psychologising discourse that stigmatises mental illness as inherently dangerous and crucially underestimates the social and collective nature of affect. As Erich Fromm (2021) suggests in his reflections on the rise of fascism in 1930s, the psychological and the social are not separate entities but are intertwined. He argues that paranoia and fear are key forces for fascist politics, as authoritarianism and racist violence can be presented as easy solutions to more complex forms of anxiety. Racist paranoia is not the outcome of individual psychology but is produced by wider social forces and given shape through political ideologies and networks. The wolf is a pack animal, after all.

The collective and organised character of this form of terrorism is clearly evident in the ways in which the terrorist attacks of Hanau, Istha and Halle were inspired and took place in relation to a wider transnational series of white supremacist terror attacks. They mirror the attacks in Christchurch, New Zealand, in which a white terrorist shooter attacked people in two Mosques, as well as the racist shootings in supermarkets in El Paso, Texas, and Buffalo, New York, in which the killers targeted Black and Latinx people. In all these cases, the killers posted manifestos online that cited the great replacement as a key inspiration for their genocidal violence. Gabriele Cosentino (2020: 65) has shown how the 'globalisation of conspiracy theories' has taken place through the 'circulation of disinformation via on-line networked communities of trolls, far-right activists, social media, alternative news outlets, fake news factories and political influencers'. Conspiracy theories like that of the great replacement are not constructed in isolation but as transnational ideologies with clear political intentions that give shape and purpose to less-ordered forms of anxiety and frustration in a precarious world. In this extreme invocation of the racial grammars of deservingness, racialised, migratised and religious minorities not only become constructed as undeserving of protection but are framed as deserving targets of genocidal violence and terror.

It is at this point that the fascist potential of fear comes to the surface. If, following Søren Kierkegaard, paranoia as an excessive form of anxiety is a generalised feeling of dread that has no clear object, fear has, or at least promises to have, a clear object (Svendsen 2008: 35). Fascist conspiracy theories are ways to project more nebulous forms of anxiety and paranoia (born from a variety of possible sources) onto a clearly demarcated enemy who gets marked as the source of negative feelings. As such, the construction of fear promises control. Rather than throwing the subject back onto itself to reflect on the actual source of bad feeling, fascist groups can use fear to propose strongmen and genocidal violence as solutions to the threat that they themselves have constructed as the root of negative affect. We can see here how, in this promise of control, fear lends itself to authoritarianism and destructiveness, which Erich Fromm defines as the two key fascist responses to the fear of freedom. This promise also helps to explain the appeal of apocalyptic conspiracies for the defence of white masculine hegemony in particular – as an institution of invulnerability sustained through rejecting and projecting affect outwards (Kimmel 2017).

Mainstreaming great replacement ideologies

The emotional underpinnings of the great replacement ideology extend beyond just right-wing terrorist networks. Indeed, many of the notions and anxieties associated with the great replacement have been formulated and popularised in a new and growing right-wing intellectual sphere in Europe (Pfahl-Traughber 2022). In France, Renaud Camus developed one of the most influential conspiracies in this genre in his book *The Great Replacement*. In his conspiratorial writing from 2011, he contends that Europe is under occupation by migrants from Northern Africa and the Middle East, and he urges white Europeans to protect their homelands. Similar ideas were developed in the outspokenly conspiratorial treaties that have been named as direct inspirations by far-right parties and even neo-Nazi groups such as Bat Ye'or's (2005) *Eurabia* and Éric Zemmour's (2014) *French Suicide*. Yet some of these ideas are also present in more academic and neutral-presenting texts such as Douglas Murray's (2017) *The Strange Death of Europe* and Eric Kaufman's (2018) *Whiteshift* as well as bestselling literary works such as Michel Houellebecq's *Submission*, which formulates the paranoid fantasy of France being governed and taken over by Islamists.

Together these texts lead to the mainstreaming and popularisation of great replacement narratives and sentiments. In their analysis of key texts on the great replacement, Sarah Bracke and Luis Manuel Hernández (2020: 695) point out how these works together construct the 'Muslim Question' as the discursive problematisation of Muslims in Europe. They argue that in these texts, the 'Muslim Question' is constructed through the 'paranoid and apocalyptic [...] – reading of the postcolonial predicament from the mindset of the former colonizer. It is an interpretation in which the postcolonial is experienced and framed as a situation of loss and of threat, and in which forces are mobilized to "fight back"'. Bracke and Hernández's analysis highlights how even the accounts of the great replacement that hide behind academic and literary debate and that are discussed, often positively, in the feuilletons, talk shows and salons of public debate feature and normalise the same fears and apocalyptic scenarios developed in the outright fascist articulations of the great replacement ideology.

This dynamic can also be observed in Germany where already in 2010, Thilo Sarrazin, the former social-democratic finance minister of the State of Berlin, published *Germany Abolishes Itself*. In this work, he warned of the higher birth rates of migrant families, particularly those of Muslim backgrounds, whom he stigmatises as being prone to terrorism and misogyny. Reaching deep into the disproven toolbox of genetic race science, he assigns them lower intelligence quotients and blames them for their reliance on the welfare system, asserting that they are detrimental to the prosperity of the German nation. Sarrazin's arguments are cloaked in the seemingly objective language of statistics and scientific evidence, yet they ultimately propagate many of the same eugenic ideas and nationalist fears that are prevalent in far-right discussions surrounding *Umvolkung* and *Überfremdung*. While scholars like Naika Foroutan (2011) have publicly refuted his ideas, exposing his work as race science in disguise, Sarrazin has become a regular guest on talk shows in Germany, and his book became one of the bestselling non-fiction works in German post-war history, selling more than 1.5 million copies.

In such discourses, we can see what María Do Mar Castro Varela and Paul Mecheril (2016) call the 'demonization of the "Other"', in which racialised and orientalist narratives are conjured to paint Muslim and other minorities as threats to European civilisation. This demonisation conjures 'one of the central legitimation strategies of the colonial civilisational mission in which it was the representation of the "Other" as barbaric, unpredictable, and dangerous' that legitimised colonial rule (2016: 10). According to Castro Varela and Mecheril, such construction of threat not only facilitates social exclusion but also legitimises and produces violence 'as an active and at times intentional attempt for the production and preservation of the social order' (2016: 7). The construction of fear works as a specifically vicious form of affective bordering, as fear can ask not only for the exclusion of a constructed threat but also for its expulsion or annihilation.

This form of affective bordering was evident in the ways in which Sarrazin's ideas were taken on in Germany over the next decades. The cautious embracement of Sarrazin's ideas across the political spectrum provided the ground from which right-wing parties mobilise their strength – an opportunity which the AFD exploited by taking on many of the central ideas expressed in ideologies of the great replacement. In the wake of the 'refugee crisis', they proclaimed that the 'population exchange (*Umvolkung*) in Germany is operating at full speed' (Schröder 2019). Their election campaigns of 2017 focused on white procreation, the protection of the white nuclear family and a stop to migration from Muslim majority countries (Hajek 2020); mobilising around the slogan 'Germany first – because we want to be able to call this country our "Heimat" in the future' (Hasselbach

2017). Constructing the idea of the homeland being overrun by migrants, the AFD pushed a narrative of *Überfremdung* as the cultural subversion of established national traditions and ways of life that, through its underlying fusing of *Land und Volk*, territory and national people, also carried the racial undertone of *Umvolkung*.

Protecting *Heimat*

While the AFD and its statements were called out as racist and conspiratorial by many political commentators, rather than challenging the wider ideas and anxieties underlying them, the renewed coalition government of the CDU and the SPD elected in 2017 tended to reaffirm them. This became particularly evident when, early in his term, the new Interior Minister Horst Seehofer renamed the Ministry of Interior (Bundesministerium des Innern) the Ministry of Interior and *Heimat* (*Bundesministerium des Innern und für Heimat*). *Heimat*, which loosely translates as 'home' or 'homeland', has a complex and troubling history in Germany. In his cultural history of the term, Peter Blickle (2004) shows that the term *Heimat* has long played a key role in the mythology of German nationalism. Developed in juxtaposition to the individualisation and alienation of industrial modernity, it describes a place of emotional security in which land, culture and its people are in harmonious unity. Grounded in early German romanticism and the nascent German nationalism of the early nineteenth century, the idea of an affective attachment to the homeland took a more sinister turn in the Third Reich, where the idea was assimilated into the 'blood and soil' ideology of Nazi fascism. Here it was the mystical idea of a German *Volk* community with a profound tie to their *Heimat* that justified some of the worst crimes of state fascism. Bilgan Ayata (2021) has further shown how the concept was also key during Germany's colonial expansion in the early twentieth century, during which the concept of *Heimat* played a central role in linking imperial territory to the German metropole.

The concept of *Heimat* has a clearly tainted history that is reproduced by far-right forces like the AFD. The renaming of the Ministry of Interior and *Heimat* shows how this discourse has made it into the centre of political discourse and power. Horst Seehofer (2018) himself was careful to point out that *Heimat* is a concept that includes everyone and that needs to be thought anew, yet his party, the CSU, as the Bavarian sibling of the CDU, has long played on nationalist romantic notions of German folklore involving white people drinking beer, eating pretzels and dancing in meadows. This mythology, made popular through German post-war *Heimatfilme* (homeland films), evokes the nostalgic construction of a time when Germany was an 'idyllic' place of heteronormative order and cultural hegemony (Schrödl 2004). The inclusion of the term in the name of the German ministry for interior security not only brings this nostalgic nationalism into the centre of power but also portrays *Heimat* as something to be defended, as an affective space that needs to be secured from outside interference and internal subversion. *Heimat* consequently is a key method of affective bordering. It is the fantasy of a warm affective space of security, belonging and simplicity that promises protection from a world of cold fear and anxiety.

Heimat, however, is offered not only as an emotional anchor but also as protection from the fear invoked by the possible threat of its destruction. As Sara Ahmed (2014: 68) argues in her dissection of racialised fears, the presence 'of the feared object also involves moving towards the loved object, through the forming of a home or enclosure'. Paradoxically, she shows that 'the turning away from the object of fear also involves *turning towards* the object of love, who becomes a defence against the death that is apparently threatened by the object of fear' (Ahmed 2014: 68). This paradoxical dynamic means that the love that *Heimat* evokes only ever works through exclusionary fears and paranoid forms of protection as it is only in the presence of its possible erosion that *Heimat* can be felt as the space promising security from this threat. The affective dynamics of proposing an emotional solution to a threat the solution constructs could also be observed on a wider European level when, in the summer of 2019, the newly appointed president of the European Commission, Ursula von der Leyen (also from the CDU) proposed to give the EU's most senior position on migration the title 'protecting our European way of life'. Given the widespread critique of the idea, the title of the European Commission in charge of migration and skilled labour was later changed to the (equally troublesome) 'promoting our European way of life' – in any case, neo-fascist figures like Marine Le Pen welcomed the step as an 'ideological victory' (Sheftalovich 2019).

Taking people's fears seriously

The renaming of the German and European Union ministries follows a common logic of affective bordering that is grounded in the political mantra that 'we need to take people's fears seriously', which we have come across at several points in this book. Long pushed by the AFD, the idea that we have to listen to the overlooked concerns of people has been taken on by representatives of the political centre, and is increasingly also expressed by left-wing populist figures, commentators and initiatives.[2] While on the political right this idea is commonly used to confirm and augment nationalist fears, in liberal and left-wing rhetoric the rationale behind this mantra is the potentially useful insight that even the most vicious and displaced racist fears and resentments originate in other forms of inequality and deprivation. It is closely linked to the German version of the 'left behind' narrative which has operated across the political spectrum in the UK and the US to, amongst others, try to explain Brexit and the election of Donald Trump. Here the idea is that white lower-class voters, mostly (ex-)blue-collar workers whose industries and social infrastructures have been destroyed through neoliberal and austerity regimes, now come to project their outrage about the economic demise onto indifferent liberal elites and racialised and ethnic minorities (for a critical discussion see Bhambra 2017b; Begum, Mondon and Winter 2021).

In Germany, this narrative is similarly constructed. Pointing to the relative strength of PEGIDA and the AFD in former Eastern states like Saxony and Brandenburg, in Germany, this narrative focuses in particular on rural and post-industrial areas in the former East. Citizens here, so the story goes, have long been disadvantaged and not been included in Germany's post-reunification economic growth, so their fear and resentment are now easily incited around migrants and refugees who are seen as receiving the attention that they have been denied. And, of course, there are legitimate fears that need to be taken seriously. Despite the common perception of Germany as the economic motor of Europe, the last decades have seen an ongoing precaritisation of the labour market which has particularly affected East Germany, long disadvantaged in an often predatory and unequal reunification process. Some employment protections were reversed, temporary and subcontracted labour increased and the German model of the coordinated market economy further liberalised and eroded (Nachtwey 2016). After the 2008 financial crisis, we can see how escalating inequalities are augmented through the global redistribution of wealth to the top, while welfare policies, health and social care are increasingly underfunded.

Yet as Naika Foroutan (2016: 99) points out, even though Germany is 'marked by intense inequality between the richest and poorest [...] economic explanations are insufficient to make sense of the racist defence and the small-minded feelings of being overrun and flooded' that are currently sprouting in Germany. Foroutan shows that public fears are commonly expressed in nationalist rather than in economic terms, and she underlines her argument by the fact that many of the AFD representatives and voters are from well-established bourgeois backgrounds, while the party proposed mostly neoliberal policies that would further augment free market logics and individual competition. In a context of remerging fascisms, narratives that explain projected fears through stories of the 'left behind' are insufficient in their explanatory power as they underestimate the nationalist and racist character of many such fears. The call to take people's fears seriously re-cements rather than challenges such fears. Drawing on the work of Leo

Löwenthal, Floris Biskamp (2017) describes such right-wing agitation as the opposite of psychoanalysis. He suggests that whereas the goal of psychoanalysis is to help individuals recognise their fears, understand their underlying causes and become independent by overcoming them, right-wing agitation strives to keep the origin of these fears hidden. It intensifies them and prevents individuals from developing autonomy and critical self-reflection.

In this context, even left-wing calls 'to take people's worries seriously' are in danger of playing into the hands of right-wing agitators. In his work on the dangers of left-wing populism, Éric Fassin (2018) has warned that alluding to the fears constructed by the political right leads left-wing actors down the wrong path, as these are not solely based on economic demise and hardship but seated in the historically established rejection of racialised minorities and the liberal elites said to protect them. Instead, as Foroutan, Biskamp and Fassin all agree, what is needed are more confrontational affective strategies in which racist fear-mongering and misinformation need to be confronted through a focus on the transnational histories and material structures that would actually help explain and tackle problems of inequality and exclusion today.

White innocence

The most important problem with the call for taking people's fears seriously, however, is the question of whose fears and worries are assumed and affirmed to matter in such speech acts. The political mantra of 'taking people's fears seriously' constructs 'the people' through what Gurminder Bhambra (2017b) describes as 'methodological whiteness'. Through this lens, both 'the people' and the 'left behind' working classes are framed as white citizens – the default figuration of the German citizen. Those erased from this performative construction are the diverse groups that make up many of the actually 'left behind' in Germany. What about the worries of migrant workers in precarious labour arrangements in agriculture, the service industry or construction across the country? What about the concerns of asylum seekers waiting for papers without which they have no right to work, those incarcerated in detention centres or stuck in transit at the coast of Libya? And what about racialised German citizens targeted by and rightfully afraid of racist violence? What about the families and friends of the victims who were killed by neo-Nazi terror attacks in the country?

Even after Germany had been shaken by some of the worst terrorist attacks in its post-war history, political will to work through and against the structural racism that made this violence possible was lacking. After the shooting in Hanau, Angela Merkel declared that 'racism is poison ... which has already caused too many crimes from the NSU, to Walter Lübcke up to the morning of Halle' and argues 'that everything, to the last bit, will be done to solve these terrible murders' (Bundesregierung 2021). Yet still, years after her speech, the families and friends of the murdered report neglect and inaction from police, the legal apparatus and social services in the wake of this catastrophe ('Drei Jahre' 2023).

Such neglect, active suppression and racialised victim-blaming by government, state services and media in the wake of right-wing terror have a long history in post-war Germany. When in the 1990s houses and residences of asylum seekers were set on fire in Solingen, Rostock and Mölln, police failed to protect the victims and covered up the traces of the perpetrators (Demirtas et al. 2023). Rather than building better protections for asylum seekers in the country, political parties from across the political spectrum came together to restrict the basic right to asylum enshrined in the German post-war constitution. The desire to prevent riots like those in Rostock in the future served as an important argument for the change in the constitution (Demirtas et al. 2023).

When over the course of 2000 and 2007, a German neo-Nazi terrorist cell, the NSU, committed ten racially motivated killings in different cities in Germany, police failure and victim-blaming continued (Karakayali et al. 2017; Schmincke and Siri 2013). Despite families of the victims alerting the police that the murders were most likely racially motivated and committed by people from the far right, the police investigated the families themselves, suspecting 'foreign' organised crime networks. In the media, the NSU murders were trivialised as the 'Kebab Murders' (Döner-Morde) and associated with mafia-like 'clan' structures. The murders were only cleared accidentally in 2011. Legal investigations into murder series were continuously blocked and sabotaged by state officials, and state complicities were coming to the surface showing that several of the neo-Nazi perpetrators received cover and support from the Federal Office for the Protection of the Constitution (Von Der Behrens 2018). Vanessa Thompson (2022: 44) has described the effects of this procedure as the 'slow violence of racial profiling' in which

> not believing family members and loved ones, closed proceedings, stressful trials lasting over many years, everyday racism during court proceedings, investigations against or lack of support for family members (as in the case of the family members of the victims of the NSU murder series in Germany or the families in Hanau, Germany) contribute to family members and friends of the victims of police violence experiencing its continuation.

The call to 'take people's fear seriously' seems a mockery in the face of the ongoing racial violence and terror. Over the last years, some work against right-wing terrorism was undertaken in the form of changes to the security apparatus and a large trial of one of the key perpetrators in the NSU killings, Beate Zschäpe. Most of these changes, however, were due to the initiatives of anti-racist activists and networks often led by families and friends families working despite, or rather against, the government (Bojadžijev 2013; Sauer 2022). Even the public trial against Beate Zschäpe focused primarily on her individual criminal activity, with little consequences for the wider terrorist networks she was embedded in, nor any mention of the Federal Office for the Protection role in allowing the Nazi complex to operate unscathed for more than ten years (Karakayali et al. 2017; Nobrega, Quent and Zipf 2021). Similarly, more current exposures of widespread Nazi networks and ideologies in the police and military forces have received scant attention and so far have had little consequences (König and Jäckle 2023). In this context, it is hard to see the public declarations of figures like Angela Merkel as more than a rhetorical plaster over a festering wound.

This plaster is based on what Gloria Wekker (2016) describes as white innocence as an active form of wilful ignorance, a political and affective mode that safeguards white privilege. The striving for white innocence helps to explain how political representatives publicly condemn the racism that infuses society and promise a thorough investigation of the crimes, while state institutions simultaneously continue to deny, suppress and sabotage such an endeavour. Wekker's lens of white innocence highlights that white dominance is reproduced not simply through the construction of migrants and racialised minorities as threats but also by the fear that the mask of innocence might slip, so that the structural violence that European societies are built upon is shown and the affective fantasy of an innocent *Heimat* and European way of life tainted. Given this contradiction, white innocence is an inherently paranoid position based on the fear that the active denial of the ongoing legacies of colonialism, enslavement and racial domination might be punctured at any point.

The paranoia of the border

The anxious character of this position can be seen in the increasingly paranoid approach to border securitisation witnessed during the last years. In the wake of the long summer of migration, efforts have been made to keep border violence out of public representation to avoid the 'border spectacle' of the long summer of migration (De Genova 2015), which worked to re-enact such border violence but also opened opportunities for people to publicly contest such violence. The statement that '2015 cannot repeat itself' is directed not only at keeping migrants out of the country but also keeping their voices and concerns out of public discussion and consideration. While the emergency logics and the hypervisibility of border violence and migrant suffering I describe in the second and third chapters of this book cannot be the answer to such violence, the invisibilisation of the border also works as a technique of affective bordering through the instalment of wilful ignorance, passivity and conformity. Ruben Andersson (2022) has described how fear has infused European border politics over the last years and has led to an increasingly diffuse and invisible border. He tracks how this process works through the creation of hotspots, violent and often clandestine pushbacks and backroom deals with buffer countries. Anouk Madörin (2022) has further shown how a range of predictive surveillance technologies have been used to liquify the border, to keep migrants movements under control and to keep solidarity activists from recording the violence taking place at the border.

While the threat of migration is being kept alive through right-wing agitation, the increasing invisibilisation of border violence makes it easier for the public to sustain the fantasy of *Heimat* and the European ways of life as innocent attachments. Hannah Jones (2021) has described this form of 'violent ignorance' as the key mechanism of how border violence operates and persists today. She argues that violent ignorance is best understood as the action of 'turning away from painful knowledge' (2021: 1). She argues that this turning away is not necessarily always intentional or conscious but 'a way to avoid negative feelings of discomfort, guilt, fear or shame' encouraged and facilitated through wider social and political processes (2021: 5). Henrike Kohpeiss (2022) has discussed a similar affective dynamic through what she calls 'bourgeois coldness' as an emotional state of the present in which citizens protect themselves from the violence they themselves have caused. She reads this affect as a racialised structure of feeling that protects white citizens from deeper engagement with the colonial and racial histories that produced the current structures of border violence and protectionism.

In this development, we can see the third authoritarian response to the fear of freedom that Erich Fromm describes in his work on the rise of fascism: conformity. Fear does not have to lead to full-fledged authoritarianism or destructiveness. It can also lead to looking away and convincing oneself that all is well as it is. This conformity is a form of affective denial which protects the self from reckoning with complicity and a sense of guilt, anger or helplessness that one might otherwise need to confront. As such, it works as a form of affective bordering, in which the refusal to challenge and confront wider social fears based in racist ideologies works to reproduce and cement border violence. In this form of affective bordering, the racial grammars of deservingness are employed to categorise migrants not only as ineligible for asylum and safeguarding but also as individuals unworthy of receiving emotional attention in the first instance.

Fear as collective world-making

What, however, about the fears of people whose concerns are framed outside of matters of public concern? What, in other words, about those who have been constructed as fearful to the nation? In the book *Your Heimat is Our Nightmare*, a group of Black, Jewish, Muslim, queer and other marginalised authors reverse the logics of *Heimat* as a site of warm and fuzzy feelings of national harmony (Aydemir and Yaghoobifarah 2019). They show how from a postmigrant perspective, *Heimat* is not an affective space of belonging and security but one of fear and violence, a nightmare that comes to haunt marginalised subjects in society. The collection contests *Heimat* as a 'a term of combat used against all those people who do not fit the ideal of a homogeneous white Christian society, denying their right to exist' (Aydemir and Yaghoobifarah 2019: 9–10). In her collective reflections on racism and border violence in the UK, Janna Abdul Zahra Aldaraji (2021) in a similar way reflects on the embodied and affective experiences that emerge from the hostile environment in the UK. Based on her work with a reading group of people affected by the racism of the UK border regime, she shows how the use of everyday technologies for border control and security, which aim to enhance national safety by excluding unwanted individuals, in contrast generates feelings of insecurity and vulnerability in subjects at the receiving end of them (see also Sterk 2023).

Both these collective interventions show how fear is produced in people subjected to the violent practices of affective bordering. Rather than conceptualising this fear as a simple form of governmental control and intimidation, however, they show how this fear can also create new communities of care and political action. The collection *Your Heimat is Our Nightmare* shows how the opposition to the nightmare of *Heimat* brings together differently marginalised subjects to discuss futures and enact collectivities that work beyond the violent feelings of paranoid nationalism. Aldaraji (2022) further suggests that paranoia is a way to anticipate forms of racialisation and racist violence and to build infrastructures and collectives that can withstand such violence. In doing so she draws on the work of Katrine Dirckinck-Holmfeld (2019: 20), who suggests that affect, in the form of fear and paranoia, 'also re-unites a passage where we become one with others; it forces us to create other affective assemblages of enunciation through a process of developing thought, practices and desires through juxtaposition and disjunction'. Fear does not only create national borders but also collectives of care and action that withstand the violence of such borders.

Both interventions speak against approaches to fear in social theory that frame fear as an inherently negative force to be overcome. It shows how the classical liberal idea of fear as the authoritarian feeling par excellence which turns subjects into childlike subjects looking for paternal protection (e.g. Nussbaum 2019) is in danger of redoing some of the violence and bordering work it aims to undo. Firstly, while authoritarianism, destruction and denial are some of the potential ways in which people can react to fear, these are not the only possible actions. As shown in the work discussed above, fear can also lead to the creation of collective action in the face of structural violence and the creation of new infrastructures of care. If in Ahmed's (2014) discussion, fear means a turning away from the object of fear and towards the object of love, which in dominant enunciations often means a turning to the nation as the site of belonging, then marginalised subjects who cannot turn to *Heimat* as an site and object of love might turn elsewhere, searching for and creating new objects of love that carry the potential to break the moulds of nationalist feeling.

Second, the assumption that fear is a primordial feeling that turns people into childlike subjects is a dangerous conceptualisation in the context of racist violence, in which victims' fears are often dismissed and belittled as overreactions. The dismissal of fear as childish easily buys into long-established infantilisation of racialised subjects in which fears are not taken seriously, as shown so violently in state and media reactions to terrorist violence in Germany.[3] The dismissal of fear in political debate and social theory can work as the mirror image of the call to 'taking people's worries seriously'. As Aldaraji (2022: 14) highlights, 'we see paranoia as a state sanctioned mode of governing, as well as a representation of irrationality when it is claimed by racialised individuals'. While some people are positioned to have legitimate concerns and worries, others are seen as simply paranoid, overly sensitive and excessive in their affectivity. The way in which fear is read differently of differently marked bodies is key to the way that fear can unfold its power in current practices of affective bordering (see also Ngai 2007).

Thirdly, the idea of fear as something to be overcome assumes that fear *can* be overcome. While fear can be exploited through its attachments to objects made sticky through racialised security discourses, fear of racist violence in a country of right-wing terror and everyday racism can (and should) not be unstuck from the structures that enable such violence in the first place. The idea that fear is a primarily negative force that people should let go of, or move beyond, can trivialise the violence and pain that has created this fear in the first place. Fear, if conceptualised as an emotional alarm system that not only reacts to but predicts possible danger, only becomes a problem, after all, if it misattributes the source of danger. In the context of neo-fascist politics and racist border violence, queer feminist calls to move beyond 'paranoid reading' practices seem facile (Sedgwick 2003). Just because the source of danger might be a familiar one and offers little excitement to the critic looking for new avenues of analysis does not make the source of violence go away. Moreover, as Aldaraji (2022: 14) points out, paranoia can also work 'as a mode of knowledge and working towards a reparative practice'. Rather than shutting or stifling critical thought, fear can lead to the examination of the source of danger through the searching for evidence, critical reflection and collective action aimed at building worlds against and beyond the source of paranoia.

The *Initiative 19th February*

The power of negative affect, including fear, in organising collective action in the face of racist violence could also be seen in the wake of the terrorist attacks of Hanau. Pushing against the inaction of the state and the infantilisation of victims by police and social services, the families and friends of the victims organised in groups like the *Initiative 19th February* and came together under the slogan 'against the forgetting, against the silencing, against the fear' (*Gegen das Vergessen, gegen das Schweigen, gegen die Angst*) ('Drei Jahre' 2023). The *Initiative* was founded to 'create a permanent space for solidarity and to demand clarification and political consequences', with the stated aim being to 'not allow February 19, 2020, to be swept under the rug – just like the countless right-wing murders before it' ('Gründungstext' 2020). The *Initiative 19th February* would organise memorials, demonstrations and public events in Hanau and across Germany calling for the memory of the victims to be honoured by #saying their names. In doing, so the *Initiative* would call out the series of state and police inactions that enabled the white supremacist to carry out his murders, and it worked with groups like Forensic Architecture to fully investigate the crimes.

The *Initiative* also focused on creating a space where families and friends of the deceased can come together with other people affected by structural racism to share their pain, grief and fear by setting up an open shop and meeting place close to the crime scene in Hanau. As the *Initiative 19th February* states in their founding text:

> We are creating a space of trust. We want political solidarity and visibility. We stand for a society of diversity. Hanau is our city, our home. It has been so, and it will remain so. Here are the relatives, families, and friends of the victims and the injured. They must be heard. In the coming weeks, months, and years, we will support each other. And ensure that consequences are drawn – and that nothing is forgotten. (Gründungstext 2020: 1)

This construction of a space of trust runs counter to the racist construction of spaces of migrant sociality as 'spaces of fear' in much of public discourse

(Biskamp 2017). Reversing the racial logic of affective bordering, Efsun Kızılay (2021: 1) points out how spaces like the Shisha bar in which the mass murder of Hanau took place 'are safer spaces because people know that nothing will happen to them there and that they will not be subjected to racism or rude comments, discrimination, or being denied entry. These are places where parts of the migrant communities come together.' The construction of a meeting space for people affected by the racist violence of Hanau was key to recreating such a space of trust in which pain, grief and fear could be shared and from which the silence and denial surrounding racist violence could be contested.

By insisting that Hanau is everywhere (#hanauistüberall), the actions of the *Initiative* further highlighted how the murderous violence of Hanau is the outcome of wider structural racism that shapes life in German society. In an interview with the mother of Ferhat Ünvar, Serpil Temiz Ünvar talks about the daily fears she and her family already faced before her son became the victim of Nazi terror. She recounts the everyday racism that her son would experience in institutional spaces like the school, stating that 'children [like him] cannot use their own potentials out of fear. And us families cannot help because of being afraid' (Kızılay, Ayboğa and Ünvar 2021). After losing her son, she discusses how she faces her fears head-on and states that her 'indignation and righteous anger has no boundaries. I am rightfully outraged. After losing my son, I am not afraid of anything and do not recognize any limits.'

Serpil Temiz Ünvar's statement and the wider anti-racist initiatives developed after the terrorist attacks in Hanau, such as the *Initiative 19th February*, show how fear does not need to lead to authoritarianism, destruction or conformity but can also lead to what Erich Fromm describes as the 'freedom to' – the unfolding of agency to no longer be subjected to oppressive forces, to be able live for oneself and others, to unfold in the face of and against the structures that create and instil fear. The counter to neo-fascist conspiracy ideologies of the great replacement, therefore, is not the white-washed idea that we need to 'take people's worries seriously' but the shifting of attention and agency to those who are constructed as fearful in its genocidal ideology. It means the construction of solidarities between marginalised subjects and the creation of an infrastructure of care that enable affected people to build worlds and spaces beyond and against the insidious violence inherent in the securing of the white homeland.

Conclusion

In their oral interviews on the affective afterlives of the racist arson attack on the house of a Turkish-German family in Solingen, Bilge Yüksel, Yahya

Alkan and Ömer Dökmeci show how the fear associated with this violence continues to shape and affect migrant communities in Germany today (see Bangel 2023). They suggest that many Turkish-Germans who lived through this time 'convey to their children: Be careful, no matter where you are, racist attacks can happen at any time' (1). In contrast to this, Yüksel, Alkan and Dökmeci suggest that 'white Germans are not even aware of the fear of being affected by racist violence [...] Especially in the younger generation, we often have to explain what exactly happened in 1993' (Bangel 2023). Their research shows how thirty years after the attacks, the fear evoked by this violence continues to structure German society and create affective borders between those who are affected by such violence and those who are not. The work of Yüksel, Alkan and Dökmeci is part of a wider intent to reverse the common calls in public and political discourse 'to take people's fears seriously', which centres white citizens as the assumed subject who deserves the protection of the nation – and that lie behind practices of affective bordering in the contemporary moment.

In this chapter, I have shown how, in the wake of the summer of migration, such calls have led to an increasing normalisation of racist fears grounded in right-wing discourse and conspiracy ideologues like that of the great replacement. As a result, the long summer of migration has itself been turned into an object of fear that legitimises ever more paranoid forms of border protection. While showing the potential of fear to fuel the neo-fascist tenets of authoritarianism, destructiveness and complicity, I have suggested that it might be counter-productive to simply think of fear as an inherently dangerous emotion. Instead, I have argued that the question of whose fears become the concerns of national attention needs to be central to political analyses and action that aims to contest the rise of authoritarianism and neo-fascist politics in the current moment. Actions like the *Initiative 19th February*, created by the families and friends of victims of racist terror, are paramount for creating community and care in the face of pain, grief and the fear of racist violence and so providing spaces from which practices of affective bordering might be reversed and eroded.

Notes

1 It is important to not here that the term 'lone wolf' is not a formally defined legal term or a widely accepted social science concept. Instead, it is a vague and disputed construct that has been used by police and political groups and constructed in media.

2 A particular prominent example in this regard is the leftist initiative 'Aufstehen' (stand up) that was founded in 2018 by Oscar Lafontaine and Sahra

Wagenknecht, the former heads of the socialist party Die Linke, who aimed to counter the surge of the political right by paying more attention to poverty and precarity in Germany. In their nationalist framing of this issue, they argued that such attention is in direct competition to more transnational concerns about migration and asylum.

3 Such construction of fear as something to be dismissed can also be seen in racialised and gendered constructions of 'snowflakes' or debates on 'trigger warnings', in which the affect of marginalised subjects, fear in particular, are framed as childish sensitivities that need to be left behind and pushed against.

Conclusion: shifting grammars
of affective bordering

The Ukrainian 'refugee crisis'

On 24 February 2022, the Russian military invaded Ukraine. Sparked by Soviet nostalgia and the imperial ambitions of Vladimir Putin, tanks assembled at the outskirts of Kyiv and a brutal drawn-out war embattled the country. Since then, more than eight million refugees fleeing Ukraine have moved to countries across Europe. Mirroring the refugee migration at the height of the civil war in Syria, another 'refugee crisis' was declared in the media. Yet despite the hesitance from the German government deeply invested in Russian gas and oil, this time the EU reacted swiftly and in relative concord. It passed wide-reaching sanctions against the Russian regime to stop its invasion, provided military and financial support to Ukraine and offered residence to refugees coming into the EU. The Temporary Protection Directive, which was introduced in the 1990s, was activated for the first time, enabling Ukrainian refugees to reside in EU countries for up to three years without the need to seek asylum through official channels (Paré 2022). Many commentators pointed out how different the European reaction was in comparison to that of the refugee migration of the years prior. Even Poland, which in 2015 still refused to take in any refugees, opened their doors and now hosts the largest group of Ukrainian people inside the EU. The empathy expressed at this moment seemed more expansive, the fear of the military invasion of Russia more acute and the pride in a shared European identity more uniting.

Meanwhile, a wave of solidarity went through Germany. Many of the solidarity infrastructures that were built in 2015 were reactivated, welcome stations at train stations opened and people organised refugee accommodations in their homes. Cautious hope built that the acceptance of Ukrainian refugees would change wider hostile attitudes towards migration by showing the universal necessity of refuge in situations of war and destitution. Yet while white Ukrainian refugees were allowed on to trains towards Central Europe for free, many Black and Ukrainians of colour, migrants and students from the African continent were denied entry at the border to Poland (Ahmed 2022). Meanwhile, the militarised border in the Mediterranean stayed shut and no temporary protections were granted to people coming from other war zones in places like Yemen, Mali or Sudan (Paré 2022). While something was different, much stayed the same in the ways in which the racialised grammars of deservingness came to structure practices of affective bordering also at this moment of crisis. The right to asylum continued to be linked to the conditional logic of affective bordering in which asylum is granted to those to whom European citizens feel a close connection and moral obligation.

These racial grammars of affective bordering not only reproduced hierarchical distinctions between white and Black and migrants of colour but also subjugated white Ukrainian refugees to the conditional logics of deservingness. As Alyosxa Tudor (2015) argues, while migrants from Eastern Europe have access to whiteness in the racial hierarchies produced by European colonialism, this access is precarious, and they are migratised and discriminated against due to their migration status, as seen in the resentment about Eastern European migration mobilised in the Brexit vote in the UK. Tudor describes 'migratism' as 'the term that names the fact that non-migration is considered the norm of nation-states and migration is always conceptualized as a potential threat to the nation or as something needing legitimization' (2015: 239–40). Tudor is careful to point out how racism and migratism intersect and co-produce each other. In this way, Ukrainian migrants are often figured as on the edge of whiteness, as 'peripheral Europeans' (Satzewich 2000), precarious in their status and 'inferiorised within Europe, but often positioned within global racialised categories of Europeanness' (Lewicki 2023: 1481).

Even the position of white Ukrainian migrants then is highly precarious as long it is based on the right feelings of the nation subject to racialised and migratised discourses of deservingness. As long as asylum policies can be legitimised through an expansive sense of empathy, the fear of Russian invasion and the pride in a shared white European identity, people's status might be relatively secure. Yet cracks are starting to show. Already in May 2022, the head of the CDU Merz would incite that 'Germany slides into a new migration crisis' and argue that the policies of the current coalition government 'push the boundaries of what society is still willing to accept' ('Flüchtlingsgipfel' 2023: 1). He would further stigmatise Ukrainian migrants going in between Germany and Ukraine as engaging in 'benefit tourism', spreading a concept popularised in Russian right-wing circles (Kordes and Stratmaan 2022). Meanwhile, the far-right spearheaded by the AFD, as well as controversial figures from the left like Sahra Wagenknecht and Alice Schwarzer (who were already key in galvanising nationalist anger after Cologne), started equalising and relativising the war crimes of the Russian regime, slowly eroding the ground from which shared feeling of concern and solidarity can be built (Reveland and Siggelkow 2023).[1] What we come across in the reactions to the Ukrainian 'refugee crisis' are similar dynamics of affective bordering in which questions of justice and rights are made conditional on the feelings of the majoritarian public. This book has shown that, as long as this conditional logic of affective bordering remains intact, the European border regime will persist, and moments of cautious hope and empathy can easily slip back into projects of protectionist re-bordering and increased nationalism.

Paradoxes of affective bordering

The book started with the puzzle of how the long summer of migration, which at least partially emerged as a moment of hope and public empathy in Germany, has increasingly turned into an object of nationalist anger, resentment and fear. It has suggested that this development cannot solely be understood as one of polarisation and competing groups and positions in society, but highlights how presumably liberal, leftist and right-wing migration politics can entangle and slip into each other through practices of affective bordering. Rather than understanding 'positive' and 'negative' emotions as oppositional forces, the analysis has revealed that different affective forces circulate within the same racial grammars of deservingness that structure contemporary migration and border politics more widely.

This insight highlights the often-paradoxical work of affective politics. Scholars like Joan Scott (1996), Wendy Brown (2000) and Sumi Madhok (2022) have used the concept of the paradox to describe politics whose proposition is true and false, useful and limiting, at the same time. The mobilisation of affect in relation to border and migration politics needs to be understood as one such paradoxical politics. Even when aimed at undoing the borders of the nation, the mobilisation of affect in contemporary migration politics often works to re-cement them. Hope can inspire and open new horizons for political action and solidarity beyond the violence of the current European border regime. Yet, as demonstrated in Chapter 1, in dominant invocations of hope such as in Angela Merkel's '*Wir schaffen das*' speeches, hope is invoked through narratives of exceptional national achievement that, while promising migrants entry to the nation, also positions them as potential threats to this delicate fantasy. Empathy similarly emerges with the powerful promise that it will create new bonds of relationality able to overcome differences of location, race, class and gender and help to include people into spheres of affective concern that have so far been excluded from them. Yet, as shown in Chapter 2, in the discourses that accompanied the publication of the image of Alan Kurdi as well as refugee travelogues that migrants shot on their way to Europe, empathy was commonly invoked through sentimental narratives of recognition and national harmony. These reinstall racialised hierarchies between the subject and object of empathy, demanding gratitude and assimilation as the appropriate answer for having received the gift of empathy. Whereas affective forces like empathy or hope can work to activate different visions of the political and enacts new bonds of solidarity, they also work as ties that bind people to the status quo of the European border regime.

More than that, practices of affective bordering are also based in the paradoxical dynamic that the mobilisation of affect can result in its opposite. As Lauren Berlant (2011) points out, the conjuring of a certain emotion does not necessarily create the emotion that is conjured. In other words, the portrayal or construction of a scene of hope does not necessarily invoke hopefulness but can also create states of depression, envy or resentment. Based on such insight, throughout this book, I have shown how 'positive' affective forces like hope and empathy do not necessarily create the affective response they intend but can also work to generate their opposite and lead to 'negative' states of anger, shame and resentment. Humanitarian campaigns focused on evoking empathy, for instance, might animate rather than contradict forces of nationalist resentment and anger. As shown in Chapters 2 and 3, if the gift of empathy bestowed upon less fortunate people is not returned through acts of gratitude and assimilation, empathy can easily lead to forms of narcissistic injury generating defensive emotions of anger and outrage, which further strengthen rather than undo border violence. Conversely, in Chapters 1 and 4, I traced how the invocation of shame and Holocaust guilt invoked in Merkel's *'Wir schaffen das'* speeches can also result in feelings of national pride based on presumably having dealt so well with these dark histories.

The paradoxical logic of affective bordering that I have uncovered in this book goes against dominant analyses of the historical present that would explain the violence of contemporary society mostly as an excess of resentment or fear and a lack of love and empathy. Instead of repeating worn-out calls for more love and hope in the face of hatred and anger, I have shown that we need analyses that pay closer attention to the paradoxical logics of affective bordering and that focus on *how* and *to what end* certain emotions are enacted and mobilised in contemporary border and migration politics. Rather than merely staying with what Aiko Holvikivi (2023: 533) calls the somewhat 'politically unsatisfactory conclusion that [something] is both "good" and "bad" feminist politics', the book has focused on uncovering the grammars of deservingness that structure these paradoxical politics.

Practices of affective bordering, I have argued, are based on deep-seated notions of who deserves affective concern and solidarity and who does not. While a child like Alan Kurdi, for instance, is commonly constructed as deserving of empathy and affective concern, adult male refugees framed as sexual invaders are not and, instead, get positioned as the source of anger and fear. Ultimately, this dynamic creates distinctions between worthy and unworthy migrants and subjugates questions of justice and rights to the emotional dynamic of deservingness.

The racial grammars of deservingness

Throughout this book, I have argued that these grammars of deservingness are racialised in the ways in which they are shaped by colonial legacies that continue to infuse whose life counts as worthy of protection and whose does not. Empathy in relation to the image of Alan Kurdi, for instance, was invoked and articulated through the racial politics of the figure of the child, which has long been a central trope for constructing the Global North as the benevolent helper of the less developed Global South (rather than an active part in its ongoing subjection and exploitation). In my reflections on anger, I have further excavated the deep stories that have long positioned racialised sexual abusers as a threat to the nation. In doing so, I have pointed out how anger emerging in the aftermath of New Year's Eve 2015 in Cologne might best be understood as a resonant echo of the colonial past that reverberates powerfully in a time of growing precariousness and challenges to enshrined entitlements in the nation. Moreover, in Chapter 5 on fear, I have shown how current constructions of migration as fearful draw on conspiracy theories of *Umvolkung*, *Überfremdung* and the great replacement based in the eugenic ideologies of the Nazis as well as the racial reproductive politics of European colonialism. What lies at the heart of practices of affective bordering then are the racialised, gendered and sexualised narratives that reproduce boundaries between citizens and non-citizens, locals and strangers, and subjects and objects of affect.

More than just positioning some people as more deserving of affective concern than others, the book has shown that practices of affective bordering interpellate some people as the *subjects of affect*, while positioning others as the *objects of affect*. Across the book, we have come across the repeated construction of 'the people', 'the Volk' and 'the nation' as a raced, gendered and classed formation. In Chapter 5 on fear, I illustrated how the racialised fears of white citizens are commonly framed as deserving of national public attention, while racialised minorities and migrant communities affected by European border violence and right-wing terror are marginalised and infantilised and become positioned as the source of fear. In Chapter 4, I have further shown how white Germans as the descendants of Nazi perpetrators become positioned as the subject of Holocaust guilt, endowed not only with negative affect but also the exceptional moral agency to act upon it. Meanwhile, migrants and racialised people in Germany are positioned as yet to learn the lessons of this dark history and are pushed to the sidelines of political action. In the logic of affective bordering, people without citizenship, as well as often racialised non-national citizens, must prove themselves not only as deserving citizens but as subjects worthy to have their own fears, concerns and desires recognised and heard the in public sphere.

The problem with practices of affective bordering thus lies not only in the kind of emotions that it produces but also in the ways in which it centres the affective experiences of national citizens and sets conditions for membership in the nation based on the affective concerns and desires of its white citizenry. Through this process, people who are migratised and/or marked as racially different are positioned as outsiders to the nation and become dependent on the right feeling and generosity of the nation. A key question for the study of affective bordering, therefore, is not simply what *kind* of emotions but *whose* emotions come to matter in public debate and policymaking. While migrants are positioned as the objects of affect, citizens, in contrast, as the assumed benefactors of the nation, are constructed and imagined as the deserving subjects of affect. They are not only positioned as rightfully indignant in their protectionist anger, resentment and fear, but also as innocent in their hope and grief, or even morally exceptional in their feelings of empathy and historical guilt.

A key tenet of affective bordering is what Gloria Wekker calls 'white innocence'. Whether it is the invocation of empathy in humanitarian campaigns or the construction of racist fears in conspiracies of the great replacement, more often than not, practices of affective bordering position the nation and its white citizenry as innocent observers overwhelmed by the sudden advent of migration rather than entangled actors whose situation is partly produced by the legacies of colonial domination and ongoing global inequality. This position of innocence is made possible through the omission of the transnational histories and structural inequalities that have made the current situation of the misnamed 'refugee crisis' possible in the first place. While this dynamic is evident in migration and border politics more widely (Danewid 2017; Ticktin 2017), it is particularly pertinent to practices of affective bordering given that, as Sara Ahmed (2014: 11) has shown, emotions operate 'through an erasure of the history of their production and circulation'. While affective bordering is crucially shaped by colonial and racial histories, the experience of affect as a feeling of the present erases its historicity. White innocence is a key mechanism in practices of affective bordering practices, as it is only in the absence of structural factors of complicity and domination that emotion can be felt as the appropriate answer to structural forms of inequality.

A key tenet of the book is to bring colonial histories into the centre of analysis. This is specifically important in the context of the misnamed 'refugee crisis', in which affective politics are commonly framed through 'crisis' and 'emergency'. Such framing leads to a depoliticisation and dehistoricisation of contemporary border violence. As Aura Lehtonen (2022) shows, the discourse of 'crisis' operates to frame certain situations as exceptional and calls for often technocratic emergency responses that treat the problem as a sudden event caused by outside forces rather than a historically and politically created situation. As such, affective bordering often leads to the disconnecting of 'connected histories' (Bhambra 2017a) and is based in narratives that explain transnational developments through an 'internalist narrative' of Europe (Hall 1991: 18). If history gets invoked in practices of affective bordering, it is usually through progress narratives that frame German history as the outcome of an exceptional achievement of overcoming post-fascist and post-socialist histories. It is only by locating these histories in their wider transnational colonial and postcolonial histories that we gain a better understanding of how affect comes to operate in the historical present.

Abolitionist horizons

By tracing the circulation of different emotions from the long summer of migration to today, the book has charted the intensification of border securitisation and the rise of increasingly authoritarian politics across Europe in its wake. This development raises the question as to what extent my analysis and critique of the paradoxical politics of affective bordering is still hitting the right target. Why should we focus on critiquing the securitising undertones of Merkel's hopeful '*Wir schaffen das*' speeches if her statement has long been diverted and overshadowed by actors further on the political right? Is it not cynical to question articulations of empathy in relation to the death of Alan Kurdi at a moment in which children crossing borders are increasingly stripped of rights, detained and deported across the globe? And what is the point in laying bare the exceptional logics that undergird activist mobilisations of shame in Germany when the underlying narratives of national guilt and responsibility are increasingly being eroded? Instead of putting the critical gaze onto the pitfalls of liberal articulations of hope, empathy or shame, maybe it would be better to defend their redeeming aspects against illiberal attacks.

While I believe that there is something integral to this line of argumentation, throughout this book I have argued that we also need to critique and think beyond the emotional politics that define the status quo of European (neo)liberal democracies. This is not to say that there is no difference between humanitarian empathy and hope and nationalist resentment or outright fascist fear. Instead, my analysis charts how one might turn into the other one – how liberal, as well as leftist, invocations of affect might not necessarily work as a counter but can also slip and coproduce nationalist forms of feeling. In her work against the humanitarian border, Miriam Ticktin (2017) has pointed out how in a context of increasing illiberalism, the challenge of the social critic is not to simply dismiss liberal forms of politics and feeling but to understand what is shared across liberal and illiberal forms of governmentality. What I have tried to delineate is to what extent liberal and left-wing, invocations of affect – whether these are the clinging to humanitarian empathy, a presumably pluralistic invocation of *Heimat* as a response to fears of *Umvolkung* or the invocation of exceptional Holocaust guilt – can actually withhold the right-wing nationalist, authoritarian and neo-fascist politics rising in front of us. My argument consequently is not one of equivalence, but an inquiry into what other forms of affective attachment there are that go beyond cruel re-attachments to contemporary border violence and nationalist politics.

If humanitarian articulations of empathy do not work as a necessary roadblock but can reinstall hierarchies between citizens and migrants, or even fuel nationalist resentment against them, we need to think harder about alternative forms of affective solidarity that might undo these power relations. If anger continues to align itself along racial, gendered and sexualised lines that secure white constructions of the nation, we need to pay attention to, and try to augment, forms of rage that break open new forms of intersectional action and analysis. Similarly, if forms of reintegrative shaming no longer work to hold state powers to account in a moment of rising shamelessness, maybe we need to think harder about forms of disintegrative forms of shaming that refuse to let go of the violent legacies of the past. To counteract practices of affective bordering, the book has argued for a shift in perspective away from the constructed emotional concerns of the national citizen and towards the affective practices enacted in the cracks of the European border regimes – often by those deemed to be the object rather than the subject of affect.

Such practices, I have suggested, not only generate critiques of the status quo of the European border regime but also gesture at forms of social organisation that go beyond it. In my reflections on hope, I posited that cross-border marches enacted by migrants and migrant solidarity actors reveal and enact practices of care, solidarity and the commons that gesture and extend beyond the humanitarian border envisioned by Merkel's politics. In the chapter on empathy, I have identified what other forms of affective solidarity are made possible when we try to move against the warm pull of empathetic engagement and turn to scenes of the abject that are usually cut out from scenes of empathetic encounter. Thinking through what it means to bear witness to refugee hunger strikes, I have suggested a different form of affective solidarity that, rather than emerging through feeling for, or with, others, arises out of a shared concern for the border regimes and systems of global inequality that are productive of violence, death and precarity. And in the chapter on fear, I have focused on initiatives by families and friends of the victims of racist terror in Germany that work to withstand the fear of racist violence.

Focusing on these alternative affective practices, I have suggested, not only highlights the critique of the current European border regime and the political demand for no or more open borders, but also gestures to a world in which the relationality of social life is not framed through threat and biopolitical control. It highlights often self-organised collective infrastructures of care that enable life to flourish and persist in the face of structural violence. Rather than seeing the current moment as one of despair, the book points to the necessity of crafting alternative affective visions that a feminist, queer and anti-racist left might mobilise to fill the void left by the gradual erosion of the liberal consensus in the historical present. As such, the contestation of affective bordering is part of a wider abolitionist project that aims to undo the binds of nationalist and liberal feeling. The paradoxical logic of affective bordering highlights the necessity of reimagining and enacting new visions of sociality that undo and go beyond the racist violence of the borders of deservingness.

Note

1 Sahra Wagenknecht and Alice Schwarzer organised a petition and demonstration 'for peace' in which they called for an end of military support for Ukraine. Their protest action and petition was heavily critiqued for the fact that they did not distance themselves from far-right actors and positions, for their naivety regarding Russian military aggression and for relativising the war crimes of the Russian regime. For a critique of such actions by parts of the international and Ukrainian left see Taras Bilous (2022) and Joey Ayoub (2022). Both of their ideas are based on Leila Al-Shami's (2018) arguments about the 'anti-imperialism of idiots' written in the context of the war in Syria.

References

Abdelmonen, Angie, Rahma Esther Bavelaar, Elisa Wynne-Hughes and Susana Galán. 2016. 'The "Taharrush" Connection: Xenophobia, Islamophobia, and Sexual Violence in Germany and Beyond'. *Jadaliyya*. Accessed 3 November 2023. https://www.jadaliyya.com/Details/33036/The-%60Taharrush%60-Connection -Xenophobia,-Islamophobia,-and-Sexual-Violence-in-Germany-and-Beyond

Abu-Lughod, Lila. 2013. *Do Muslim Women Need Saving?* Cambridge, MA: Harvard University Press.

Adler-Nissen, Rebecca, Katrine Emilie Andersen and Lene Hansen. 2020. 'Images, Emotions, and International Politics: The Death of Alan Kurdi'. *Review of International Studies* 46(1): 75–95.

Adopt a Revolution. 2015. 'Days of Hope: Marsch der Syrischen Revolution nach Europa'. *Adopt a Revolution* (blog). Accessed 3 November 2023. https:// adoptrevolution.org/march-of-hope-erlebnisse/

Adorno, Theodor W. 1959. 'Was bedeutet Aufarbeitung der Vergangenheit?' *Gesammelte Schriften* 10(2): 555–72.

Åhäll, Linda. 2018. Affect as Methodology: Feminism and the Politics of Emotion. *International Political Sociology* 12(1): 36–52.

Ahmed, Asiya. 2022. 'Nigerian Students Share Their Journey of Fleeing War in Ukraine'. *Gal Dem*, 1 March. Accessed 15 March 2024. https://gal-dem.com/ african-students-ukraine-war/

Ahmed, Asiya. 2023. '"We Were on Our Own from the Beginning": Nigerian Students Share Their Journey of Fleeing War in Ukraine'. *Gal Dem*. Accessed 3 November 2023. https://gal-dem.com/african-students-ukraine-war/

Ahmed, Sara. 2004. 'Affective Economies'. *Social Text* 22(2): 117–39.

Ahmed, Sara. 2014. *Cultural Politics of Emotion*. Edinburgh: Edinburgh University Press.

Ahmed, Sara. 2016. 'Living a Feminist Life'. In *Living a Feminist Life*. Durham, NC: Duke University Press.

Ahmed, Sara. 2020. *The Promise of Happiness*. Durham, NC: Duke University Press.

Ajour, Ashjan. 2021. *Reclaiming Humanity in Palestinian Hunger Strikes: Revolutionary Subjectivity and Decolonizing the Body*. London: Palgrave.

Al-Shami, Leila. 2018. 'The "Anti-Imperialism" of Idiots'. *Libcom.org* (blog). Accessed 3 November 2023. https://libcom.org/article/anti-imperialism-idiots -leila-al-shami

Aldaraji, Janna Abdul Zahra. 2021. 'Feeling Bodies, Feeling Borders: A Collective Exploration of Racialisation & Bordering in Britain'. *New Sociological Perspectives* 1(1): 6–22.

Alonso, Alexandra Délano and Benjamin Nienass. 2016. 'Introduction: Borders and the Politics of Mourning'. *Social Research* 83(2): xix–xxxi.

Anderson, Bridget. 2013. *Us and Them? The Dangerous Politics of Immigration Control*. Oxford: Oxford University Press.

Anderson, Bridget and Rutvica Andrijasevic. 2008. 'Sex, Slaves and Citizens: The Politics of Anti-Trafficking'. *Soundings* 40: 135–45.

Anderson, Bridget, Nandita Sharma and Cynthia Wright. 2009. 'Why No Borders? No Borders as Practical Politics: Editorial'. *Refuge: Canada's Journal on Refugees* 26(2): 5–18.

Andersson, Ruben. 2014. *Illegality, Inc.: Clandestine Migration and the Business of Bordering Europe*. Oakland, CA: University of California Press.

Andersson, Ruben. 2022. *No Go World: How Fear Is Redrawing Our Maps and Infecting Our Politics*. Oakland, CA: University of California Press.

Andrijasevic, Rutvica. 2007. 'Beautiful Dead Bodies: Gender, Migration and Representation in Anti-Trafficking Campaigns'. *Feminist Review* 86(1): 24–44.

Angulo-Pasel, Carla. 2018. 'The Journey of Central American Women Migrants: Engendering the Mobile Commons'. *Mobilities* 13(6): 894–909.

'Annual Report 2006'. *UNITED for Intercultural Action*. Accessed 3 November 2023. https://s3.eu-central-1.amazonaws.com/unitedfia.org/wp-media-folder-united-for-intercultural-action/wp-content/uploads/2019/11/AnnualReport2006.pdf

Arendt, Hannah. 1973. *The Origins of Totalitarianism*. Boston, MA: Houghton Mifflin Harcourt.

Arendt, Hannah. 1977. *On Revolution*. New York: Penguin Books.

Assmann, Aleida. 2012. 'Weltmeister im Erinnern? Über das Unbehagen an der Deutschen Erinnerungskultur'. *Vorgänge: Zeitschrift für Bürgerrechte und Gesellschaftspolitik* 51(2): 24–32.

'Asylbewerber Demonstrieren Für Bessere Zustände in Deutschland'. 2015. *News Cam*. Accessed 3 November 2023. https://www.youtube.com/watch?v=W0u6fN4zfCY

Ayata, Bilgin. 2021. 'Heimat oder Rassismus? Affektive Verhandlungen von Zugehörigkeit und Vielfalt nach der NSU-Mordserie'. In *Umkämpfte Vielfalt: Affektive Dynamiken institutioneller Diversifizierung*, edited by Hansjörg Dilger and Matthias Warstat, 49–65. Frankfurt am Main: Campus Verlag.

Ayata, Bilgin. 2022. 'Affective Citizenship: Differential Regimes of Belonging in Plural Societies'. In *Affect, Power, and Institutions*, edited by Millicent Churcher, Sandra Calkins, Jandra Böttger and Jan Slaby, 47–58. London: Routledge.

Aydemir, Fatma and Hengameh Yaghoobifarah (eds). 2019. *Eure Heimat ist unser Albtraum*. München: Ullstein Verlag.

Ayoub, Joey. 2022. 'On Ukraine–Syria Solidarity and the "Anti-Imperialism of Idiots"'. *Shado Magazine*. Accessed 3 November 2023. https://shado-mag.com/opinion/on-ukraine-syria-solidarity-and-the-anti-imperialism-of-idiots/

Azoulay, Ariella A. 2015. *Civil Imagination: A Political Ontology of Photography*. London: Verso.

Balibar, Étienne. 2015. 'Stunde der Wahrheit'. *Die Zeit*. Accessed 3 November 2023. https://www.zeit.de/2015/41/asypolitik-europa-fluechtlinge-angela-merkel

Bangel, Christian. 2023. 'Anschlag von Solingen: "Diese Angst wird nie weggehen"'. *Die Zeit*. Accessed 3 November 2023. https://www.zeit.de/gesellschaft/ zeitgeschehen/2023-05/solingen-brandanschlag-30-jahre-zeitzeugen

Bargetz, Brigitte. 2015. 'The Distribution of Emotions: Affective Politics of Emancipation'. *Hypatia* 30(3): 580–96.

Barrett, Lisa Feldman. 2017. *How Emotions Are Made*. London: Pan Macmillan.

Bauder, Harald. 2017. 'Sanctuary Cities: Policies and Practices in International Perspective'. *International Migration* 55(2): 174–87.

Bayramoğlu, Yener. 2023. 'Border Countervisuality: Smartphone Videos of Border Crossing and Migration'. *Media, Culture & Society* 45(3): 595–611.

Begum, Neema, Aurelien Mondon and Aaron Winter. 2021. 'Between the "Left Behind" and "the People": Racism, Populism, and the Construction of the "White Working Class" in the Context of Brexit'. In *Routledge Handbook of Critical Studies in Whiteness*, edited by Shona Hunter and Christi van der Westhuizen. London: Routledge.

Bellacasa, María Puig de la. 2017. *Matters of Care: Speculative Ethics in More Than Human Worlds*. Minneapolis, MN: University of Minnesota Press.

Berardi, Franco. 2011. *After the Future*. Chico, CA: AK Press.

Berlant, Lauren. 1998. 'Intimacy'. *Critical Inquiry* 24(2): 281–88.

Berlant, Lauren. 2004. *Compassion: The Culture and Politics of an Emotion*. London: Routledge.

Berlant, Lauren. 2011. *Cruel Optimism*. Durham, NC: Duke University Press.

Berlant, Lauren. 2016a. 'The Commons: Infrastructures for Troubling Times'. *Environment and Planning D: Society and Space* 34(3): 393–419.

Berlant, Lauren. 2016b. 'Trump, or Political Emotions'. *The New Inquiry* (blog). Accessed 3 November 2023. https://thenewinquiry.com/trump-or-political -emotions/

Bhambra, Gurminder. 2017a. 'The Current Crisis of Europe: Refugees, Colonialism, and the Limits of Cosmopolitanism'. *European Law Journal* 23(5): 395–405.

Bhambra, Gurminder. 2017b. 'Brexit, Trump, and "Methodological Whiteness": On the Misrecognition of Race and Class'. *The British Journal of Sociology* 68(1) Supplement 1: 214–32.

Bhattacharyya, Gargi. 2009. *Dangerous Brown Men: Exploiting Sex, Violence and Feminism in the 'War on Terror'*. London: Bloomsbury Publishing.

Bigo, Didier. 2002. 'Security and Immigration: Toward a Critique of the Governmentality of Unease'. *Alternatives: Global, Local, Political* 27(1): 63–92.

Bild. 2018. 'Wiedereinreise-Wahnsinn: Terroristen durften ganz legal zu uns kommen'. *Die Bild Zeitung*, 19 June. Accessed 15 March 2024. https://www .bild.de/politik/inland/asylrecht/islamisten-durften-ganz-legal-nach-deutschland -kommen-56060690.bild.html

Bilous, Taras. 2022. 'A Letter to the Western Left from Kyiv'. *Dissent* 69(2): 88–94.

Birnbaum, Robert. 2016. 'Jahresklausur der CDU: "Köln hat alles verändert"'. *Der Tagesspiegel Online*. Accessed 30 May 2023. Accessed 3 November 2023. https:// www.tagesspiegel.de/politik/koln-hat-alles-verandert-5205370.html

Biskamp, Floris. 2017. 'Angst-Traum "Angst-Raum": Über den Erfolg der AfD, "die Ängste der Menschen" und die Versuche, sie "ernst zu nehmen"'. *Forschungsjournal Soziale Bewegungen* 30(2): 91–100.

Bissenbakker, Mons and Lene Myong. 2019. 'The Affective Biopolitics of Migration'. *Nordic Journal of Migration Research* 9(4): 417–24.

Blickle, Peter. 2004. *Heimat: A Critical Theory of the German Idea of Homeland.* London: Camden House.

Bloch, Ernst. 1954. *The Principle of Hope.* Oxford: Blackwell.

Boatcă, Manuela. 2016. *Global Inequalities Beyond Occidentalism.* London: Routledge.

Boccagni, Paolo and Loretta Baldassar. 2015. 'Emotions on the Move: Mapping the Emergent Field of Emotion and Migration'. *Emotion, Space and Society* 16: 73–80.

Bojadžijev, Manuela. 2013. 'Wer von Rassismus Nicht Reden Will: Einige Reflexionen Zur Aktuellen Bedeutung von Rassismus Und Seiner Analyse'. In *NSU-Terror*, edited by Imke Schmincke and Jasmin Siri, 145–54. Bielefeld: Transcript Verlag.

Boulila, Stefanie C. and Christiane Carri. 2017. 'On Cologne: *Gender*, Migration and Unacknowledged Racisms in Germany'. *European Journal of Women's Studies* 24(3): 286–93.

Bracke, Sarah, and Luis Manuel Hernández Aguilar. 2020. '"They Love Death as We Love Life": The "Muslim Question" and the Biopolitics of Replacement'. *The British Journal of Sociology* 71(4): 680–701.

Bradley, Gracie Mae and Luke de Noronha. 2022. *Against Borders: The Case for Abolition.* London: Verso.

Braithwaite, John. 1989. *Crime, Shame and Reintegration.* Cambridge: Cambridge University Press.

Braithwaite, John. 2000. 'Shame and Criminal Justice'. *Canadian Journal of Criminology* 42(3): 281–98.

Braun, Stefan and Evelyn Roll. 2016. 'Angela Merkel: "Deutschland wird Deutschland bleiben"'. *Süddeutsche Zeitung.* Accessed 3 November 2023. https://www .sueddeutsche.de/politik/kanzlerin-merkel-im-sz-interview-deutschland-wird -deutschland-bleiben-1.3141520

Breger, Claudia. 2020. *Making Worlds: Affect and Collectivity in Contemporary European Cinema.* New York: Columbia University Press.

Brock, Alexander. 2015. 'Hallplatz-Hungerstreik Beendet: Flüchtlinge Sind Umgezogen'. *Nordbayern Kurier.* Accessed 3 November 2023. https://www .nordbayern.de/region/nuernberg/hallplatz-hungerstreik-beendet-fluchtlinge-sind -umgezogen-1.4677593?rssPage=bm9yZGJheWVVybi5kZQ%3D%3D

Bröcker, Michael. 2015. 'Kommentar: Das Bild der Krise'. *Rheinische Post.* Accessed 3 November 2023. https://rp-online.de/politik/das-bild-der-krise_aid-22036409

Bronner, Stephen E. 2020. 'Conspiracy Fetishism, Community, and the Antisemitic Imaginary'. *Antisemitism Studies* 4(2): 371–87.

Brown, Wendy. 1993. 'Wounded Attachments'. *Political Theory* 21(3): 390–410.

Brown, Wendy. 2000. 'Suffering Rights as Paradoxes'. *Constellations* 7(2): 208–29.

Buckel, Sonja, Laura Graf, Judith Kopp, Neva Löw and Maximilian Pichl (eds). 2021. *Kämpfe um Migrationspolitik seit 2015: Zur Transformation des europäischen Migrationsregimes.* Bielefeld: Transcript Verlag.

Bundesregierung. 2015. 'Sommerpressekonferenz von Bundeskanzlerin Merkel'. Speech delivered 31 August. Accessed 3 November 2023. https://www .bundesregierung.de/bregde/aktuelles/pressekonferenzen/

Bundesregierung. 2021. 'Kanzlerin Merkel: "Rassismus ist ein Gift. Der Hass ist ein Gift"' Podcast delivered 13 February. Accessed 3 November 2023. https://www .bundesregierung.de/breg-de/mediathek/podcast-jahrestag-hanau-gs-1853566

Burger, Reiner. 2016. 'Übergriffe in Köln: "Straftaten einer neuen Dimension"'. *Frankfurter Allgemeine Zeitung*. Accessed 3 November 2023. https://www.faz .net/aktuell/gesellschaft/kriminalitaet/uebergriffe-in-koeln-straftaten-einer-neuen -dimension-13997272.html

Butler, Judith. 1997. *The Psychic Life of Power: Theories in Subjection*. Stanford, CA: Stanford University Press.

Butler, Judith. 2002. *Antigone's Claim: Kinship between Life and Death*. New York: Columbia University Press.

Butler, Judith. 2009. *Frames of War: When Is Life Grievable?* London: Verso.

Butler, Judith. 2015. *Notes Toward a Performative Theory of Assembly*. Cambridge, MA: Harvard University Press.

Butler, Judith, Zeynep Gambetti and Leticia Sabsay (eds). 2016. *Vulnerability in Resistance*. Durham, NC: Duke University Press.

Calloway-Thomas, Carolyn. 2010. *Empathy in the Global World: An Intercultural Perspective*. London: Sage Publishing.

Campt, Tina. 2005. *Other Germans: Black Germans and the Politics of Race, Gender, and Memory in the Third Reich*. Ann Arbor, MI: University of Michigan Press.

Casas-Cortes, Maribel, Sebastian Cobarrubias, Nicholas De Genova, Glenda Garelli, Giorgio Grappi, Charles Heller and Sabine Hess. 2015. 'New Keywords: Migration and Borders'. *Cultural Studies* 29(1): 55–87.

Castañeda, Claudia. 2002. *Figurations: Child, Bodies, Worlds*. Durham, NC: Duke University Press.

Castro Varela, María do Mar and Paul Mecheril. 2016. *Die Dämonisierung der Anderen: Rassismuskritik der Gegenwart*. Bielefeld: Transcript Verlag.

Castro Varela, María Do Mar and Nikita Dhawan. 2010. 'Mission Impossible: Postkoloniale Theorie im deutschsprachigen Raum'. In *Postkoloniale Soziologie: Empirische Befunde, theoretische Anschlüsse, politische Intervention*, edited by Julia Reuter and Paula-Irene Villa, 303–30. Bielefeld: Transcript Verlag.

Cattien, Jana. 2021. 'What Is Leitkultur?' *New German Critique* 48(1): 181–209.

Chauvin, Sébastien and Blanca Garcés-Mascareñas. 2014. 'Becoming Less Illegal: Deservingness Frames and Undocumented Migrant Incorporation'. *Sociology Compass* 8(4): 422–32.

Chin, Rita. 2007. *The Guest Worker Question in Postwar Germany*. Cambridge: Cambridge University Press.

Chin, Rita, Heide Fehrenbach, Geoff Eley and Atina Grossmann. 2010. *After the Nazi Racial State: Difference and Democracy in Germany and Europe*. Ann Arbor, MI: University of Michigan Press.

Chouliaraki, Lilie. 2006. *The Spectatorship of Suffering*. London: Sage Publishing.

Chouliaraki, Lilie. 2017. 'Symbolic Bordering: The Self-Representation of Migrants and Refugees in Digital News'. *Popular Communication* 15(2): 78–94.

Chouliaraki, Lilie and Tijana Stolic. 2017. 'Rethinking Media Responsibility in the Refugee "Crisis": A Visual Typology of European News'. *Media, Culture & Society* 39(8): 1162–77.

Chouliaraki, Lilie and Rafal Zaborowski. 2017. 'Voice and Community in the 2015 Refugee Crisis: A Content Analysis of News Coverage in Eight European Countries'. *International Communication Gazette* 79(6–7): 613–35.

Code, Lorraine. 1994. *Rhetorical Spaces: Essays on Gendered Locations*. London: Routledge.

Coleman, Rebecca and Debra Ferreday. 2013. *Hope and Feminist Theory*. London: Routledge.

Collins, Patricia Hill. 1993. 'Toward a New Vision: Race, Class, and Gender as Categories of Analysis and Connection'. *Race, Sex and Class* 1(1): 25–45.

Cooper, Davina. 2014. *Everyday Utopias: The Conceptual Life of Promising Spaces*. Durham, NC: Duke University Press.

Coplan, Amy and Peter Goldie. 2011. *Empathy: Philosophical and Psychological Perspectives*. Oxford: Oxford University Press.

Cosentino, Gabriele. 2020. 'From Pizzagate to the Great Replacement: The Globalization of Conspiracy Theories'. In *Social Media and the Post-Truth World Order*, 59–86. Cham: Palgrave Pivot.

Crenshaw, Kimberlé. 2011. 'From Private Violence to Mass Incarceration: Thinking Intersectionally about Women, Race, and Social Control'. *UCLA Law Review* 59(6): 1418–73.

Crenshaw, Kimberlé. 2017. *On Intersectionality: Essential Writings*. New York: The New Press.

Cvetkovich, Ann. 2003. *An Archive of Feelings: Trauma, Sexuality, and Lesbian Public Cultures*. Durham, NC: Duke University Press.

Cvetkovich, Ann. 2012a. *Depression: A Public Feeling*. Durham, NC: Duke University Press.

Cvetkovich, Ann. 2012b. 'Depression Is Ordinary: Public Feelings and Saidiya Hartman's Lose Your Mother'. *Feminist Theory* 13(2): 131–46.

Czollek, Max. 2020. *Gegenwartsbewältigung*. Munich: Carl Hanser Verlag.

d'Aoust, Anne-Marie. 2013. 'In the Name of Love: Marriage Migration, Governmentality, and Technologies of Love'. *International Political Sociology* 7(3): 258–74.

Dadusc, Deanna, Margherita Grazioli and Miguel A. Martínez. 2019. 'Introduction: Citizenship as Inhabitance? Migrant Housing Squats versus Institutional Accommodation'. *Citizenship Studies* 23(6): 521–39.

Danewid, Ida. 2017. 'White Innocence in the Black Mediterranean: Hospitality and the Erasure of History'. *Third World Quarterly* 38(7): 1674–89.

Danewid, Ida. 2022. 'Policing the (Migrant) Crisis: Stuart Hall and the Defence of Whiteness'. *Security Dialogue* 53(1): 21–37.

Dathan, Matt. 2015. 'Cameron Finally Breaks Silence on Refugee Crisis'. *The Independent*. Accessed 3 November 2023. https://www.independent.co.uk/news /uk/politics/aylan-kurdi-david-cameron-says-he-felt-deeply-moved-by-images -of-dead-syrian-boy-but-gives-no-details-of-plans-to-take-in-more-refugees -10484641.html

Davey, Jacob and Julia Ebner. 2019. '"The Great Replacement": The Violent Consequences of Mainstreamed Extremism'. *Institute for Strategic Dialogue* 7: 1–36.

Davis, Angela Y. 1981. *Women, Race, & Class*. New York: Knopf Doubleday Publishing Group.

Davis, Angela Y. 2000. 'The Color of Violence against Women'. *Colorlines* 3(3): 4.

Davis, Angela Y. 2011. *Are Prisons Obsolete?* New York: Seven Stories Press.

De Genova, Nicholas. 2015. 'Spectacles of Migrant "Illegality": The Scene of Exclusion, the Obscene of Inclusion'. In *The Language of Inclusion and Exclusion in Immigration and Integration*, edited by Marlou Schrover and Willem Schinkel, 58–76. London: Routledge.

De Genova, Nicholas. 2017. *The Borders of 'Europe': Autonomy of Migration, Tactics of Bordering*. Durham, NC: Duke University Press.

De Genova, Nicholas. 2023. 'A Racial Theory of Labour: Racial Capitalism from Colonial Slavery to Postcolonial Migration'. *Historical Materialism* 1: 1–33.

De Vries, L.A. and Guild, E. 2019. 'Seeking Refuge in Europe: Spaces of Transit and the Violence of Migration Management'. *Journal of Ethnic and Migration Studies* 45(12): 2156–66.

De Vries, Leonie Ansems, Nora Stel and Nadine Voelkne. 2024. 'Methodological Reflections on Migration Governance through Uncertainty and Affect'. In *Collective Movements and Emerging Political Spaces*, edited by Agharad Closs Stephens and Martina Tazzioli. London: Routledge.

Dean, Carolyn Janice. 2004. *The Fragility of Empathy after the Holocaust*. Ithaca, NY: Cornell University Press.

Demirtas, Birgül, Adelheid Schmitz, Derya Gür-Seker and Çagri Kahveci (eds). 2023. *Solingen, 30 Jahre nach dem Brandanschlag: Rassismus, extrem rechte Gewalt und die Narben einer vernachlässigten Aufarbeitung*. Bielefeld: Transcript Verlag.

Derrida, Jacques. 2000. 'Hospitality'. *Angelaki* 5(3): 3–18.

Devichand, Mukul. 2016. 'Alan Kurdi's Aunt: "My Dead Nephew's Picture Saved Thousands of Lives"'. *BBC News*. Accessed 3 November 2023. https://www.bbc.com/news/blogs-trending-35116022

Dhawan, Nikita. 2013. 'The Empire Prays Back: Religion, Secularity, and Queer Critique'. *Boundary 2* 40(1): 191–222.

Dhawan, Nikita. 2014. *Decolonizing Enlightenment: Transnational Justice, Human Rights and Democracy in a Postcolonial World*. Leverkusen: Verlag Barbara Budrich.

Di Gregorio, Michael and Jessica L. Merolli. 2016. 'Introduction: Affective Citizenship and the Politics of Identity, Control, Resistance'. *Citizenship Studies* 20(8): 933–42.

Dietze, Gabriele. 2016a. 'Deutscher Exzeptionalismus'. *Transversal Texts* (blog). Accessed 3 November 2023. https://transversal.at/pdf/blog/404/

Dietze, Gabriele. 2016b. 'Ethnosexismus. Sex-Mob-Narrative um die Kölner Sylvesternacht'. *Movements: Journal for Critical Migration and Border Regime Studies* 2(1).

Diner, Dan. 1996. *Zivilisationsbruch: Denken nach Auschwitz*. Frankfurt am Main: S. Fischer Verlag.

Dirckinck-Holmfeld, Katrine. 2019. '(Para) Paranoia: Affect as Critical Inquiry'. *Diffractions* 1: 1–24.

Doughan, Sultan. 2022. 'Desiring Memorials: Jews, Muslims, and the Human of Citizenship'. In *Jews and Muslims in Europe*, 46–70. Leiden: Brill.

Douthat, Ross. 2016. 'Germany on the Brink'. *The New York Times*. Accessed 3 November 2023. https://www.nytimes.com/2016/01/10/opinion/sunday/germany -on-the-brink.html

'Drei Jahre nach dem rassistischen Anschlag in Hanau: Wir trauern und erinnern'. 2023. *Initiative 19*. Februar (blog). Accessed 3 November 2023. https://19feb -hanau.org/2023/01/24/3-jahre-nach-dem-rassistischen-anschlag-in-hanau-wir -trauern-und-erinnern/

Eagleton, Terry. 2019. *Hope Without Optimism*. New Haven, CT: Yale University Press.

Edelman, Lee. 2004. *No Future: Queer Theory and the Death Drive*. Durham, NC: Duke University Press.

Edwards, Maxim. 2021. 'One Year after the Hanau Massacre, Victims' Families Fight for Justice'. *Open Democracy*. Accessed 3 November 2023. https://www .opendemocracy.net/en/one-year-after-the-hanau-massacre-victims-families-fight -for-justice/

Ehrenberg, Markus. 2016. 'Wie Flüchtlinge mit dem Handy ihre Odyssee filmen'. *Der Tagesspiegel*. Accessed 3 November 2023. https://www.tagesspiegel.de/ gesellschaft/medien/wie-fluchtlinge-mit-dem-handy-ihre-odyssee-filmen-5466586 .html

'Einhundert Asylbewerber demonstrieren in Nürnberg'. 2015. *Bayerischer Rundfunk*. Accessed 3 November 2023. https://www.br.de/nachrichten/bayern/100 -asylbewerber-demonstrieren-in-nuernberg,70t3gc1j70v36c1g70tkgcht6wv0

El-Enany, Nadine. 2016. 'Aylan Kurdi: The Human Refugee'. *Law and Critique* 27(1): 13–15.

El-Enany, Nadine. 2020. *Bordering Britain: Law, Race and Empire*. Manchester: Manchester University Press.

El-Tayeb, Fatima. 1999. '"Blood Is a Very Special Juice": Racialized Bodies and Citizenship in Twentieth-Century Germany'. *International Review of Social History* 44(7): 149–69.

El-Tayeb, Fatima. 2016. *Undeutsch: Die Konstruktion des Anderen in der postmigrantischen Gesellschaft*. Bielefeld: Transcript Verlag.

El-Tayeb, Fatima. 2017. 'The European Refugee Crisis: Neoliberal Racial Capitalism and Queer of Color Activism'. Keynote lecture presented at *Challenges in Queer and Feminist Migration and Diaspora Studies*. London, SOAS: 24–25.

Eribon, Didier. 2004. *Insult and the Making of the Gay Self*. Durham, NC: Duke University Press.

Eribon, Didier. 2018. *Returning to Reims*. London: Penguin.

'Erschreckende Zahlen – Der Bevölkerungsaustausch läuft'. 2017. *Alternative für Deutschland* (blog). Accessed 3 November 2023. https://www.afd.de/alexander -gauland-erschreckende-zahlen-der-bevoelkerungsaustausch-laeuft/

'Ex-Minister Friedrich spricht von "Schweigekartell"'. 2016. *Die Welt.* Accessed 3 November 2023. https://www.welt.de/politik/deutschland/article150686468/Ex -Minister-Friedrich-spricht-von-Schweigekartell.html

Faller, Heike. 2016. 'Alan Kurdi: Ohne ihn'. *Die Zeit.* Accessed 3 November 2023. https://www.zeit.de/zeit-magazin/2016/03/alan-kurdi-fluechtlingsjunge-strand -familie

Fanon, Frantz. 2017. *Black Skin, White Masks.* London: Pluto Press.

Farris, Sara R. 2017. *In the Name of Women's Rights: The Rise of Femonationalism.* Durham, NC: Duke University Press.

Fassin, Didier. 2005. 'Compassion and Repression: The Moral Economy of Immigration Policies in France'. *Cultural Anthropology* 20(3): 362–87.

Fassin, Didier. 2011. *Humanitarian Reason: A Moral History of the Present.* Oakland, CA: University of California Press.

Fassin, Didier. 2013. 'On Resentment and Ressentiment: The Politics and Ethics of Moral Emotions'. *Current Anthropology* 54(3): 249–67.

Fassin, Éric. 2012. 'Sexual Democracy and the New Racialization of Europe'. *Journal of Civil Society* 8(3): 285–88.

Fassin, Éric. 2017. 'The Neo-Fascist Moment in Neoliberalism'. *Open Democracy.* Accessed 3 November 2023. https://www.opendemocracy.net/en/can-europe -make-it/neo-fascist-moment-of-neoliberalism/

Fassin, Éric. 2018. *Populism Left and Right.* Chicago, IL: Prickly Paradigm Press.

Fassin, Éric and Aurélie Windels. 2016. 'The German Dream: Neoliberalism and Fortress Europe'. *Near Futures – Europe at a Crossroads.* Accessed 3 November 2023. http://nearfuturesonline.org/the-german-dream-neoliberalism-and-fortress -europe/

Fehrenbach, Heide. 2005. *Race after Hitler: Black Occupation Children in Postwar Germany and America.* Princeton, NJ: Princeton University Press.

Fekete, Liz. 2007. *They Are Children Too. A Study of Europe's Deportation Policies.* Nottingham: Russell Press.

Feldman, Allen. 2008. *Formations of Violence: The Narrative of the Body and Political Terror in Northern Ireland.* Chicago, IL: University of Chicago Press.

Filipovič, Alexander. 2015. 'Foto ist kaum auszuhalten'. *Der Spiegel.* Accessed 3 November 2023. https://www.spiegel.de/kultur/gesellschaft/medienethiker -alexander-filipovic-foto-ist-kaum-auszuhalten-a-1051262.html

Fitting, Peter. 2009. 'A Short History of Utopian Studies'. *Science Fiction Studies* 121–31.

Fleischmann, Larissa and Elias Steinhilper. 2017. 'The Myth of Apolitical Volunteering for Refugees: German Welcome Culture and a New Dispositif of Helping'. *Social Inclusion* 5(3): 17–27.

Florvil, Tiffany. 2020. *Mobilizing Black Germany: Afro-German Women and the Making of a Transnational Movement.* Champaign, IL: University of Illinois Press.

Florvil, Tiffany. 2021. 'Queer Memory and Black Germans'. *The New Fascism Syllabus* (blog). Accessed 3 November 2023. https://newfascismsyllabus.com/ opinions/the-catechism-debate/queer-memory-and-black-germans/

'Flüchtlinge in Deutschland: Sigmar Gabriels Video-Podcast Zu Flüchtlingspolitik'. *SPD*. Accessed 3 November 2023. https://www.youtube.com/watch?v =EMDVu0x6KNo

'Flüchtlingsgipfel: CDU-Chef Merz schlägt Bundesregierung Zusammenarbeit vor'. 2023. *Die Zeit*. Accessed 3 November 2023. https://www.zeit.de/politik/ deutschland/2023-03/union-friedrich-merz-fluechtlingsgipfel-kommunen

Follis, Karolina. 2019. 'Rejecting Refugees in Illiberal Poland: The Response from Civil Society'. *Journal of Civil Society* 15(4): 307–25.

Foroutan, Naika. 2010. 'Neue Deutsche, Postmigranten und Bindungs-Identitäten. Wer gehört zum neuen Deutschland?' *Aus Politik und Zeitgeschehen* 46/47: 9–15.

Foroutan, Naika. 2015. 'Über Stereotype in Flüchtlingsfragen: Interview mit Karen Krüger'. *Frankfurter Allgemeine Zeitung*. Accessed 3 November 2023. https:// www.faz.net/aktuell/feuilleton/debatten/naika-foroutan-ueber-stereotype-in -fluechtlingsfragen-13886917.html

Foroutan, Naika. 2016. 'Nationale Bedürfnisse und soziale Ängste'. In *Die Dämonisierung des Anderen*, edited by María do Mar Castro Varela and Paul Mecheril, 97–106. Bielefeld: Transcript Verlag.

Foroutan, Naika, Korinna Schäfer, Coskun Canan and Benjamin Schwarze. 2011. *Sarrazins Thesen auf dem Prüfstand*. Berlin: Humboldt-Universität zu Berlin, Universitätsbibliothek der Humboldt-Universität. https://doi.org/10.18452/5094

Fortier, Anne-Marie. 2010. 'Proximity by Design? Affective Citizenship and the Management of Unease'. *Citizenship Studies* 14(1): 17–30.

Fortier, Anne-Marie. 2016. 'Afterword: Acts of Affective Citizenship? Possibilities and Limitations'. *Citizenship Studies* 20(8): 1038–44.

'Fortress Europe: Death by Policy'. 2016. *UNITED for Intercultural Action*. Accessed 3 November 2023. https://unitedagainstrefugeedeaths.eu/about-the -campaign/fortress-europe-death-by-policy/

Foucault, Michel. 2003. *'Society Must Be Defended'*: Lectures at the Collège de France, 1975–1976. *Vol. 1*. London: Macmillan.

Frevert, Ute. 2020. *Mächtige Gefühle: Von A wie Angst bis Z wie Zuneigung – Deutsche Geschichte seit 1900*. Frankfurt am Main: S. Fischer Verlag.

Fried, Nico. 2016. 'Ein Wort zu viel'. *Süddeutsche Zeitung*. Accessed 3 November 2023. https://www.sueddeutsche.de/politik/politiker-ein-wort-zu-viel-1.2808096

Fröhlich, Alexander. 2018. 'Kleidung weg: AfD-Chef Gauland beim Baden in Potsdam bestohlen'. *Der Tagesspiegel*. Accessed 3 November 2023. https://www .tagesspiegel.de/potsdam/landeshauptstadt/afd-chef-gauland-beim-baden-in -potsdam-bestohlen-7825099.html

Fromm, Erich. 2021 [1941]. *The Fear of Freedom*. London: Routledge.

Ghadban, Ralph. 2016. 'Migration importiert ein archaisches Frauenbild'. *Die Welt*, 1 February. Accessed 10 March 2023. https://www.welt.de/debatte/kommentare/ article151741148/Migration-importiert-ein-archaisches-Frauenbild.html

Giddens, Anthony. 1991. *Modernity and Self-Identity: Self and Society in the Late Modern Age*. Stanford, CA: Stanford University Press.

Gilmore, Ruth Wilson. 2007. *Golden Gulag: Prisons, Surplus, Crisis, and Opposition in Globalizing California*. Oakland, CA: University of California Press.

Goldberg, David T. 2009. *The Threat of Race: Reflections on Racial Neoliberalism*. Hoboken, NJ: John Wiley & Sons.

Gordon, Avery. 1997. *Ghostly Matters: Haunting and the Sociological Imagination*. Minneapolis, MN: University of Minnesota Press.

Gould, Deborah B. 2009. *Moving Politics: Emotion and ACT UP's Fight against AIDS*. Chicago, IL: University of Chicago Press.

Gray, Harriet and Anja K Franck. 2019. 'Refugees as/at Risk: The Gendered and Racialized Underpinnings of Securitization in British Media Narratives'. *Security Dialogue* 50(3): 275–91.

Gregg, Melissa and Gregory J. Seigworth. 2010. *The Affect Theory Reader*. Durham, NC: Duke University Press.

'Gründungstext der Initiative 19. Februar Hanau'. 2020. *Initiative 19*. Februar (blog). Accessed 3 November 2023. https://19feb-hanau.org/ueber-uns/

Gully, Jennifer M. and Lynn Mie Itagaki. 2017. 'The Migrant Is Dead, Long Live the Citizen!: Pro-Migrant Activism at EU Borders'. *PhiloSOPHIA* 7(2): 281–304.

Gümüşay, Kübra et al. 2016. 'Against Sexualised Violence and Racism. Always. Anywhere. #ausnahmslos'. *Ausnahmslos*. Accessed 3 November 2023. https://ausnahmslos.org/english

Gunaratnam, Yasmin. 2003. *Researching 'Race' and Ethnicity: Methods, Knowledge, and Power*. London: Sage Publishing.

Gunaratnam, Yasmin. 2013. *Death and the Migrant: Bodies, Borders, and Care*. London: Bloomsbury Academic.

Gunaratnam, Yasmin and Gail Lewis. 2001. 'Racialising Emotional Labour and Emotionalising Racialised Labour: Anger, Fear and Shame in Social Welfare'. *Journal of Social Work Practice* 15(2): 131–48.

Habermas, Jürgen. 1986. 'Eine Art Schadensabwicklung'. *Die Zeit* 29.

Habermas, Jürgen. 1991. *The Structural Transformation of the Public Sphere: An Inquiry into a Category of Bourgeois Society*. Cambridge, MA: MIT Press.

Habermas, Rebekka. 2016. *Skandal in Togo: Ein Kapitel deutscher Kolonialherrschaft*. Frankfurt am Main: S. Fischer Verlag.

Hage, Ghassan. 2003. *Against Paranoid Nationalism: Searching for Hope in a Shrinking Society*. London: Pluto Press.

Hagen, Kevin. 2016. 'Sahra Wagenknecht zum Asylrecht: Die Gast-Rechte'. *Der Spiegel*. Accessed 3 November 2023. https://www.spiegel.de/politik/deutschland/sahra-wagenknecht-zum-asylrecht-die-gast-rechte-a-1071614.html

Hajek, Katarina. 2020. 'The AfD and Right-Wing (Anti-)Gender Mobilisation in Germany'. Accessed 3 November 2023. *Engenderings* (blog). https://blogs.lse.ac.uk/gender/2020/02/27/the-afd-and-right-wing-anti-gender-mobilisation-in-germany/

Hall, Stuart. 1978. *Policing the Crisis: Mugging, the State, and Law and Order*. London: Holmes & Meier.

Hall, Stuart. 1991. 'Europe's Other Self'. *Marxism Today* 18: 18–19.

Hall, Stuart. 1997. *Representation: Cultural Representations and Signifying Practices*. London: Sage.

Halperin, David M. and Valerie Traub. 2009. *Gay Shame*. Chicago, IL: University of Chicago Press.

Hamann, Ulrike and Serhat Karakayali. 2016. 'Practicing Willkommenskultur: Migration and Solidarity in Germany'. *Intersections* 2(4): 69–86.

Hamid, Mohsin. 2018. *Exit West*. London: Penguin.

Hark, Sabine and Paula-Irene Villa. 2015. *Anti-Genderismus: Sexualität und Geschlecht als Schauplätze aktueller politischer Auseinandersetzungen*. Bielefeld: Transcript Verlag.

Hark, Sabine and Paula-Irene Villa. 2020. *The Future of Difference: Beyond the Toxic Entanglement of Racism, Sexism and Feminism*. London: Verso.

Hartman, Saidiya. 2022. *Scenes of Subjection: Terror, Slavery, and Self-Making in Nineteenth-Century America*. New York: W.W. Norton.

Harvey, David. 2020. *Spaces of Hope*. Berkeley, CA: University of California Press.

Hasselbach, Christoph. 2017. 'Die Politik entdeckt die Heimat für sich'. *Deutsche Welle*. Accessed 3 November 2023. https://www.dw.com/de/die-politik-entdeckt -die-heimat-f%C3%BCr-sich/a-40840865

Heidenreich, Ulrike. 2016. 'Ein Gespräch mit fünf Frauen in Flüchtlingsheimen'. *Süddeutsche Zeitung*. Accessed 3 November 2023. https://www.sueddeutsche.de/ leben/fluechtlinge-nicht-erst-seit-koeln-schliessen-sie-die-tuer-ab-1.2870295

Hemmings, Clare. 2005. 'Invoking Affect: Cultural Theory and the Ontological Turn'. *Cultural Studies* 19(5): 548–67.

Hemmings, Clare. 2011. *Why Stories Matter: The Political Grammar of Feminist Theory*. Durhan, NC: Duke University Press.

Hemmings, Clare. 2012. 'Affective Solidarity: Feminist Reflexivity and Political Transformation'. *Feminist Theory* 13(2): 147–61.

Hemmings, Clare. 2021. 'Unnatural Feelings: The Affective Life of 'Anti-Gender'- Mobilisations'. *Radical Philosophy* 2: 27–39.

Herzog, Dagmar. 2007. *Sex after Fascism: Memory and Morality in Twentieth-Century Germany*. Princeton, NJ: Princeton University Press.

Hess, Sabine. 2021. 'Umkämpfte Neuordnung.: Europas neues-altes Grenzregime fünf Jahre später'. In *Jahrbuch für Europäische Ethnologie*, 183–208. Paderborn: Brill Schöningh.

Hess, Sabine, Bernd Kasparek, Stefanie Kron, Mathias Rodatz, Maria Schwertl and Simon Sontowski. 2017. *Der Lange Sommer Der Migration: Grenzregime III*. Hamburg: Assoziation A.

Hickmann, Christoph and Kurbjuweit, Dirk. 2023. Interview with Olaf Scholz: 'We Have to Deport People More Often and Faster'. *Der Spiegel*. Accessed 3 November 2023. https://www.spiegel.de/international/germany/interview-with -german-chancellor-olaf-scholz-we-have-to-deport-people-more-often-and-faster -a-790a033c-a658-4be5-8611-285086d39d38

Hill, Jenny. 2015. 'Migrant Crisis: How Long Can Merkel Keep German Doors Open?' *BBC News*. Accessed 3 November 2023. https://www.bbc.com/news/ world-europe-34402001

Hochschild, Arlie Russell. 1979. 'Emotion Work, Feeling Rules, and Social Structure'. *American Journal of Sociology* 85(3): 551–75.

Hochschild, Arlie Russell. 2018. *Strangers in Their Own Land: Anger and Mourning on the American Right*. New York: The New Press.

Hoffmann, Jule. 2021. 'NS-Vergangenheit: Deutsch und damit nicht normal'. *Die Zeit*. Accessed 3 November 2023. https://www.zeit.de/kultur/2021-03/ns -vergangenheit-nazihintergrund-she-said-buchladen-emilia-von-senger

Hofmann, Laura and Matthias Meisner. 2017. 'Brandrede in Dresden: Der totale Höcke'. *Der Tagesspiegel*. Accessed 3 November 2023. https://www.tagesspiegel .de/politik/der-totale-hocke-4912966.html

Höijer, Birgitta. 2004. 'The Discourse of Global Compassion: The Audience and Media Reporting of Human Suffering'. *Media, Culture & Society* 26(4): 513–31.

Holmes, Seth M. and Heide Castañeda. 2016. 'Representing the "European Refugee Crisis" in Germany and Beyond: Deservingness and Difference, Life and Death'. *American Ethnologist* 43(1): 12–24.

'Holocaust Memorial Bornhagen'. 2019. Centre for Political Beauty. Accessed 3 November 2023. https://politicalbeauty.com/memorial.html

Holst, Sina and Johanna Montanari (eds). 2017. *Wege zum Nein. Emanzipative Sexualitäten und queer-feministische Visionen. Beiträge für eine radikale Debatte nach der Sexualstrafrechtsreform in Deutschland nach 2016*. Münster: Edition Assemblage.

Holvikivi, Aiko. 2015. 'Contending with Paradox: Feminist Investments in Gender Training'. *Signs: Journal of Women in Culture and Society* 48(3): 533–55.

Holvikivi, Aiko. 2023. 'Contending with Paradox: Feminist Investments in Gender Training'. *Signs: Journal of Women in Culture and Society* 48(3): 533–55.

Holvikivi, Aiko, Tomás Ojeda and Billy Holzberg. 2024. *Transnational Anti-Gender Politics: Feminist Solidarity in Times of Global Attacks*. London: Palgrave Macmillan.

Holzberg, Billy. 2018. 'The Multiple Lives of Affect: A Case Study of Commercial Surrogacy'. *Body & Society* 24(4): 32–57.

Holzberg, Billy. 2024. 'The Great Replacement Ideology as Anti-Gender Politics: Affect, White Terror and Reproductive Racism in Germany and Beyond'. In *Transnational Anti-Gender Politics: Feminist Solidarity in Times of Global Attacks*, edited by Aiko Holvikivi, Billy Holzberg and Tomás Ojeda. London: Palgrave Macmillan.

Holzberg, Billy, Kristina Kolbe and Rafal Zaborowski. 2018. 'Figures of Crisis: The Delineation of (Un)Deserving Refugees in the German Media'. *Sociology* 52(3): 534–50.

Holzberg, Billy, Anouk Madörin and Michelle Pfeifer. 2021. 'The Sexual Politics of Border Control: An Introduction'. *Ethnic and Racial Studies* 44(9): 1485–506.

Holzberg, Billy and Priya Raghavan. 2020. 'Securing the Nation Through the Politics of Sexual Violence: Tracing Resonances between Delhi and Cologne'. *International Affairs* 96(5): 1189–208.

hooks, bell. 1992. *Black Looks: Race and Representation*. London: Routledge.

Howard, Marc M. 2008. 'The Causes and Consequences of Germany's New Citizenship Law'. *German Politics* 17(1): 41–62.

Huysmans, Jef. 2006. *The Politics of Insecurity: Fear, Migration and Asylum in the EU*. London: Routledge.

Huysmans, Jef and Vicki Squire. 2016. 'Migration and Security'. In *Routledge Handbook of Security Studies*, 161–71. London: Routledge.

Ibrahim, Yasmin. 2018. 'The Unsacred and the Spectacularized: Alan Kurdi and the Migrant Body'. *Social Media + Society* 4(4): 1–9.

Illouz, Eva. 2007. *Cold Intimacies: The Making of Emotional Capitalism*. London: Polity.

'Im Wortlaut: "Wenn wir nicht gerade aus Stein sind"'. 2016. *Der Tagesspiegel*. Accessed 3 November 2023. https://www.tagesspiegel.de/politik/wenn-wir-nicht -gerade-aus-stein-sind-3758905.html

Irom, Bimbisar. 2018. 'Virtual Reality and the Syrian Refugee Camps: Humanitarian Communication and the Politics of Empathy'. *International Journal of Communication* 12: 23.

Isin, Engin F. and Greg M. Nielsen. 2008. *Acts of Citizenship*. London: Bloomsbury.

Jasper, James M. 1998. 'The Emotions of Protest: Affective and Reactive Emotions in and around Social Movements'. *Sociological Forum* 13: 397–424.

Jasper, James M. 2018. *The Emotions of Protest*. Chicago, IL: University of Chicago Press.

Jaspers, Karl. 1946. *Die Schuldfrage*. Munich: Piper.

Jasser, Greta, Megan Kelly and Ann-Kathrin Rothermel. 2020. 'Male Supremacism and the Hanau Terrorist Attack: Between Online Misogyny and Far-Right Violence'. Den Haag: ICCT – International Centre for Counter-Terrorism.

Jones, Hannah. 2021. *Violent Ignorance: Confronting Racism and Migration Control*. London: Bloomsbury.

Jones, Hannah, Yasmin Gunaratnam, Gargi Bhattacharyya, William Davies, Sukhwant Dhaliwal, Kirsten Forkert, Emma Jackson and Roiyah Saltus. 2017. *Go Home? The Politics of Immigration Controversies*. Manchester: Manchester University Press.

Kade, Claudia. 2016. 'Boris Palmer: "Unsere großzügige Hilfe wurde missbraucht"'. *Die Welt*. Accessed 3 November 2023. https://www.welt.de/politik/deutschland/ article156969128/Unsere-grosszuegige-Hilfe-wurde-missbraucht.html

Kallius, Annastiina, Daniel Monterescu and Prem Kumar Rajaram. 2016. 'Immobilizing Mobility: Border Ethnography, Illiberal Democracy, and the Politics of the "Refugee Crisis" in Hungary'. *American Ethnologist* 43(1): 25–37.

Kapoor, Nisha. 2018. *Deport, Deprive, Extradite: 21st Century State Extremism*. London: Verso.

Kappert, Ines. 2021. '"2015 darf sich nicht wiederholen": Das ist der Satz'. *Heinrich-Böll-Stiftung*. Accessed 3 November 2023. https://www.gwi-boell.de/de/2021/08 /19/2015-darf-sich-nicht-wiederholen-das-ist-der-satz

Kapur, Ratna. 2013. 'Gender, Sovereignty and the Rise of a Sexual Security Regime in International Law and Postcolonial India'. *Melbourne Journal of International Law* 14: 317–45.

Karakayali, Juliane, Çagri Kahveci, Doris Liebscher and Carl Melchers. 2017. *Den NSU-Komplex analysieren: Aktuelle Perspektiven aus der Wissenschaft*. Bielefeld: Transcript Verlag.

Karakayali, Serhat. 2017. 'Feeling the Scope of Solidarity: The Role of Emotions for Volunteers Supporting Refugees in Germany'. *Social Inclusion* 5(3): 7–16.

Kasparek, Bernd, and Marc Speer. 2015. 'Of Hope. Hungary and the Long Summer of Migration'. *Bordermonitoring*. Accessed 3 November 2023. https://bordermonitoring.eu/ungarn/2015/09/of-hope-en/

Kasper-Claridge, Manuela. 2021. 'Deutsche Welle Interview with Olaf Scholz'. *Deutsche Welle*. Accessed 3 November 2023. https://www.dw.com/en/olaf-scholz-its-imperative-that-we-return-to-the-rule-of-law/a-58834963

Kaya, Asiye. 2013. '(Re)Considering the Last Fifty Years of Migration and Current Immigration Policies in Germany'. *German Politics and Society* 31(2): 1–12.

Kehrl, Oliver. 2017. 'Wie mich die Silvesternacht zum Politiker machte'. *Focus*. Accessed 3 November 2023. https://www.focus.de/regional/koeln/kommentar-aus-koeln-landtagsabgeordneter-oliver-kehrl-ueber-die-silvesternacht-vor-zwei-jahren_id_8149496.html

Kelle, Birgit. 2016. 'Gastkommentar: Wir wollen Helden! Männer sollen Frauen mit der Faust verteidigen'. *Focus*. Accessed 3 November 2023. https://www.focus.de/politik/experten/bkelle/gastkommentar-von-birgit-kelle-ja-wir-wollen-helden-maenner-sollen-ihre-frauen-mit-der-faust-verteidigen_id_5561612.html

Keskinen, Suvi. 2013. 'Antifeminism and White Identity Politics'. *Nordic Journal of Migration Research* 3(4): 225–32.

Khanna, Ranjana. 2003. *Dark Continents: Psychoanalysis and Colonialism.* Durham, NC: Duke University Press.

Khorana, Sukhmani. 2022. *Mediated Emotions of Migration: Reclaiming Affect for Agency*. Bristol: Bristol University Press.

Kimmel, Michael. 2017. *Angry White Men: American Masculinity at the End of an Era*. London: Hachette.

Kinnvall, Catarina. 2015. 'Borders and Fear: Insecurity, Gender and the Far Right in Europe'. *Journal of Contemporary European Studies* 23(4): 514–29.

Kızılay, Efsun. 2021. 'Haunau hätte verhindert werden können'. *Edition F*, 19 February. Accessed 15 March 2024. https://editionf.com/efsun-kizilay-wenn-deutschland-sich-mit-seinem-rassismusproblem-auseinandergesetzt-haette-haette-hanau-verhindert-werden-koennen-2/

Kızılay, Efsun. 2023. 'Interview: "Hanau hätte verhindert werden können, wenn Deutschland sich mit seinem Rassismusproblem auseinandergesetzt hätte"'. *Edition F* (blog). Accessed 3 November 2023. https://editionf.com/efsun-kizilay-wenn-deutschland-sich-mit-seinem-rassismusproblem-auseinandergesetzt-haette-haette-hanau-verhindert-werden-koennen-2/

Kızılay, Efsun, Ercan Ayboğa and Serpil Temiz Ünvar. 2021. 'Im Gespräch mit Serpil Temiz Ünvar: "Warum haben sie uns voller Hass das Leben weggenommen?"' *Rosa-Luxemburg-Stiftung*. Accessed 3 November 2023. https://www.rosalux.de/news/id/44424/anschlag-von-hanau-warum-haben-sie-uns-voller-hass-das-leben-weggenommen

Kleist, Nauja and Stef Jansen. 2016. 'Introduction: Hope over Time – Crisis, Immobility and Future-Making'. *History and Anthropology* 27(4): 373–92.

Knight, Ben. 2018. 'German Parliament Rows over UN Migration Compact'. *Deutsche Welle*. Accessed 3 November 2023. https://www.dw.com/en/german-parliament-rows-over-un-migration-compact/a-46213002

Kohut, Heinz. 1972. 'Thoughts on Narcissism and Narcissistic Rage'. *The Psychoanalytic Study of the Child* 27(1): 360–400.

Kolbe, Kristina. 2024. *The Sound of Difference: Race, Class and the Politics of 'Diversity' in Classical Music*. Manchester: Manchester University Press.

'Köln: Angela Merkel verlangt harte Antwort des Rechtsstaats'. 2016. *Der Spiegel*. Accessed 3 November 2023. https://www.spiegel.de/politik/deutschland/koeln-angela-merkel-verlangt-harte-antwort-des-rechtsstaats-a-1070609.html

König, Pascal and Sebastian Jäckle. 2023. *Contemporary Germany and the Fourth Wave of Far-Right Politics*. London: Routledge.

Konrad-Adenauer-Stiftung. 2015. 'Protokoll 28. Parteitag Der CDU Deutschlands'. Konrad-Adenauer-Stiftung. Accessed 3 November 2023. https://www.kas.de/c/document_library/get_file?uuid=51820aaa-2f21-e948-9544-ffbf29dc9499&groupId=252038

Kordes, Herbert and Lara Straatman. 2022. 'Aussage zu Ukrainern: Wie CDU-Chef Merz Kreml-Propaganda verbreitete'. *Tagesschau*. Accessed 3 November 2023. https://www.tagesschau.de/faktenfinder/merz-sozialtourismus-101.html

Korteweg, Anna and Gökçe Yurdakul. 2009. 'Islam, Gender, and Immigrant Integration: Boundary Drawing in Discourses on Honour Killing in the Netherlands and Germany'. *Ethnic and Racial Studies* 32(2): 218–38.

Korteweg, Anna and Gökçe Yurdakul. 2014. *The Headscarf Debates: Conflicts of National Belonging*. Stanford, CA: Stanford University Press.

Korvensyrjä, Aino. 2024. 'Criminalizing Black Solidarity: Dublin Deportations, Raids, and Racial Statecraft in Southern Germany'. *Identities* 31(1): 104–22.

Krautkrämer, Felix. 2021. 'Wenn die Generation Widerstand dem eigenen Nazi-Hintergrund nachforscht'. *Junge Freiheit*. Accessed 3 November 2023. https://jungefreiheit.de/debatte/kommentar/2021/nazi-hintergrund/

Krüger, Karen. 2015. 'Naika Foroutan über Stereotype in Flüchtlingsfragen'. *Frankfurter Allgemeine Zeitung*, 3 November. Accessed 19 March 2023. https://www.faz.net/aktuell/feuilleton/debatten/naika-foroutan-ueber-stereotype-in-fluechtlingsfragen-13886917.html

Krznaric, Roman. 2015. *Empathy: Why It Matters, and How to Get It*. New York: Tarcher Perigee.

Kuhar, Roman and David Paternotte. 2017. *Anti-Gender Campaigns in Europe: Mobilizing against Equality*. London: Rowman & Littlefield.

Kumar, Krishan. 1987. *Utopia and Anti-Utopia in Modern Times*. Oxford: Basil Blackwell.

Kunz, Sarah. 2022. 'Learning via Instagram: Interview with Sinthujan Varatharajah'. *Andragoška Spoznanja* 28(2): 123–36.

Kurt, Seyda. 2023. *Hass: Von der Macht eines widerständigen Gefühls*. Hamburg: Harper Collins.

Kurth, Cornelia. 2016. 'Flucht-Doku mit Handy-Fotos'. *Schaumburger Zeitung*. Accessed 3 November 2023. https://www.szlz.de/region/rinteln_artikel,-fluchtdoku-mit-handyfotos-_arid,834213.html

Kymlicka, Will. 2012. 'Multiculturalism: Success, Failure, and the Future'. Report from the *Migration Policy Institute*. Accessed 3 November 2023. http://www .miguelcarbonell.com/artman/uploads/1/kymlicka.pdf

Landtag Nordrhein-Westfalen. 2017. Schlussbericht Des Parlamentarischen Untersuchungsausschusses IV. *Landtag Nordrhein-Westfalen*. Accessed 3 November 2023. https://www.landtag.nrw.de/portal/WWW/dokumentenarchiv/ Dokument/MMD16–14450.pdf

Lang, Juliane. 2021. '10 Jahre Nach Dem NSU. Vom Reden Über Frauenhass Und Rechten Terror'. *Soziale Probleme* 32: 167–81.

Leboucq, Fabien. 2018. 'Une liste de migrants noyés a-t-elle été déroulée au Parlement européen pour que les députés marchent dessus ?' *Libération*. Accessed 3 November 2023. https://www.liberation.fr/checknews/2018/10/16/une-liste -de-migrants-noyes-a-t-elle-ete-deroulee-au-parlement-europeen-pour-que-les -deputes-marchen_1685614/

Lehtonen, Aura. 2022. *The Sexual Logics of Neoliberalism in Britain: Sexual Politics in Exceptional Times*. London: Routledge.

Lentin, Alana. 2014. 'Post-Race, Post Politics: The Paradoxical Rise of Culture after Multiculturalism'. *Ethnic and Racial Studies* 37(8): 1268–85.

Lentin, Alana. 2020. *Why Race Still Matters*. Hoboken, NJ: John Wiley & Sons.

Leurs, Koen. 2017. 'Communication Rights from the Margins: Politicising Young Refugees' Smartphone Pocket Archives'. *International Communication Gazette* 79(6–7): 674–98.

Levitas, Ruth. 2010. *The Concept of Utopia*. Lausanne: Peter Lang.

Lewicki, Aleksandra. 2017. '"The Dead Are Coming": Acts of Citizenship at Europe's Borders'. *Citizenship Studies* 21(3): 275–90.

Lewicki, Aleksandra. 2018. 'Race, Islamophobia and the Politics of Citizenship in Post-Unification Germany'. *Patterns of Prejudice* 52(5): 496–512.

Lewicki, Aleksandra. 2023. 'East–West Inequalities and the Ambiguous Racialisation of "Eastern Europeans"'. *Journal of Ethnic and Migration Studies* 49(6): 1481–99.

Leys, Ruth. 2011. 'The Turn to Affect: A Critique'. *Critical Inquiry* 37(3): 434–72.

'List of Refugee Deaths'. 2023. *UNITED for Intercultural Action*. Accessed 3 November 2023. https://unitedagainstrefugeedeaths.eu/about-the-campaign/ about-the-united-list-of-deaths/

Lohaus, Stefanie and Anne Wizorek. 2016. 'Die Rape Culture wurde nicht importiert – sie war schon immer da'. *Vice*. Accessed 3 November 2023. https://www .vice.com/de/article/xdk9dw/die-rape-culture-wurde-nicht-nach-deutschland -importiert-sie-war-schon-immer-da-aufschrei-118

Lorde, Audre. 1997. 'The Uses of Anger'. *Women's Studies Quarterly* 25(1/2): 278–85.

Luibhéid, Eithne. 2002. *Entry Denied: Controlling Sexuality at the Border*. Minneapolis, MN: University of Minnesota Press.

Luibhéid, Eithne. 2013. *Pregnant on Arrival: Making the Illegal Immigrant*. Minneapolis, MN: University of Minnesota Press.

Lutz, Catherine A. and Lila E. Abu-Lughod. 1990. *Language and the Politics of Emotion*. Cambridge: Cambridge University Press.

Machin, Amanda. 2016. 'Hunger Power: The Embodied Protest of the Political Hunger Strike'. *Interface: A Journal on Social Movements* 8(1): 157–80.

Madhok, Sumi. 2022. *On Vernacular Rights Cultures: The Politics of Origins, Human Rights, and Gendered Struggles for Justice*. Cambridge: Cambridge University Press.

Madörin, Anouk. 2021. 'Fungibility at the Border: Selfies, Proxies, and (Faux) Self-Representations in the European Border Regime'. *Global Media Journal* 11(2).

Madörin, Anouk. 2022. *Postcolonial Surveillance: Europe's Border Technologies Between Colony and Crisis*. London: Rowman & Littlefield.

Mai, Nicola and Russell King. 2009. 'Love, Sexuality and Migration: Mapping the Issue(s)'. *Mobilities* 4(3): 295–307.

Mainwaring, Ċetta and Daniela DeBono. 2021. 'Criminalizing Solidarity: Search and Rescue in a Neo-Colonial Sea'. *Environment and Planning C: Politics and Space* 39(5): 1030–48.

Malkki, Liisa H. 1996. 'Speechless Emissaries: Refugees, Humanitarianism, and Dehistoricization'. *Cultural Anthropology* 11(3): 377–404.

Malkki, Liisa H. 2010. 'Children, Humanity, and the Infantilization of Peace'. In *In the Name of Humanity: The Government of Threat and Care*, edited by Ilana Feldman and Miriam Ticktin, 58–85. Durham, NC: Duke University Press.

Mandel, Ruth. 2008. *Cosmopolitan Anxieties: Turkish Challenges to Citizenship and Belonging in Germany*. Durham, NC: Duke University Press.

'March of Hope'. 2015. *Moving Europe*. Accessed 3 November 2023. http://moving -europe.org/march-of-hope-3/

Maroldt, Lorenz and Stephan-Andreas Casdorff. 2017. '"Die Liste" von Banu Cennetoglu: Künstlerin dokumentiert das Sterben von 33.293 Geflüchteten'. *Der Tagesspiegel*. Accessed 3 November 2023. https://www.tagesspiegel.de/politik/ kunstlerin-dokumentiert-das-sterben-von-33293-gefluchteten-3892450.html

Martenstein, Harald. 2016. 'Es geht um den Islam, nicht um Flüchtlinge'. *Der Tagesspiegel*. Accessed 3 November 2023. https://www.tagesspiegel.de/politik/es -geht-um-den-islam-nicht-um-fluchtlinge-5205283.html

Mason, Paul. 2021. *How to Stop Fascism: History, Ideology, Resistance*. London: Penguin.

Massumi, Brian. 1995. 'The Autonomy of Affect'. *Cultural Critique* 31: 83–109.

Massumi, Brian. 2010. 'The Political Ontology of Threat'. In *The Affect Theory Reader*, edited by Melissa Gregg and Gregory J. Seigworth, 52–70. Durham, NC: Duke University Press.

Massumi, Brian. 2021. *Parables for the Virtual: Movement, Affect, Sensation*. Durham, NC: Duke University Press.

Mayblin, Lucy and Joe Turner. 2020. *Migration Studies and Colonialism*. Hoboken, NJ: John Wiley & Sons.

Meier, Isabel. 2020. 'Affective Border Violence: Mapping Everyday Asylum Precarities across Different Spaces and Temporalities'. *Emotion, Space and Society* 37: 100702.

Mendel, Meron. 2021. 'Identitätspolitik versus Erinnerung an den Holocaust'. *Frankfurter Allgemeine Zeitung*. Accessed 3 November 2023. https://www.faz .net/aktuell/feuilleton/debatten/identitaetspolitik-versus-erinnerung-an-den -holocaust-17256208.html

Merrill, Samuel. 2018. 'The Dead Are Coming: Political Performance Art, Activist Remembrance and Dig(ital) Protests'. In *Performance and Civic Engagement*, edited by Ananda Breed and Tim Prentki, 159–85. Cham: Springer International.

Mezzadra, Sandro, and Brett Neilson. 2013. *Border as Method, or, the Multiplication of Labor*. Durham, NC: Duke University Press.

Mills, China and Brenda A. Lefrançois. 2018. 'Child as Metaphor: Colonialism, Psy-Governance, and Epistemicide'. *World Futures* 74(7–8): 503–24.

Moeller, Susan D. 2002. *Compassion Fatigue: How the Media Sell Disease, Famine, War and Death*. London: Routledge.

Mohanty, Chandra Talpade. 2003. '"Under Western Eyes" Revisited: Feminist Solidarity through Anticapitalist Struggles'. *Signs: Journal of Women in Culture and Society* 28(2): 499–535.

Monforte, Pierre. 2021. 'Protestors' Emotional Work in Contexts of Marginalisation: The Emancipation of "Forced Migrants" in Germany'. *Antipode* 53(2): 445–64.

Mortensen, Mette. 2017. 'Constructing, Confirming, and Contesting Icons: The Alan Kurdi Imagery Appropriated by #humanitywashedashore, Ai Weiwei, and *Charlie Hebdo*'. *Media, Culture & Society* 39(8): 1142–61.

Moses, Dirk. 2019. '"White Genocide" and the Ethics of Public Analysis'. *Journal of Genocide Research* 21(2): 201–13.

Moses, Dirk. 2021a. 'The German Catechism'. *Geschichte der Gegenwart* (blog). Accessed 3 November 2023. https://geschichtedergegenwart.ch/the-german-catechism/

Moses, Dirk. 2021b. 'Dialectic of Vergangenheitsbewältigung'. *The New Fascism Syllabus* (blog). Accessed 3 November 2023. http://newfascismsyllabus.com/opinions/the-catechism-debate/dialectic-of-vergangenheitsbewaltigung/

Mouffe, Chantal. 2022. *Towards a Green Democratic Revolution: Left Populism and the Power of Affects*. London: Verso.

Mpofu, Phillip, Moses O. Asak and Abiodun Salawu. 2022. 'Facebook Groups as Transnational Counter Public Sphere for Diasporic Communities'. *Cogent Arts & Humanities* 9(1): 2027598.

Muñoz, José Esteban. 2009. *Cruising Utopia: The Then and There of Queer Futurity*. New York: New York University Press.

Munt, Sally R. 2017. *Queer Attachments: The Cultural Politics of Shame*. London: Routledge.

Mushaben, Joyce Marie. 2017. 'Wir Schaffen Das! Angela Merkel and the European Refugee Crisis'. *German Politics* 26(4): 516–33.

Myong, Lene and Mons Bissenbakker. 2016. 'Love Without Borders? White Transraciality in Danish Migration Activism'. *Cultural Studies* 30(1): 129–46.

'Nach Köln – Kritik an Titelseiten von "Focus" und "Süddeutscher Zeitung"'. *Migazin*. Accessed 3 November 2023. https://www.migazin.de/2016/01/12/nach-koeln-kritik-titelseiten-focus/

Nachtwey, Oliver. 2016. *Die Abstiegsgesellschaft: Über Das Aufbegehren in Der Regressiven Moderne*. Frankfurt am Main: Suhrkamp Verlag.

Nakamura, Lisa. 2020. 'Feeling Good about Feeling Bad: Virtuous Virtual Reality and the Automation of Racial Empathy'. *Journal of Visual Culture* 19(1): 47–64.

Nash, Jennifer C. 2008. 'Re-Thinking Intersectionality'. *Feminist Review* 89(1): 1–15.

Ngai, Sianne. 2007. *Ugly Feelings*. Cambridge, MA: Harvard University Press.

Nobrega, Onur Suzan, Matthias Quent and Jonas Zipf (eds). 2021. *Rassismus. Macht. Vergessen.: Von München über den NSU bis Hanau: Symbolische und materielle Kämpfe entlang rechten Terrors*. Bielefeld: Transcript Verlag.

'Nürnberg: Flüchtlinge Am Hallplatz Im Hungerstreik'. 2015. *Karawane – Für die Rechte der Flüchtlinge und MigrantInnen*. Accessed 3 November 2023. http://thecaravan.org/node/4359

Nussbaum, Martha C. 1996. 'Compassion: The Basic Social Emotion'. *Social Philosophy and Policy* 13(1): 27–58.

Nussbaum, Martha C. 2013. *Political Emotions*. Cambridge, MA: Harvard University Press.

Nussbaum, Martha C. 2016a. *Anger and Forgiveness: Resentment, Generosity, Justice*. Oxford: Oxford University Press.

Nussbaum, Martha C. 2016b. 'There's No Emotion We Ought to Think Harder about Than Anger'. *Aeon* (blog). Accessed 3 November 2023. https://aeon.co/essays/there-s-no-emotion-we-ought-to-think-harder-about-than-anger

Nussbaum, Martha C. 2019. *The Monarchy of Fear: A Philosopher Looks at Our Political Crisis*. London: Simon and Schuster.

Olesen, Thomas. 2010. *Power and Transnational Activism*. London: Routledge.

Olesen, Thomas. 2018. 'Memetic Protest and the Dramatic Diffusion of Alan Kurdi'. *Media, Culture & Society* 40(5): 656–72.

Olufemi, Lola. 2021. *Experiments in Imagining Otherwise*. London: Hajar Press.

Özyürek, Esra. 2023. *Subcontractors of Guilt: Holocaust Memory and Muslim Belonging in Postwar Germany*. Stanford, CA: Stanford University Press.

Pallister-Wilkins, Polly. 2022. *Humanitarian Borders: Unequal Mobility and Saving Lives*. London: Verso.

Papadopoulos, Dimitris and Vassilis S. Tsianos. 2013. 'After Citizenship: Autonomy of Migration, Organisational Ontology and Mobile Commons'. *Citizenship Studies* 17(2): 178–96.

Papoulias, Constantina, and Felicity Callard. 2010. 'Biology's Gift: Interrogating the Turn to Affect'. *Body & Society* 16(1): 29–56.

Paré, Céline. 2022. 'Selective Solidarity? Racialized Othering in European Migration Politics'. *Amsterdam Review of European Affairs* 1(1): 42–61.

Parvulescu, Anca. 2010. *Laughter: Notes on a Passion*. Cambridge, MA: MIT Press.

Patel, Leigh. 2015. 'Deservingness: Challenging Coloniality in Education and Migration Scholarship'. *Association of Mexican American Educators Journal* 9(3): 11–21.

Pedwell, Carolyn. 2014a. *Affective Relations: The Transnational Politics of Empathy*. London: Palgrave.

Pedwell, Carolyn. 2014b. 'On Empathy, Accuracy and Transnational Politics'. *Theory, Culture & Society* (blog). Accessed 3 November 2023. https://www.theoryculturesociety.org/blog/carolyn-pedwell-on-empathy-accuracy-and-transnational-politics

Petter, Jan. 2018. 'Alexander Gauland: Chef der AfD verharmlost Nazi-Zeit als "Vogelschiss in der Geschichte"'. *Der Spiegel*. Accessed 3 November 2023. https://www.spiegel.de/politik/deutschland/alexander-gauland-chef-der-afd-verharmlost-nazi-zeit-als-vogelschiss-in-der-geschichte-a-00000000-0003-0001-0000-000002462132

Pfahl-Traughber, Armin. 2022. *Intellektuelle Rechtsextremisten: Das Gefahrenpotenzial der Neuen Rechten*. Bonn: Verlag JHW Dietz.

Pfeifer, Michelle. 2018. 'Becoming Flesh: Refugee Hunger Strike and Embodiments of Refusal in German Necropolitical Spaces'. *Citizenship Studies* 22(5): 459–74.

Phillips, Anne. 2015. *The Politics of the Human*. Cambridge: Cambridge University Press.

Phillips, Anne. 2016. 'Are We Not Both Human Beings?' *Paul Hirst Memorial Lecture*. Accessed 3 November 2023. https://player.fm/series/birkbeck-politics/are-we-not-both-human-beings-professor-anne-phillips

Phipps, Alison. 2020. *Me, Not You: The Trouble with Mainstream Feminism*. Manchester: Manchester University Press.

Pichl, Maximilian. 2021. 'Rechtskämpfe gegen die Asylrechtsverschärfungen. In *Kämpfe um Migrationspolitik seit 2015: Zur Transformation des europäischen Migrationsregimes*, edited by Sonja Buckel, Laura Graf, Judith Kopp, Neva Löw and Maximilian Pichl, 125–56. Bielefeld: Transcript Verlag.

Pidd, Helen. 2018. 'List of Refugee Deaths Displayed by Artist in Liverpool Torn down Again'. *The Guardian*. Accessed 3 November 2023. https://www.theguardian.com/uk-news/2018/aug/15/liverpool-artwork-listing-refugee-deaths-is-torn-down-again

Piers, Gerhart and Milton B. Singer. 1954. 'Shame and Guilt: A Psychoanalytic and a Cultural Study'. *Philosophy and Phenomenological Research* 15(2).

'Political Resistance in the 21ˢᵗ Century: Weaponizing the Power of History'. 2016. Centre for Political Beauty. Accessed 3 November 2023. https://politicalbeauty.com/about.html

Pollmer, Cornelius and Jens Schneider. 2015. 'Pegidas Partei'. *Süddeutsche Zeitung*. Accessed 3 November 2023. https://www.sueddeutsche.de/politik/afd-im-aufschwung-pegidas-partei-1.2683289

Ponzanesi, Sandra. 2018. 'Digital Strangers at Our Door: Moral Panic and the Refugee Crisis'. *EuropeNow – A Journal of Research and Art* 19.

Probyn, Elspeth. 2005. *Blush: Faces of Shame*. Minneapolis, MN: University of Minnesota Press.

Puar, Jasbir K. 2007. *Terrorist Assemblages: Homonationalism in Queer Times*. Durham, NC: Duke University Press.

Puar, Jasbir K. 2013. 'Rethinking Homonationalism'. *International Journal of Middle East Studies* 45(2): 336–39.

Raffelhüschen, Bernt. 2015. 'Der größte Fehler der vergangenen Jahrzehnte'. *Focus*. Accessed 3 November 2023. https://www.focus.de/finanzen/news/wer-soll-das-bezahlen-der-groesste-fehler-der-vergangenen-jahrzehnte_id_5045092.html

Rai, A. 2002. *Rule of Sympathy: Sentiment, Race, and Power 1750–1850*. London: Springer.

Ramadani, Zana. 2016. '"Der Islam macht unsere Werte kaputt"'. *Die Welt*. Accessed 3 November 2023. https://www.welt.de/vermischtes/article150989935/Seid-wuetend-auf-die-muslimischen-Frauen.html

'Rassismus bei Rathjen nicht Hauptmotiv? Attentäter von Hanau wollte offenbar vor allem Aufmerksamkeit'. 2020. *Der Tagesspiegel*. Accessed 3 November 2023. https://www.tagesspiegel.de/politik/attentater-von-hanau-wollte-offenbar-vor-allem-aufmerksamkeit-4156264.html

'Rassistische Titelbilder: Eine Entschuldigung, eine Rechtfertigung für Titel'. 2016. *Der Spiegel*. Accessed 3 November 2023. https://www.spiegel.de/kultur/gesellschaft/focus-und-sueddeutsche-zeitung-eine-entschuldigung-eine-rechtfertigung-fuer-titel-a-1071334.html

Rechavia-Taylor, Howie. 2022. *Coming to Terms with Namibia in the Federal Republic: Race, Reckoning, and Reparation in a Fractured Europe*. PhD Dissertation submitted to Columbia University in the City of New York.

Rechavia-Taylor, Howie. 2023. 'German Colonialism in the Courtroom – Law, Reparation, and the Grammars of the Shoah'. *Humanity: An International Journal of Human Rights, Humanitarianism, and Development* 14(2): 212–29.

Rechavia-Taylor, Howie and Dirk Moses. 2021. 'The Herero and Nama Genocide, the Holocaust, and the Question of German Reparations'. *E-International Relations* (blog). Accessed 3 November 2023. https://www.e-ir.info/2021/08/27/the-herero-and-nama-genocide-the-holocaust-and-the-question-of-german-reparations/

Rensmann, Lars. 2004. 'Collective Guilt, National Identity, and Political Processes in Contemporary Germany'. In *Collective Guilt*, edited by Nyla R. Branscombe and Bertjan Doosje, 169–90. Cambridge: Cambridge University Press.

Reynolds, James. 2018. 'Matteo Salvini: Can Italy's Populist Leader Return to Power?' BBC News. Accessed 3 November 2023. https://www.bbc.com/news/world-europe-44921974

Risam, Roopika. 2018. 'Now You See Them: Self-Representation and the Refugee Selfie'. *Popular Communication* 16(1): 58–71.

Rothberg, Michael. 2009. *Multidirectional Memory: Remembering the Holocaust in the Age of Decolonization*. Stanford, CA: Stanford University Press.

Rothberg, Michael. 2021. '"People with a Nazi Background": Race, Memory, and Responsibility'. *Los Angeles Review of Books*. Accessed 3 November 2023. https://lareviewofbooks.org/article/people-with-a-nazi-background-race-memory-and-responsibility/

Rothberg, Michael. 2022. 'Lived Multidirectionality: "Historikerstreit 2.0" and the Politics of Holocaust Memory'. *Memory Studies* 15(6): 1316–29.

Rothberg, Michael and Hanno Hauenstein. 2021. 'Nazi-Hintergrund, NS-Erbe und materielle Kontinuität: Das Schweigen brechen'. *Berliner Zeitung*. Accessed 3 November 2023. https://www.berliner-zeitung.de/wochenende/nazi-hintergrund-ns-erbe-und-materielle-kontinuitaet-das-schweigen-brechen-li.150838

Rothberg, Michael and Yasemin Yildiz. 2011. 'Memory Citizenship: Migrant Archives of Holocaust Remembrance in Contemporary Germany'. *Parallax* 17(4): 32–48.

Ruch, Philipp. 2013. 'Aggressiver Humanismus. Von der Unfähigkeit der Demokratie, große Menschenrechtler hervorzubringen'. In *Wege aus der Krise: Ideen und Konzepte für Morgen*, edited by Elias Bierdel and Maximilian Lakitsch, 105–119. Münster: LIT Verlag.

Ruch, Philipp. 2015. *Wenn nicht wir, wer dann? Ein politisches Manifest*. Munich: Ludwig Verlag.

Rudkin, Hayley. 2012. 'Self-Starvation as Performance'. *Cultural Studies Review* 18(1): 308–13.

Sabsay, Leticia. 2012. 'The Emergence of the Other Sexual Citizen: Orientalism and the Modernisation of Sexuality'. *Citizenship Studies* 16(5–6): 605–23.

Sabsay, Leticia. 2016. 'Permeable Bodies: Vulnerability, Affective Powers, Hegemony'. In *Vulnerability in Resistance*, edited by Judith Butler, Zeynep Gambetti and Leticia Sabsay, 278–302. Durham, NC: Duke University Press.

Sahin, Reyhan. 2014. *Die Bedeutung des muslimischen Kopftuchs: Eine kleidungssemiotische Untersuchung*. Münster: LIT Verlag.

Said, Edward W. 1995. *Orientalism*. London: Penguin.

Salem, Sara. 2018. 'Intersectionality and Its Discontents: Intersectionality as Traveling Theory'. *European Journal of Women's Studies* 25(4): 403–18.

Salem, Sara and Vanessa Thompson. 2016. 'Old Racisms, New Masks: On the Continuing Discontinuities of Racism and the Erasure of Race in European Contexts'. *Nineteen Sixty Nine: An Ethnic Studies Journal* 3(1).

Samudzi, Zoé. 2021. 'In Absentia of Black Study'. *The New Fascism Syllabus* (blog). Accessed 3 November 2023. http://newfascismsyllabus.com/opinions/the-catechism-debate/in-absentia-of-black-study/

Santos, Fabio. 2021. *Bridging Fluid Borders: Entanglements in the French-Brazilian Borderland*. London: Routledge.

Satzewich, Vic. 2000. 'Whiteness Limited: Racialization and the Social Construction of "Peripheral Europeans"'. *Histoire Sociale/Social History* 33(66): 271–89.

Sauer, Madlyn. 2022. *Wir klagen an! NSU-Tribunale als Praxis zwischen Kunst, Recht und Politik*. Münster: Unrast Verlag

Sauter, Dominik. 2016. 'Wir müssen die Sorgen der Bürger ernst nehmen'. *Bayernkurier*. Accessed 3 November 2023. https://www.bayernkurier.de/inland/9473-wir-muessen-die-sorgen-der-buerger-ernst-nehmen/

Scheel, Stephan. 2017. 'Appropriating Mobility and Bordering Europe through Romantic Love: Unearthing the Intricate Intertwinement of Border Regimes and Migratory Practices'. *Migration Studies* 5(3): 389–408.

Schirmbeck, Samuel. 2016. 'Gastbeitrag von Samuel Schirmbeck zum muslimischen Frauenbild'. *Frankfurter Allgemeine Zeitung*. Accessed 3 November 2023. https://www.faz.net/aktuell/politik/inland/gastbeitrag-von-samuel-schirmbeck-zum-muslimischen-frauenbild-14007010.html

Schlüter, Nadja. 2016. 'In Syrien ist es nicht normal, dass Frauen im Bus stehen'. *Jetzt – Süddeutsche Zeitung*. Accessed 3 November 2023. https://www.jetzt.de/fluechtlinge/nach-silvester-in-koeln-interview-mit-einem-syrischen-fluechtling

Schmincke, Imke and Jasmin Siri (eds). 2013. *NSU-Terror: Ermittlungen Am Rechten Abgrund. Ereignis, Kontexte, Diskurse*. Bielefeld: Transcript Verlag.

Schmitz-Berning, Cornelia. 2010. *Vokabular des Nationalsozialismus*. Berlin: De Gruyter.

Schröder, Christian. 2019. 'Anschlag in Neuseeland: Die Verschwörungstheorie des Todesschützen'. *Der Tagesspiegel*, 19 March. Accessed 1 March 2023. https://www.tagesspiegel.de/kultur/die-verschworungstheorie-des-todesschutzen-4048306.html

Schrödl, Barbara. 2004. 'Heimatfilme Und Die Neuordnung Des Nationalen'. *FKW Zeitschrift Für Geschlechterforschung und Visuelle Kultur* 37: 29–37.

Schüßler, Michael. 2020. 'Judenhass und der Kampf um männliche Vorherrschaft'. *Wissen schafft Demokratie* 8: 156–67.

Schultz, Tanjev. 2021. *Auf dem rechten Auge blind?: Rechtsextremismus in Deutschland*. Stuttgart: Kohlhammer Verlag.

Scott, Joan Wallach. 1996. *Only Paradoxes to Offer: French Feminists and the Rights of Man*. Cambridge, MA: Harvard University Press.

Sedgwick, Eve K. 2003. *Touching Feeling: Affect, Pedagogy, Performativity*. Durham, NC: Duke University Press.

Sedgwick, Eve K. and Adam Frank. 1995. 'Shame in the Cybernetic Fold: Reading Silvan Tomkins'. *Critical Inquiry* 21(2): 496–522.

Seehofer, Horst. 2018. 'Warum Heimatverlust die Menschen umtreibt'. *Frankfurter Allgemeine Zeitung*. Accessed 3 November 2023. https://www.faz.net/aktuell/politik/inland/innenminister-horst-seehofer-zum-thema-heimat-15565980.html

'Seehofer will Rechtsstaat "der Biss hat"'. 2016. *Merkur*. Accessed 3 November 2023. https://www.merkur.de/politik/seehofer-muenchner-presseclub-reaktion-koeln-rechtsstaat-zaehne-hat-zr-6023868.html

Seigworth, Gregory J. and Carolyn Pedwell (eds). 2023. *The Affect Theory Reader 2: Worldings, Tensions, Futures*. Durham, NC: Duke University Press.

Sharpe, Christina. 2016. *In the Wake: On Blackness and Being*. Durham, NC: Duke University Press.

Shefer, Tamara and Sally R Munt. 2019. 'A Feminist Politics of Shame: Shame and Its Contested Possibilities'. *Feminism & Psychology* 29(2): 145–56.

Sheftalovich, Zoya. 2019. 'Von Der Leyen on "European Way of Life": We Can't Let Others "Take Away Our Language"'. *Politico*. Accessed 3 November 2023. https://www.politico.eu/article/von-der-leyen-on-european-way-of-life-we-cant-let-others-take-away-our-language/

Siddiqui, Sophia. 2021. 'Racing the Nation: Towards a Theory of Reproductive Racism'. *Race & Class* 63(2): 3–20.

Siggelkow, Pascal and Carla Reveland. 2023. 'Ukraine-Krieg: Debatte um Wagenknecht-Schwarzer-Petition'. *Tagesschau*. Accessed 3 November 2023. https://www.tagesschau.de/faktenfinder/russland-ukraine-manifest-101.html

Sirriyeh, Ala. 2018. *The Politics of Compassion: Immigration and Asylum Policy*. Bristol: Bristol University Press.

Slaby, Jan and Christian von Scheve. 2019. *Affective Societies: Key Concepts*. London: Routledge.

Smith, Nicholas H. 2006. 'Hope and Critical Theory'. *Critique Today* 45–61.

Snyder, Jack. 2020. 'Backlash against Human Rights Shaming: Emotions in Groups'. *International Theory* 12(1): 109–32.

Solomon, Robert C. 1993. *The Passions: Emotions and the Meaning of Life*. Indianapolis, IN: New Hackett Publishing.

Sorenson, Claire, Beth Bolick, Karen Wright and Rebekah Hamilton. 2016. 'Understanding Compassion Fatigue in Healthcare Providers: A Review of Current Literature'. *Journal of Nursing Scholarship* 48(5): 456–65.

Spelman, Elizabeth V. 1998. *Fruits of Sorrow*. Boston, MA: Beacon Press.

Spivak, Gayatri C. 1988. 'Can the Subaltern Speak?' In *Marxism and the Interpretation of Culture*, edited by C. Nelson and L. Grossberg. Urbana, IL: University of Illinois Press.

Squire, Vicki. 2018. 'Mobile Solidarities and Precariousness at City Plaza: Beyond Vulnerable and Disposable Lives'. *Studies in Social Justice* 12(1): 111–32.

'Staatsanwaltschaft ermittelt gegen Zentrum für Politische Schönheit'. 2019. *Die Zeit*. Accessed 3 November 2023. https://www.zeit.de/gesellschaft/2019-04/aktionskuenstler-zentrum-fuer-politische-schoenheit-staatsanwaltschaft-gera

Steinhagen, Martín. 2021. *Rechter Terror: Der Mord an Walter Lübcke Und Die Strategie Der Gewalt*. Hamburg: Rowohlt Verlag.

Steinhilper, Elias. 2021. *Migrant Protest: Interactive Dynamics in Precarious Mobilizations*. Amsterdam: Amsterdam University Press.

Sterk, Pippa. 2023. '"They Always Want to Argue with You": Navigating Raciolinguistic Ideologies at Airport Security'. *Journal of Sociolinguistics* 27(4): 364–83.

Stierl, Maurice. 2015. 'The WatchTheMed Alarm Phone. A Disobedient Border-Intervention'. *Movements. Journal for Critical Migration and Border Regime Studies* 1(2).

Stierl, Maurice. 2016. 'Contestations in Death – the Role of Grief in Migration Struggles'. *Citizenship Studies* 20(2): 173–91.

Stockton, Kathryn Bond. 2006. *Beautiful Bottom, Beautiful Shame: Where 'Black' Meets 'Queer'*. Durham, NC: Duke University Press.

Stoler, Ann Laura. 2002. *Carnal Knowledge and Imperial Power: Race and the Intimate in Colonial Rule*. Oakland, CA: University of California Press.

Surkis, Judith. 2019. *Sex, Law, and Sovereignty in French Algeria, 1830–1930*. Ithaca, NY: Cornell University Press.

Svendsen, Lars. 2008. *A Philosophy of Fear*. London: Reaktion Books.

'Syrer demonstrieren in Köln gegen Sexismus: "Es geht um den Respekt füreinander!"'. 2016. *Kölnische Rundschau*. Accessed 3 November 2023. https://www.rundschau-online.de/koeln/syrer-demonstrieren-in-koeln-gegen-sexismus-es-geht-um-den-respekt-fuereinander-318711

Tazzioli, Martina. 2015. *Border Abolitionism: Migrants' Containment and the Genealogies of Struggles and Rescue*. Manchester: Manchester University Press.

Tazzioli, Martina. 2019. 'The Politics of Counting and the Scene of Rescue'. *Radical Philosophy* 192: 2–6.

Tazzioli, Martina. 2023. *Border Abolitionism: Migration Containment and the Genealogies of Struggles and Rescue*. Manchester: Manchester University Press.

'The Dead Are Coming'. 2015. Centre for Political Beauty. Accessed 3 November 2023. https://politicalbeauty.com/dead.html

'Thomas de Maizière fordert "Ankommenskultur" der Flüchtlinge'. 2015. *Der Spiegel*. Accessed 3 November 2023. https://www.spiegel.de/politik/deutschland/de-maiziere-fordert-ankommenskultur-der-fluechtlinge-a-1055837.html

Thompson, Vanessa E. 2022. 'Policing Blackness in Europe: Colonial Entanglements and Contemporary Articulations of Struggle'. *European Yearbook of Minority Issues Online* 19(1): 27–48.

Thorleifsson, Cathrine. 2017. 'Disposable Strangers: Far-Right Securitisation of Forced Migration in Hungary'. *Social Anthropology/Anthropologie Sociale* 25(3): 318–34.

Ticktin, Miriam. 2006. 'Where Ethics and Politics Meet'. *American Ethnologist* 33(1): 33–49.

Ticktin, Miriam. 2008. 'Sexual Violence as the Language of Border Control: Where French Feminist and Anti-Immigrant Rhetoric Meet'. *Signs: Journal of Women in Culture and Society* 33(4): 863–89.

Ticktin, Miriam. 2011. *Casualties of Care: Immigration and the Politics of Humanitarianism in France*. Oakland, CA: University of California Press.

Ticktin, Miriam. 2016. 'Thinking Beyond Humanitarian Borders'. *Social Research* 83(2): 255–71.

Ticktin, Miriam. 2017. 'A World Without Innocence'. *American Ethnologist* 44(4): 577–90.

Timur, Safak. 2016. 'Two Men Sentenced in Death of Alan Kurdi, Syrian Boy Who Drowned in September'. *The New York Times*. Accessed 3 November 2023. https://www.nytimes.com/2016/03/05/world/europe/syrians-sentenced-aylan -alan-kurdi.html

'Totes Flüchtlingskind: Steuerte Aylans Vater selbst das Schlepperboot?' 2015. *Bild*. Accessed 3 November 2023. https://www.bild.de/politik/ausland/fluechtling/ arbeitete-aylans-vater-mit-den-schleppern-zusammen-42550358.bild.html

Tsianos, Vassilis, and Serhat Karakayali. 2010. 'Transnational Migration and the Emergence of the European Border Regime: An Ethnographic Analysis'. *European Journal of Social Theory* 13(3): 373–87.

Tudor, Alyosxa. 2015. *From [al'manja] with love: Trans/feministische Positionierungen zu Rassismus und Migratismus*. Frankfurt am Main: Brandes & Apsel Verlag.

Tudor, Alyosxa. 2018. 'Cross-Fadings of Racialisation and Migratisation: The Postcolonial Turn in Western European Gender and Migration Studies'. *Gender, Place & Culture* 25(7): 1057–72.

Tudor, Alyosxa. 2023. 'Ascriptions of Migration: Racism, Migratism and Brexit'. *European Journal of Cultural Studies* 26(2): 230–48.

Tyler, Imogen. 2013. *Revolting Subjects: Social Abjection and Resistance in Neoliberal Britain*. London: Zed Books.

Tyler, Imogen. 2020. *Stigma: The Machinery of Inequality*. London: Bloomsbury.

Van Houtum, Henk. 2010. 'Human Blacklisting: The Global Apartheid of the EU's External Border Regime'. *Environment and Planning D: Society and Space* 28(6): 957–76.

Varoufakis, Giannis. 2015. 'Deutschland: Die moralische Nation'. *Frankfurter Allgemeine Zeitung*. Accessed 3 November 2023. https://www.faz.net/aktuell/ feuilleton/deutschland-die-moralische-nation-13799629.html

Von Der Behrens, Antonia. 2018. 'Lessons from Germany's NSU Case'. *Race & Class* 59(4): 84–91.

Vu, Vanessa. 2018. Kein Witz. *Die Zeit*. Accessed 3 November 2023. https://www .zeit.de/gesellschaft/zeitgeschehen/2018-07/horst-seehofer-69-abschiebung -afghanistan-69-geburtstag-fluechtlinge

Walia, Harsha. 2021. *Border and Rule: Global Migration, Capitalism, and the Rise of Racist Nationalism*. Chicago, IL: Haymarket Books.

Walkerdine, Valerie, and Luis Jimenez. 2012. *Gender, Work and Community after De-Industrialisation: A Psychosocial Approach to Affect*. London: Palgrave.

Walters, William. 2010. 'Foucault and Frontiers: Notes on the Birth of the Humanitarian Border'. In *Governmentality*, edited by Ulrich Bröckling, Susanne Krasmann and Thomas Lemke, 146–72. London: Routledge.

Weeks, Kathie. 2011. *The Problem with Work: Feminism, Marxism, Antiwork Politics, and Postwork Imaginaries*. Durham, NC: Duke University Press.

Weiland, Severin. 2018. 'Wirbel um Merkel-Äußerung von FDP-Vize Kubicki'. *Der Spiegel*. Accessed 3 November 2023. https://www.spiegel.de/politik/deutschland/chemnitz-wirbel-um-aeusserung-von-fdp-vize-wolfgang-kubicki-zu-angela-merkel-a-1225553.html

Wekker, Gloria. 2016. *White Innocence: Paradoxes of Colonialism and Race*. Durham, NC: Duke University Press.

Wetherell, Margaret. 2012. *Affect and Emotion*. London: Sage.

Wetherell, Margaret. 2013. 'Affect and Discourse – What's the Problem? From Affect as Excess to Affective/Discursive Practice'. *Subjectivity* 6: 349–68.

Wetherell, Margaret. 2015. 'Trends in the Turn to Affect: A Social Psychological Critique'. *Body & Society* 21(2): 139–66.

'Wiedereinreise-Wahnsinn – Terroristen durften ganz legal zu uns kommen'. 2018. *Bild*. Accessed 3 November 2023. https://www.bild.de/politik/inland/asylrecht/islamisten-durften-ganz-legal-nach-deutschland-kommen-56060690.bild.html

Wieners, Karin and Marion Winterholler. 2016. 'Häusliche und sexuelle Gewalt gegen Frauen'. *Bundesgesundheitsblatt – Gesundheitsforschung – Gesundheitsschutz* 59(1): 73–80.

Wildenthal, Lora. 2001. *German Women for Empire, 1884–1945*. Durham, NC: Duke University Press.

Wilhelmsen, Fredrik. 2021. '"The Wife Would Put on a Nice Suit, Hat, and Possibly Gloves": The Misogynistic Identity Politics of Anders Behring Breivik'. *Fascism* 10(1): 108–33.

Wilson, Chris. 2022. 'Nostalgia, Entitlement and Victimhood: The Synergy of White Genocide and Misogyny'. *Terrorism and Political Violence* 34(8): 1810–25.

Wilson, Kalpana. 2011. '"Race", Gender, and Neoliberalism: Changing Visual Representations in Development'. *Third World Quarterly* 32(2): 315–31.

Winston, Andrew S. 2021. '"Jews Will Not Replace Us!": Antisemitism, Interbreeding and Immigration in Historical Context'. *American Jewish History* 105(1): 1–24.

Wirth, Hans-Jürgen. 2022. *Gefühle machen Politik*. Giessen: Psychosozial-Verlag.

Wodak, Ruth. 2020. *The Politics of Fear: The Shameless Normalization of Far-Right Discourse*. London: Sage Publishing.

Wolfe, Patrick. 2002. 'Race and Racialisation: Some Thoughts'. *Postcolonial Studies: Culture, Politics, Economy* 5(1): 51–62.

Younes, Anna-Esther. 2020. 'Fighting Anti-Semitism in Contemporary Germany'. *Islamophobia Studies Journal* 5(2): 249–66.

Yuval-Davis, Nira. 1997. *Gender and Nation*. London: Sage Publishing.

Yuval-Davis, Nira, Georgie Wemyss and Kathryn Cassidy. 2019. *Bordering*. London: John Wiley & Sons.

Ziai, Aram. 2016. *Postkoloniale Politikwissenschaft: Theoretische und empirische Zugänge*. Bielefeld: Transcript Verlag.

Zschaler, Mathias. 2015. 'Günther Jauch mit Björn Höcke: Nicht zum Lachen – und trotzdem komisch'. *Der Spiegel*. Accessed 3 November 2023. https://www .spiegel.de/kultur/tv/guenther-jauch-mit-bjoern-hoecke-afd-nicht-zum-lachen -und-trotzdem-komisch-a-1058418.html

'Zug der Verzweifelten: Massentreck auf der M1'. 2015. *Der Spiegel*. Accessed 3 November 2023. https://www.spiegel.de/fotostrecke/fluechtlinge-in-bicske-im -zug-der-verzweifelten-fotostrecke-129798.html

Index

EU authorised representative for GPSR:
Easy Access System Europe, Mustamäe tee 50,
10621 Tallinn, Estonia
gpsr.requests@easproject.com

www.ingramcontent.com/pod-product-compliance
Lightning Source LLC
Chambersburg PA
CBHW052008270326
41929CB00015B/2831